The Empire of Lies

The Truth About China in the Twenty-First Century

Guy Sorman

Translated by Asha Puri

ENCOUNTER BOOKS
NEW YORK · LONDON

Encounter Books website address: www.encounterbooks.com

Manufactured in the United States and printed on acid-free paper. The paper used in this publication meets the minimum requirements of ANSI/NISO Z39.48-1992 (R 1997) (Permanence of Paper).

FIRST AMERICAN EDITION

Library of Congress Cataloging-in-Publication Data

Sorman, Guy.
  The empire of lies : the truth about China in the twenty-first century / Guy Sorman. — American ed.
     p. cm.
  Includes bibliographical references and index.
  ISBN-13: 978-1-59403-216-5 (hardcover : alk. paper)
  ISBN-10: 1-59403-216-5 (hardcover : alk. paper)
  1. China—Politics and government—2002- 2. China—Politics and government—1976-2002. 3. China—Social conditions—2000- 4. China—Social conditions—1976-2000. I. Title.
  DS779.46.S68 2008
  951.06—dc22

                                                    2008001916

Table of Contents

Foreword
to the American Edition

The Western press is full of stories these days on China's arrival as a superpower, some even heralding, or warning, that the future may belong to it. Western political and business delegations stream into Beijing, confident of China's economy, which continues to grow rapidly. Investment pours in. Crowning China's new status, Beijing will host the 2008 Summer Olympics.

But China's success is, at least in part, a mirage. True, 200 million of its subjects, fortunate to be working for an expanding global market, increasingly enjoy a middle-class standard of living. The remaining billion, however, remain among the poorest and most exploited people in the world, lacking even minimal rights and public services. Popular discontent simmers, especially in the countryside, where it often flares into violent confrontation with Communist Party authorities. China's economic "miracle" is rotting from within.

The Party's primary concern is not improving the lives of the downtrodden; it seeks power more than it seeks social development. It expends extraordinary energy in suppressing Chinese freedoms—the media operate under suffocating censorship, and political opposition can result in expulsion or prison—even as it tries to seduce the West, which has conferred greater legitimacy on it than do the Chinese themselves.

The West's tendency to misread China dates back to the seventeenth century, when French and Italian Jesuit travelers formed stereotypes that clutter our minds even today. We learned then—or thought we learned—that the Chinese were not like us. They had no religion, and the notion of freedom was alien to them. They naturally gravitated toward enlightened despotism, as embodied by the philosopher-emperor. Such misconceptions link up across time: Voltaire sang the praises of the mandarins, wishing a similar elite class could rule Europe; leftist intellectuals in the Sixties and Seventies celebrated the heroism of Mao Zedong; and today's business elites happily go along with the Communist propaganda that democracy and free speech are contrary to the Chinese ethos.

Yet with enough patience and will, one can plunge into the real China. Since 1967, I have visited the country regularly, and I spent all of 2005, part of 2006—the Year of the Rooster*—and then part of 2007 traveling through its teeming cities as well as its innermost recesses, where few Westerners go. I make no claim to know China fully, an impossibly ambitious task. I merely want to record the words and impressions of some exceptional Chinese men and women, who mostly suffer in silence, raising when they can the demand for a free nation—a "normal" nation.

Before the totalitarian reign of Mao Zedong and his immediate successors, never before had an entire nation experienced such intense surveillance. The Chinese not only had to speak alike; they had to **think** alike with the Communist Party regulating every aspect of private life. Millions were imprisoned and killed.

Things have obviously changed, much for the better. China is no longer totalitarian. Yet the 60-million-member Communist Party, if subtler, remains cruel and omnipresent. I have visited Henan Province, for example, where thousands of families in far-flung villages have died of AIDS. The Party does not merely leave them to perish. It initially denied the epidemic. It arrests Beijing students trying to bring food and medicine to the affected villagers, and accuses

---

*The first edition of this book was originally published in French in 2006 under the title *L'anné du Coq: Chinois et rebelles.*

them of being enemies of the state. One of these—Hu Jia, a thirty-four-year-old human rights activist—was illegally sentenced to house arrest for 300 days in 2006 and 2007 for daring to distribute medicine to Henan's suffering villages. Now that the Party finally acknowledges the plague, it claims that it is under control, which unfortunately is far from the truth.

I also managed to visit the city of Linyi in Shandong Province. In 2005, government agents responsible for enforcing China's family-planning laws kidnapped 12,000 women from the area, forcing abortions on those who were pregnant—in some cases, immersing seven- to eight-month-old fetuses in boiling water—and sterilizing those who weren't. Chen Guangcheng, a self-taught blind lawyer, has been languishing in solitary confinement since 2006 because he protested legally against this atrocity. Such acts of cruelty take place throughout the country, especially in the rural areas, where 800 million Chinese live. If the regime works as well as it claims, I often wonder, why does it need to resort to so much violence?

From the point of view of its members, of course, the Communist Party has been successful. It has maintained its grip over China, initiated economic growth, won legitimacy for the country, and lined its members' pockets; why should it undertake the risky business of permitting political debate or democratization? Instead it keeps a close watch on any attempt to change its perfect system, brutally suppressing peasant and worker rebellions and imprisoning political bloggers—or branding them terrorists and executing them. The real purpose of family planning is not so much to limit the number of children as to keep the rural population on a tight leash. Besides, it provides easy income for officials willing to turn a blind eye to wrongdoing for a consideration. Corruption is rampant at all levels; peasant and entrepreneur alike indulge in it. Every Chinese has to endure some form of extortion.

Whenever I meet a Communist official, I never fail to point this out. The standard reply: "We are in a period of transition." Transition to what? Treated as second-class citizens, those living in the rural areas have little hope of escaping their plight. Currently, the economy generates no more than 20 million jobs a year, which means that it will require forty years to restore some dignity to the countryside. Schools and health care could improve the lot of the villagers substantially, but little is being done. The government makes all the right noises about removing injustice and promoting social development, but its deeds don't match its words. Social harmony, the new buzzword of the Communist Party, remains nothing more than a slogan.

The fact is that in the absence of democracy, there is no compulsion for the Party to help the three-quarters of China's population living in its rural villages. Will the new urban middle class press for democracy the way the Koreans and the Taiwanese did? It seems unlikely: city dwellers are wary of peasants, fearing that they would seize power under a democratic government. Will the peasants revolt? Uprisings take place all over the country, but they are sporadic, spontaneous outbursts against corrupt officials, lacking coordination, leadership, and a political agenda. The Party's special police force is ruthlessly efficient in quelling these protests and has no qualms about killing their leaders. The revival of religion in China, Westerners often say, will bring about change: many Chinese human-rights activists are either Buddhist or Christian, and students who convert to evangelical denominations usually get involved in humanitarian activities. But to imagine that their isolated actions will bring about major political change is wishful thinking.

Two things could threaten the regime: a downturn in the global economy or an uncontrolled epidemic. The regime's legitimacy is closely linked to China's growth rate, which in turn is pegged to world consumption, especially U.S. consumption. If for any reason Americans began to consume less, the Communist Party would lurch into disarray, and the new middle class might want a regime change—but not necessarily a democracy. A pandemic more devastating than the SARS outbreak of 2003 is also quite possible, given the lack of proper health-care facilities in rural China and the country's massive internal migration, and history suggests that it could take several months for the central authorities and the international community to learn of it and respond.

None of this is to suggest that the West boycott China. In fact, we must continue to engage with it not only through trade but also through cultural exchange. China's renaissance, however imperfect, is good news. Hundreds of millions of people are shaking off the yoke of poverty; the process is slow and chaotic, but it is better than total-itarianism and hunger. Importing Chinese goods also helps the economies of the West, for it forces us to raise our productivity and offers our consumers cheaper goods. Of course, there is the other side of the coin—cheap Chinese goods hasten the destruction of some Western low-tech industries—but doesn't creative destruction drive the free market? China is still a poor country. Its economy can hardly be called sophisticated, and the possibility of it overtaking the U.S., Europe, or Japan is remote. Neither is there any threat from China in the international arena yet: its army is still lagging, and its diplomatic clout is limited. We need not fear it, though we must con-tinue to innovate to stay ahead.

We also would do well to back pro-democracy and human rights activists in China, as we did in the erstwhile Soviet Union. In the Seventies and Eighties, the West continued to trade with the USSR while supporting dissidents there. There is no reason to treat China differently. We must not be swayed by the Communist leadership's claims that China has a distinct cultural ethos and that its people are not committed to freedom. Our course will compel the Chinese leadership, desperately seeking international legitimacy, to listen. And they will listen, since their economy would collapse if our con-sumers and investors abandoned them.

The Communist Party's Propaganda Department, helped by a plethora of public-relations consultants and politically articulate emissaries, does all it can to woo foreign critics. The ham-handed methods of Maoist China are a thing of the past. After my year in China, when I returned to Paris and published my views, I spoke with Yan Yfan (a pseudonym)—a scholar on the payroll of a Beijing foundation, an extension of the Party, who had been assigned my case. "Do you dare deny China's success story, its social stability, economic growth, cultural renaissance, and international restraint?"

he asked me. I responded that political and religious oppression, censorship, entrenched rural poverty, family-planning excesses, and rampant corruption were just as real as economic growth in today's China. "What you are saying is true but affects only a minority yet to benefit from reforms," he asserted.

Yet nothing guarantees that this so-called minority—a billion people!—will integrate with modern China. It is just as possible that the "minority" will remain poor, since it has no say in determining its fate, even as Party members get richer. Yan Yfan underscores my fundamental error: "You don't have any confidence in the Party's ability to resolve the pertinent issues you have raised." He's right; I don't.

I think it is time we listened to other voices than the Party's strident one—those of the humble, the poor, the meek, and the oppressed. To give voice to the voiceless: this, in all humility, is what I have set out to do in *The Empire of Lies.* The book explores individual destinies and then discusses the ongoing debate on the nature of the Chinese regime, attempting to disprove the theory, put forth by Eastern and Western scholars, that China is a class apart. I refuse to accept that the Party is China. I have visited the country frequently for long stretches and have always been struck by the fact that the Chinese, like us, desire prosperity and freedom. Their supposed proclivity for an enlightened Communist Party is an ideological artifact.

The Chinese leadership would like the world to believe that they have found an alternative to Western liberal democracy, a balance between a free market and enlightened despotism—a view shared by those in the West who prize economic efficiency above political freedom. Unfortunately, this claim does not stand up to scrutiny. The Chinese economy has only succeeded when the basic principles of the free market were applied: entrepreneurship, competition, free trade, and a stable currency. These principles are universal, not just Chinese. Whenever China has not adhered to them, it has had to pay the price. A behemoth public sector is dragging down its economy, and unsound banks are issuing bad loans and promoting unhealthy speculation. In the absence of the rule of law, corruption is rampant, and the scant respect for intellectual property is hampering innovation. The so-called Chinese characteristics of the market economy are neither Chinese nor progressive: they are merely symptomatic of the transition from socialism to the market economy.

There is nothing innovative about China's political institutions. Though the Communist Party has 60 million members, it can hardly claim to represent the Chinese people as a whole: it recruits only educated men from the cities, and it has very few women and virtually no peasants or workers on its rolls. The educated technocracy, the backbone of the Party, thinks that it knows what is best for the people and does not think it fit to ask them what they want. It is perhaps for this reason that countless decisions made at the top, without consultation at the grassroots, have failed to yield results. The Party prefers grandiose political gestures and high-sounding rhetoric to actual implementation. Though they use a Marxist vocabulary, China's leaders tend to identify more and more with the ancient mandarin class. They are as arrogant and corrupt as the mandarins before 1911, when the Republican revolution put an end to their dominance.

As things stand, rebellion is the only recourse left for people to express their discontent. What is even more worrisome is the question of succession. So far, Mao's successors, beginning with Deng Xiaoping, have—despite Tiananmen—behaved rationally. But even if the Party has succeeded in generating four relatively enlightened despots, its process of choosing a leader remains obscure. There is no telling what the next one will be like. Internecine factionalism will make the outcome unpredictable. Without elections, China can only count on luck for an orderly succession.

Until now, fortune has favored China. If its lucky streak continues, so will the status quo. The Party has a well-oiled machinery for dealing with protest; moreover, the Chinese abhor disorder, their history having nurtured in them a deep-seated fear of civil strife, and the Party leadership knows how to play on this fear. But fortune is transient, and so is fear. Eventually, the enlightened despotism of the

Party will be replaced by military dictatorship, chaos, or, if one is optimistic, a liberal democracy. I personally believe that there is no reason, cultural or otherwise, for China not to become a free nation like any other.

Guy Sorman, New York, February 2008

The Myth of China

In the words of Napoleon Bonaparte, "When China awakens, the world will tremble." The world will tremble because the myth of China is far more potent than its reality: image, it would seem, prevails over truth. Western observers of China have always proved singularly inept, forever seeing what is not. And down the ages, the Chinese leadership, from the Empire to the Communist Party, has successfully cultivated an air of inscrutability that has taken in a credulous West. The idea of a powerful China submerging the rest of the world is far-fetched; it is a poor nation, its economy barely the size of the French or Italian economy.

The world trembles because it feeds on fantasies. The reality on the ground is far less awesome, if only an attempt were made to understand it. The failure to do so, as we shall see, is not new but part of a long story.

What the Jesuits, Jean-Paul Sartre, and today's businessmen have in common

Four hundred years ago, when Italian and French Jesuits went to China, they saw all that was trivial and missed all that was essential. Should one go by their accounts, chiefly responsible for the larger-than-life image of China in the European imagination, there was no place for religion in a country ruled by a philosopher-emperor. In *Les*

Lettres édifiantes et curieuses, a 1702 bestseller written by French Jesuits, the Chinese people were portrayed as an amorphous superstitious mass whereas the Confucian mandarins were deemed by our great travelers to be delightful men of letters. So deep was the imprint they left on the Enlightenment philosophers, Leibniz and Voltaire in particular, that Voltaire lived in the hope of Europe being ruled by an enlightened despot and enjoying a godless morality. Voltaire's Supreme Being has Chinese genes. A portrait of Confucius, bearing the inscription "To Master Kong who was a prophet in his own land" presided over his Ferney study. And so the reality of China was supplanted by the myth of China and sinology founded as an ideology.

The reality of Chinese society lay elsewhere, however. The mandarins, not always chosen on merit, were often corrupt and made the people submit to their exactions. The people suffered Confucianism as an anticlerical ideology, inimical to their belief in the Buddha and the immortal Daoists. As for the legitimacy of dynastic rule and emperors, no fewer than twenty-six dynasties and numerous palace coups came before the Republican Revolution of 1911.

Understanding the real China seems to be the least of our concerns. Until very recently, most universities in France taught Confucian philosophy and court manners, paying scant attention to contemporary Chinese society. Over the last few years, it is true, a shift has occurred. The fascination for the mandarins, a legacy of the Jesuits and Voltaire, is waning, though slowly. Language courses are being offered, with Chinese being taught like any other living language, for purposes other than sinology. Economists, lawyers, sociologists, and others have started venturing into China and viewing it like any another country, which is how it should be. And yet the tendency to mystify China persists, with scholars hard put to come to grips with flesh-and-blood Chinese. From 1973 to 1994, the French statesman and prolific writer Alain Peyrefitte almost single-handedly shaped our perception of China, with his exotically titled books—*When China Awakens, the World Will Tremble; The Immobile Empire;* and *The Chinese Tragedy*—firing the public imagination. The ordinary Chinese people were of no interest to Peyrefitte; his China was an organic mass lost in slumber or steeped in tragedy. I wonder if there is any other country on which we could have projected our hopes and fears as freely as we have on China.

The conservatives were the first to mystify China; a few hundred years later, the progressives, hardly more levelheaded, did exactly the same thing. The Jesuits had dreamed of universal evangelization and philosopher-emperors, and found both in China. In the Seventies, our much vaunted intellectuals, in search of a mentor and a universal revolution, gravitated naturally toward China.

Three hundred years after the Jesuit priests, Roland Barthes, Philippe Sollers, Jacques Lacan, and many others of the same ilk made their pilgrimage to China; like their predecessors, they saw only what they wanted to—that is, nothing at all. When the so-called Cultural Revolution, a euphemism for a civil war, was at its peak, Maria-Antonietta Macciocchi, a self-styled intellectual authority on the subject in Italy and France, wrote: "After three years of trouble, the Cultural Revolution will usher in a thousand years of happiness." The "New Philosophers" Guy Lardreau and Christian Jambet saw in Mao a resurrection of Christ and compared *The Little Red Book* to the Gospels. This metaphorical approach to Maoism, very much in line with the Jesuit interpretation of Confucianism, was yet another journey in the realm of the imaginary. And Jean-Paul Sartre, receptive at all times to the aesthetics of violence, embraced Maoism without even having gone to China. "A learned fool," said Molière, "is twice as foolish as an ignorant fool."

A discerning few refused to be mesmerized by this second invention of China. In the Seventies, the Belgian writer Pierre Ryckmans, alias Simon Leys, spoke of how he saw bodies, tied together, floating down the Pearl River to Victoria Harbor. There was also a substantial amount of documentary evidence of the massacres for anyone who wished to consult it. But the perceptive observer's condemnation of Maoism made for dreary reading compared with the fabulous tales of the Jesuits and the Leftists. In 1971, René Viénet and Chang Hing-ho published Simon Leys's *The New Clothes of President Mao* in their collection "The Asian Library," and it went on to become a classic in the analysis of the Maoist dictatorship. The generation of the Seventies turned a blind eye to the blatant crimes of the Maoist regime in the same way that earlier generations had chosen not to see the horrors of the Soviet Gulag or the Nazi death camps.

In the eighteenth century, Europe was enamored of all things Chinese, in the Fifties of all things Stalinist, and in the Seventies of all things Maoist. Nothing seems to have changed, for today we have simply invented a new myth in place of the old.

The steady stream of political and business delegations visiting Beijing these days wears the same kind of blinkers as its Jesuit and progressive predecessors, it seems. Business interests and profit motivate the visitors, but these interests hardly make them more clearsighted. They are just as overawed as the progressive intellectuals of the Seventies and believe China cannot be judged by the same yardstick as its Asian neighbors such as Korea and Japan. Western delegations visiting the country move as if in a trance, a feeling heightened by their Communist hosts, past masters, like the emperors and Mao, in the art of stage management. When it comes to China, the mindlessness of Westerners is truly astounding. The country is no more "exotic" than Africa or India; in fact, over the last twenty years, it is even less so. Yet our fascination for the slumbering giant remains unabated.

Like their Jesuit and intellectual forerunners, today's businessmen deal only with officialdom, though the current set of leaders lacks the refinement of the earlier mandarins. The Communist Party believes in brutal methods, and this is reflected in their style of governance. The gullibility of the hurried visitor is excusable to a certain extent: China is a vast country, access to several regions is forbidden, information is censored, and people are reluctant to talk or are under surveillance. In their individual capacity, the Chinese may express themselves and criticize the regime, provided that what they say does not spread and take on any form of organization. Other than the Communist Party, no form of political, social, religious, or cultural organization is allowed, the leaders of such groups often languishing in jail without trial. The ordinary Chinese are ruled by an authoritarian party, according to the dictates of the Security and Propaganda Departments. The Propaganda Department functions with ruthless efficiency, making gullible foreigners accept unquestioningly whatever it chooses to put out: economic statistics that cannot be verified, trumped-up elections, blanked-out epidemics, imaginary labor harmony, and the purported absence of any aspiration for democracy.

The voice of the common man in China

What does the 95 percent of the Chinese population that does not belong to the Communist Party think? We are talking about more than a billion people, poor peasants and free spirits. In a totalitarian country, it is not easy to measure public discontent with the Communist establishment. But it is possible to meet men and women who have the courage to express their desire for freedom. This is what I did, and the task, though difficult, was not insurmountable. Others—journalists, sociologists, economists—are conducting the same inquiry and coming to the same conclusion: the Chinese people do not like the Communist Party, and the vast majority wish for a less corrupt, more equitable regime. An infinitesimal number of people have benefited from economic development; for most Chinese, the feeling of deep injustice is far greater than the hope for a better tomorrow.

From January 2005 to January 2006, the Year of the Rooster according to the Chinese calendar, and on other trips in 2006 and 2007, I listened to these free-spirited Chinese; it was the least I could do. Though I was in no danger, the people who spoke to me did so at great personal risk. These men and women who cherish freedom and who occupy the center stage of my inquiry were perplexed by the collusion of Western governments with the Communist Party. They wondered how we could have forgotten the Tiananmen massacre so quickly. They wondered if we knew that the authorities had not even bothered to return the bodies of the victims to their families—and that whenever the Party felt threatened, it would not hesitate to call in the army and employ the same brutality. They wondered whether we had heard of the peasant revolts in the countryside and worker unrest in the factories in protest against the Party. The questions kept pouring in. Did we not know that religion was put down and thousands of priests, pastors, and followers of various sects were interned in so-called labor reeducation centers without any trial? Did we not care about the fate of the hundreds of thousands of AIDS victims left to fend for themselves or of the millions of young peasant girls forced into prostitution for—among other reasons—gratifying foreign investors? Did the massive migratory flow—millions of Chinese from the most educated to the humblest—to other countries convey nothing? Did we not know that corrupt Party officials had embezzled most of the foreign investment, leaving workers in foreign companies with a pittance for a salary? Were we unaware of the extent to which Party cadres were fleecing foreign investors and Chinese workers? Had we no inkling about the billions stashed away overseas where families of officials had already fled in anticipation of a coup?

We simply cannot afford to ignore these questions on the pretext that these are China's internal affairs. The fate of the country hangs to a large extent on decisions made in the West. Should foreign investment and imports begin to peter out, the Chinese economy would come to a grinding halt. Sixty percent of Chinese exports are carried out by foreign companies, and the Communist Party's survival depends on its ability to maintain a favored relationship with Western decision makers. It is precisely for this reason that the Propaganda Department assiduously woos Western public opinion and tries to buy it off.

Is China a country to be feared?

Western realpolitik with respect to China is clearly immoral; what is debatable is whether the West stands to gain by it. Chinese goods flooding Western markets are a matter of concern but can hardly be considered a serious threat. In any international division of labor, cheap imports may lead to a loss of jobs, but they also raise standards of living and compel firms to become more innovative. The challenge of cheap imports is by no means insurmountable.

The real danger of this cozy relationship with the Communist Party lies elsewhere: we are allowing a totalitarian state to build an arsenal, fraught with consequences for China's neighbors, Asia, and the rest of the world. Nobody is threatening China, so why does the Party put such store by military might? What is the purpose of maintaining 700 fighter jets and nuclear weapons capable of striking not just Taiwan but also Japan, Korea, and the United States? And more immediately, what is the purpose of the hundreds of medium-range missiles targeting the people of Taiwan from the Fujian and Jiangxi mountains? The Party's intentions are abundantly clear. It is equally clear that the real threat, both to the Chinese people and to the rest of the world, is the Party. Like citizens everywhere, the ordinary Chinese only want peace and a secure future for their children.

The West has an alternative, and that is to support the Chinese democrats. On the one hand, the Communist Party, dependent as it is on foreign investors, is especially vulnerable to outside pressure in the run-up to the Olympic Games to be held in Beijing in 2008. The Party is pinning all its hopes on these games: if they go off successfully, it will be a consecration of the Party. On the other hand, there is the constant fear of some untoward incident (a revolt, epidemic, or other event) bringing it into disrepute. Two precedents underscore the importance of the 2008 Games: the Berlin Olympics of 1936 that consecrated Nazi ideology; and the Seoul Olympics in 1988 that opened Korea to the rest of the world, heralding the country's democratization. What will Beijing 2008 be: Berlin or Seoul? The answer depends on the approach of the West, on whether it remains in awe of Chinese might or whether it shares with the Chinese the values of freedom and liberty.

The time is thus ripe to put pressure on the Communist Party to stop jailing democrats and religious leaders, to let political exiles return, to give teeth to the human rights of which the constitution speaks, to allow other political parties to emerge, and to free information from the control of the Propaganda Department. Hu Ping, a

Chinese democrat exiled in the United States, says: "We are not asking the Party to do anything, we are asking it to do nothing." If the Communist leaders are so sure of their popularity, let them prove it in a free and fair election. The West should press for universal suffrage, as it did in the case of South Africa at the time of apartheid. The principle of "one man, one vote" would not do China any harm. Stripped of its mystique, China would then become a country like any other.

Do the Chinese really want freedom?

Were the Chinese free to express themselves, they would certainly ask for freedom. They are no different from any other people in their hatred of tyranny, so why should they want to remain oppressed by the Communist Party? We in the West, blinded by our economic and political prejudices, are happy to go along with the Communist propaganda that democracy in China is an aberration, inconceivable at present and, in any case, contrary to the Chinese ethos. The Chinese are as much citizens of our times as they are of their country; they know what democracy is. Having suffered for so long the oppression of the Communist Party, they are just waiting for it to collapse.

Are the people not grateful to the Party for loosening somewhat its grip on society? It is true that with the restoration of the right to live in a family, choose their lifestyle, and, for a small minority, acquire wealth, they are less subjugated. But they are still held on a tight leash by the Party and continue to bear the brunt of its whims and factional quarrels at all levels—in the neighborhood or the village or the factory, everyone is at the mercy of the local chieftain. If the Chinese could, they would consign these apparatchiks to the dustbins of history. Some actually dare to say so openly, displaying great courage.

In the West, we call these democrats dissidents. The term is reductionist: these "dissidents" are not marginal but speak for the entire Chinese nation. Ever since China has been under the sway of the Communist Party, these extraordinary men and women have worked tirelessly from one generation to the next to spread the message of democracy. The Party may use its coffers to stifle their voices; the purpose of this inquiry is to listen to what they have to say. I would go as far as to state that they are the pride of China, perhaps its future.

A normal China is what the Chinese democrats are asking for. Let us pay heed to what they are saying, so that what follows is not, or so I hope, yet another book on China. It is meaningless to write about China in general, just as it serves no purpose to write about the West in general. Prophesying about China is equally futile, inhabited as it is by an unpredictable multitude of peoples whose situation is becoming increasingly volatile by the day. My aim was to listen, not to all the Chinese but to a few exceptional Chinese, who, I believe, are representative of the present debate between the authoritarian power structure and its opponents; they are men and women of sterling character, convinced of the righteousness of their cause. The present work is not intended as a book on China but as a series of encounters with these indomitable Chinese. The least I felt I could do, in the Year of the Rooster and after, was to listen to China's democrats as they waged their valiant struggle against tyranny. It was also a way of not falling prey to the strange fascination that sometimes grips the West in the face of tyrants.

CHAPTER ONE

The Dissenters

O n the first day of the Year of the Rooster, in a fast-food joint located in the Chinese quarters of Washington, Wei Jingsheng was chain-smoking under a "No Smoking" sign. People looked on indulgently as he used the butt of the cigarette he had finished to light the next. They all knew about his eighteen-year ordeal in a Chinese prison. The lady who ran the place and the clients were happy to see him, and rushed to greet him. Wei told me over a bowl of steaming wonton soup, "The rule of law gives me the freedom to break the law." In a democracy, that is, the law is clear and can be broken without running undue risks.

Wei currently lives in exile in the United States. He is a staunch advocate of democracy despite its flaws and imperfections. He wants democracy for China because he has no illusions about it being perfect; for him, democracy is not a substitute for Marxism but the end of ideology.

The story of Wei, the most well-known and unrelenting of the Chinese dissidents, began on December 5, 1978. That day he pasted a handwritten poster "in small letters" titled "The Fifth Modernization" on a wall in Beijing. Deng Xiaoping, the new Party chief, had asked people to put up posters on that particular wall in Xidan, an outlying locality of Beijing, in order to drum up support for his reforms and get rid of the leftists led by Mao Zedong's widow. Deng favored what in Communist Party parlance is referred to as the four

1

modernizations: agriculture, industry, education, and science. Twenty-nine-year-old Wei, an electrician like Solidarity's Lech Walesa in Poland, thought it fit to propose a fifth modernization, political modernization. Until that fateful day, the only political activity Wei had indulged in was the mandatory Friday afternoon discussion circle of his work unit at the Beijing zoo.

In his private life, though, he had displayed an independent streak, living with a Tibetan girl born to a "counterrevolutionary" family. A marriage in China has to be sanctioned by the work unit. Wei was not granted the necessary permission. He had to choose between abstinence, the only course open to him under socialist law, or cohabitation, which was not legal. It goes without saying that the Party leadership is released from such legalities. The sexual pursuits of Mao Zedong are well-known.

The man who isn't afraid to tell the truth

"People need democracy," wrote Wei. "The demand for democracy is simply asking for the restoration of what belongs to the people. Whoever dares deny them their rights is nothing but a shameless bandit, more despicable than the capitalist who lives off the blood and sweat of the worker." A little later, he wrote: "We need neither God nor emperor, we have no faith in any savior and we want to be masters of our own destiny." Soon after the first poster, he wrote another one: "History shows that there must be a limit to the power conferred on any one individual. Those who ask for the unreserved trust of the people are consumed by unrestrained ambition. We must choose people whom we can trust and, more importantly, make them accountable to ensure that the will of the majority is carried out. We can only trust such representatives as those we elect ourselves and who are accountable to us."

In the West, such statements would appear commonplace, but in Beijing, they created a stir. Every day, crowds gathered in front of the Democracy Wall and someone would read out the text for the benefit of the bystanders; many wept, overcome with emotion. After thirty years of propaganda, Wei had touched a chord and put in words what they all felt deep inside. His words were simple, stripped of all jargon, Marxist or otherwise. What made his posters provocative was that he had signed them. He told me that signing his name was his way of restoring the dignity of the Chinese individual and putting a symbolic end to servitude.

For a few weeks, the Communist Party did not react. Then, as soon as Deng Xiaoping got rid of his rivals, he had the Democracy Wall razed to the ground. Wei was accused of selling state secrets abroad and arrested. All he had done was to give an interview to a British journalist. His public trial was held in front of a carefully chosen audience, but a Chinese journalist managed to smuggle the soundtrack out and it was heard around the world. The journalist—Liu Qing—was sentenced to ten years of hard labor. Xinhua agency photos showed Wei, skinny arms and shaven head, reading a text admonishing his judges. He cited the Chinese constitution, which, in principle, guarantees the independence of the judiciary; the judges looked embarrassed but sentenced him to fifteen years of prison nonetheless.

In a windowless dungeon, on a mean bed in a labor camp, the *laogaï,* or Chinese gulag that French sinologist Jean-Luc Domenach aptly called the "forgotten archipelago," Wei suffered the worst kind of humiliation, unbearable ordeals, and horror of the kind experienced by victims and prisoners of the Stalin and Hitler eras. In the West, people are convinced that nothing could be worse than the Holocaust, but many Chinese intellectuals compare the *laogaï* and massacres of the Cultural Revolution with Auschwitz.

I could not help staring at Wei, looking for the scars of loneliness, torture, and humiliation that were his lot. His teeth fell out because of malnutrition and have been replaced by inexpensive dentures. For the rest, he seems to be in good health, lively and pink like the immortal gods of popular Chinese religion. The years of solitude, the hunger strikes, and hard labor do not seem to have touched his body, but the scars he bears inside have desensitized him. He has lost the capacity to experience pain, to suffer, feel, and love. Except for his struggle, Wei has nothing to live for.

How did he survive? Like Nelson Mandela, by the sheer strength of his conviction. Wei kept telling himself in prison that he was freer than his jailers because he had the courage to say what he thought. "I was happier than them because I lived out my conviction whereas the others just did what they were told." After his incarceration, Wei was rearrested in 1994, and again sent off to the *laogaï,* this time for trying to organize a union. Western human rights organizations demanded Wei's release, for he had become the best-known Chinese dissident; in 1997, he was expelled from China and sent to the United States on health grounds. In this way, neither the Party nor Wei lost face.

At the age of twenty-nine in Communist China, what did Wei know of democracy? "At that time," he explained, "I hadn't read Western philosophers like Montesquieu or John Locke; but I was sufficiently informed to know that democracy was better than communism." Young Wei had been a Red Guard at sixteen. During the course of his travels across the country, he discovered the yawning gap between the glorious discourse of the Revolution and its sordid reality—famine, fear, and the massacres of the Cultural Revolution. He added, "My state of mind then was what the Chinese are experiencing now: they know enough to know that democracy is by far the best system."

Wei Jingsheng's tribulations are now a closed chapter. This at least is the official line in China. The Party wants to forget Wei and others like him and have us believe that his story belongs to a bygone era. So does Wei still represent a threat to the communists? It is hard to say: China in 2006 is no longer the totalitarian nightmare Wei lived through. Even so, the Party is firmly entrenched; it is tyrannical and unwilling to admit its mistakes. Wei's struggle therefore continues to be meaningful. The excesses of the past and the daily violations of human rights cannot be wished away. If China is to have a *normal* future, the struggle must go on.

Wei Jingsheng claims that he can feel the pulse of the people better than any journalist or diplomat in Beijing. They can only see what the Party wants them to see. Wei uses the telephonic and Internet feedback to his *Voice of America* broadcasts to gauge public opinion. He says that people ring him up from all over China because the *Voice of America* is the only credible source of information. Is it really that popular? Whenever I asked people in China, the replies I got were evasive. "They speak excellent Chinese," "The sound quality is good," "I never listen, it's the voice of George Bush" were some of the standard comments. At the Guangzhou Sun Yat-sen University, one professor told me, "All my students listen to it," while another said, "No one listens." Whatever the case may be, the *Voice of America* is recognized. Those who listen in—the politicized minority—know that Wei, the man who did not hesitate to tell off his judges, will not lie to them in exile.

Do the Chinese really want democracy? Would they not be content with an enlightened despot? Wei disagrees. "Democracy," he says, "may be a relatively new idea in China, but so it is in Europe." Moreover, the preference for democracy is not the result of an ideological conversion but of a pragmatic choice, opting for "what works rather than what does not work." Wei, who has never been part of the academic establishment, rejects all theories that the meaning of freedom in Chinese civilization is different. He holds that for too long, Communist leaders have twisted tradition and Confucianism to suit their own ends. The teachings of Confucius can be interpreted any way one wants. They can be used to oppress the people or to guarantee their rights. Wei defends Confucianism: "At the time of the Empire, Confucianism ensured social peace by respecting the independence of families and clans; the emperor did not interfere in the private life of the Chinese. Maoists replaced Confucianism with constant police surveillance, leaving the people with no choice but to become robots in the service of the Party." Confucius hijacked by Wei the democrat? Master Kong, so dear to Voltaire, seems to be the quintessential man for all seasons.

I think of Nelson Mandela, Václav Havel, and all those who came to power after years of incarceration. In 1911, Sun Yat-sen returned from his exile in London to become president of the first Republic of China. Is Wei a likely candidate for president in China? "Impossible," he exclaims. "I have no desire to perpetuate central rule in China." Countering the argument of tyrants, who maintain that centralized power is the only form of governance possible in order to justify their existence, Wei believes that any democratic renewal must recognize the diversity of the Chinese. "China," he says, "is more diverse than the United States, which has a common language, but less so than the European Union." The institutions of democratic China could thus incorporate some elements of the American model and some of the European Union. Such an arrangement could easily accommodate Hong Kong, Taiwan, Tibet, Xinjiang, and Inner Mongolia—inconceivable in a centralized China.

Is such a scenario unlikely? How would the transition from a dictatorship to a democratic federation take place? Wei is waiting for the differences between the pragmatists and dogmatists in the Communist Party to erupt. This, he feels, is bound to happen. With the inevitable economic debacle and rising unemployment, change must come. A day will arrive, he concludes, when the police and the army will get tired of being despised. He is also counting on the United States, "the only democratizing force in the world." For the moment, however, the American government has abandoned the cause of Chinese dissidents. Wei, who met President Clinton after his release, no longer enjoys official support. Even the innumerable American foundations for freedom have succumbed to Communist Party pressure. After discarding Wei, the Ford Foundation was allowed to finance local elections in the villages of China. The extent to which the West stands in awe of a powerful China is nothing short of madness.

Wei Jingsheng says that the fear of losing the vast Chinese market is making people cowards. He feels, however, that this situation will not last for long. "Sooner or later, the Americans will realize that the Communist Party has been lying to them about everything, be it intellectual property, human rights, Taiwan, or its support to North Korea." Is a conflict between the United States and China inevitable? Wei replies that a showdown is inevitable with the Communist Party but not with the Chinese people. He reminds us that so far, twenty-six dynasties have ruled over China. Now the time for democracy has come. China will be a nation like any other, its people at last able to lead the normal life to which they aspire. Will the Chinese forgive those who succumbed to the pressure and the lures of the Communist Party, believing them to be one and the same? Yes, provided that Wei Jingsheng, or someone like him, becomes president.

The Tiananmen survivor

In Taipei, I mentioned my meeting with Wei Jingsheng to Wuer Kaixi. He immediately distanced himself from Wei's approach. He said, "Wei is a symbol I respect but he never took the plunge. I was at the forefront of the protesting crowd at Tiananmen Square; I led the Tiananmen Revolution; I was its commander." Wuer Kaixi likes being called the commander, a title given to him by Western journalists present in Beijing at the time, and he uses it often when referring to himself.

In the portly gentleman before me, I found it hard to recognize the slender young boy who, in May 1989, led half a million students, heckled the Chinese prime minister, talked with journalists from all over the world, started a hunger strike, and unwittingly led his troops to disaster.

At present, Wuer Kaixi lives peacefully with his wife and children in Taiwan. But when he speaks, there are still sparks of the old fire that galvanized the crowds and shook the establishment in China. The Chinese army had to be called in to silence him. His black eyes are as intense as ever, and in his gaze are shades of Genghis Khan. Chinese by culture, Wuer Kaixi is not a Han but an Uigur, born to a Muslim family from Xinjiang. Wuer Kaixi is the Chinese transcription of the Turkish name Uerkesh Daolet. His story is startlingly similar to that of another famous revolutionary, Daniel Cohn-Bendit, the leader of the May 1968 uprising in Paris.

Both men were outsiders—one a German Jew, the other an Asian Turk. They stood out in the crowd; perhaps this aloofness explained their charisma and large following. Both were powerful orators, displaying the same irreverence for the establishment, refusing to accept its legitimacy or might. They could be dispassionate precisely because they were outsiders. Unlike their fellow citizens, neither Cohn-Bendit nor Wuer Kaixi stood in awe of the state. No doubt, it was easier for Wuer than for a Chinese of old stock not to submit to authority in the name of an eternal China. He holds that in the struggle for democracy, the notion of "Chineseness" has to be dispensed with; from time immemorial, tyrants, unable to tolerate dissent in any form, have conjured "a certain idea of China" to quell protest. The communists were no different and used the same strategy to put down democrats.

The communists said that the temerity to ask for freedom was shameful, since it went against the grain of the Chinese ethos. When Wuer Kaixi was "commanding" his troops at Tiananmen Square, Alain Peyrefitte shared the communists' view and thought it appropriate to tell his French readers that Kaixi "was not Chinese." The idea of the Chinese ethos was dear to Peyrefitte; as he wrote his piece he must have been thinking of that other foreigner, Cohn-Bendit, who had crossed swords with him when he was minister of education. Had Wuer Kaixi been a respecter of "Chineseness," he would have submitted his complaint to the "emperor." If this elicited no response and heightened his indignation, he would have committed suicide. Such interpretations, however, are not borne out by Chinese history. Confucius is dead and gone, and the last 2,500 years have been marked by numerous instances of popular revolt.

Both Cohn-Bendit and Wuer Kaixi took the escape route of exile, but here the similarity ends. The former embarked on a conventional political career, the latter, cramped and homesick in Taiwan, clings on to his dreams of revolution and a greater China. "A revolution would be ideal," he says. He imagines himself returning under cover to Beijing to stage a grand reentry at Tiananmen Square under the nose of the police. Then the dream fades away in the tropical heat of Taipei. In anticipation of the great evening, Wuer Kaixi cherishes the memory of Tiananmen. In defense of his action, he says that the Beijing government recognized its political, thus legal, character. His students were not aiming to overthrow the Communist Party; they were only asking it to enter into a dialogue with them and respect the freedom of expression granted in the constitution. Perhaps the students were naïve. It was the time of velvet revolutions in Eastern Europe and perestroika in the Soviet Union. General Secretary Zhao Ziyang embodied the liberal school in the Party. The students hoped for a Chinese Gorbachev, not a coup d'état. Obviously, they had misread the character of the Chinese Party, which was far more totalitarian than its Soviet counterpart.

Wuer Kaixi knows that the Party is not going to change, but the least the Chinese democrats can do is to acknowledge the positive nature of Tiananmen. But democrats both in China and in exile have remained divided on the issue. Did the 1989 revolt hasten or slow China's march toward freedom? This question exercises the exiles, putting them at loggerheads with one another.

Kaixi is clear in his mind. Since Tiananmen, "the Chinese have gained in self-respect, both in the way they view themselves and in the way the world views them." That Beijing spring was also a reminder that whenever the Chinese gathered it was in support of political freedom: from the first student demonstration at Tiananmen Square of May 4, 1919, to April 1989, the demand for democracy is what brought the demonstrators out on the streets. The Communist Party has never been able to get public support. When its members convene at the People's Palace, next to Tiananmen Square, tens of thousands of policemen and soldiers stand guard outside. Does the Party fear the people? In March 2005, 65,000 policemen were deployed at the annual meeting of the National People's Congress, the puppet parliament of the regime.

How many people were killed at Tiananmen Square on June 4, 1989? The Chinese government maintains that not a single death took place on the square; it was only later that the army gunned down 3,000 demonstrators trying to flee on the nearby streets. Nineteen years later, there is complete silence on the subject: speaking about Tiananmen or carrying out any research on it is strictly forbidden. An organization of the parents of the Beijing victims, headed by Madam Ding Zilin, is being hounded by the police for trying to draw up a list of the missing. All reference to Tiananmen is banned even in literary works. At the same time, the Cultural Revolution is discussed in literature and cinema, though not in school textbooks. In Beijing, I asked the novelist Mo Yan, known both in the West and in China for *Red Sorghum* and the film based on it, when he would deal with the 1989 massacre. "Not before fifteen years," he whispered, embarrassed by my question.

In comparison with the millions of victims of the civil war, the Great Leap Forward, the Cultural Revolution, and the *laogaï*, the Tiananmen carnage appears insignificant. Deng Xiaoping, who gave the order to shoot, was surprised by the Western outrage. Public opinion in Europe and the United States had been far less critical during Mao's time. But that was before television. Captured on camera, Tiananmen will remain inside and outside China as the indelible stamp of the Communist Party. When China becomes a democracy, June 4 will be celebrated as a day of national commemoration. The Party fears this, for every year on this day security is reinforced in Beijing. As June 4 approaches, police cordons in the city center are tightened, mobile phones of democratic intellectuals stop working, SMS and Internet communication gets jammed, and sensitive websites are blocked. Yet despite all its might, the Communist government seems afraid of a handful of dissenters.

Our memory is short-lived

It did not take us long to forget Tiananmen. June 4, 1989, a day on which the Western world was filled with righteous anger at the massacre of students, is not so long ago. On July 14 of that year, the bicentenary of the French Revolution, dissidents who had fled from China led the parade on the Champs-Elysées. The image of Chinese students in Paris leading the parade produced as strong an emotion among the Chinese as the emotion we felt when we saw a boy standing up to a row of tanks lined along the boulevard with nothing more than his schoolbag. Europe and the United States, it appeared, had learned their lesson: there would be no repetition of the previous indifference to fascism, Nazism, Stalinism, and the Khmer Rouge. Western governments decided to take punitive action against the Chinese Communist government and placed an embargo on the sale of arms; this was the least that they could do. In France, only Alain Peyrefitte tried to rationalize the behavior of the Chinese leaders, though he did not support the repression. He said that one injustice was better than disorder and that one massacre was better than a new civil war. Simon Leys, always far more clear-sighted than the rest, anticipated that Western indignation would be short-lived; he had also been the first European to condemn the Cultural Revolution. In June 1989, he had prophesized in an epitaph to the victims that "the heads of state and businessmen would flock back to Beijing to sit again at the banquet of the assassins." Chinese democrats who had chosen to group together in Paris realized that France valued trade more than human rights, so they left for the United States and Taiwan.

Do the dissidents in exile have any influence in China? Yes, but only with people of their own generation, bound by a common history. The younger generations have a hazy picture of what happened. Some democratic activists have chosen to merge with Western society, leading a normal life as teachers (Fang Lizhi, called the "Chinese Sakharov"), CEOs (Chai Ling), and academics (Wang Dan). No one can blame them for doing so. Wuer Kaixi says, "In China, we had no notion of individualism, love, or consumerism; everything was political and for the community. When we came to the West, we discovered all this; we were twenty and we enjoyed it." The Communist leaders were confident that these dissidents would be incapable of finding common ground and constituting in exile a credible alternative to communism. In point of fact, the dissidents are a divided lot, of different generations, with different strategies and ambitions. The Communist Party, active outside China, does its best to maintain these divisions and ensure that the democrats gain no influence. Pressure is put on governments and organizations willing to receive Wei Jingsheng, Wuer Kaixi, and the Dalai Lama: the threat of canceling a business contract or the simple refusal to grant a visa suffices. The French president Jacques Chirac had consistently refused to meet the Dalai Lama and Wei Jingsheng when they visited France. Even so, Jacques Chirac, as the mayor of Paris, had lavished praise on the very same Dalai Lama! The Communist Party also makes sure that the overseas Chinese media do not support the dissidents. In 2004, the Communist Party discreetly bought off the New York Chinese press, influential among the Chinese community in the United States, and changed its political stance. The Party, however, cannot stop people like Wei Jingsheng and Wuer Kaixi from speaking the truth, even as it continues to lie shamelessly. The dissidents whom I met live in exile, not out of choice but out of compulsion. But there are still others who are keeping the struggle alive in China itself.

Feng Lanrui, a veteran of democracy

It was a January morning in Beijing. Some thirty-odd dishes revolved on a central tray. Heaven knows what they contained! The congealed sauces were far from appetizing, and hygiene seemed not to have been a consideration. We dug into common bowls with plastic chopsticks and, like our hosts, slurped noisily, dropping the sauce on a dirty tablecloth that no one had bothered to change. We were in one of the many cheap eating houses that have sprung up in Beijing since the Chinese opted for private enterprise.

I remembered the formal banquets of Mao's time. The few Western travelers were shown every courtesy, to make sure that they went back with wonderful memories. While millions of Chinese starved, foreign delegations—one could only travel to China in a group—enjoyed lavish feasts. Dishes of all kinds—sweet, sour, salted—were served to the accompaniment of the same monotonous speech, faithfully regurgitated by the local apparatchik. "Chinese cuisine and French cuisine," he would begin ingratiatingly, "are the best cuisines in the world." The guests would lap up these trite utterances, translated word for word by the interpreter, repeat them wondrously in French, and hear themselves translated into Chinese, after which it was time to toast. The etiquette was to down one's drink at one go and show the empty glass; failure to do so meant having to drink three glasses. The custom has endured. One was also required to clink glasses with every guest at every table, a feat that taxed one's ingenuity, since one had to think of a new toast each time.

The Chinese, too, would look forward to these visits, for it was the only time that they could eat to their hearts' content, and the French, needless to say, were delighted; mellowed by compliments and delicacies, including bird's-nest soup, they listened beatifically to Chinese propaganda. We were told that French and Chinese cuisines were better than any other in the world and that the superiority of our two civilizations was unquestionable. As the Chinese held us in such high regard, is it any wonder we went into raptures about everything Chinese? During that period, delegations of friends of China, woolly-headed intellectuals, fellow travelers of the Communist Party, and other such easy targets were happy to feast on the culinary and ideological fare offered by the regime, the massacre of millions of Chinese not troubling their pleasure in the least. We should have looked more carefully at the scullery and the chef. Now businessmen and tourists have replaced political onlookers, but the bill of fare, ladled by the minions of the Communist Party, remains unchanged. Our hostess of the day, Madam Feng Lanrui, is, however, quick to dissipate all our illusions. Madam Feng is the very embodiment of the Chinese intellectual's endless march on the road to freedom.

"Democracy," she said, "is a value common to all civilizations, the undivided legacy of mankind as a whole." An innocuous remark in itself, daring only because of the place it was made. That Madam Feng chose to speak loudly and clearly in a public place was astonishing. Does the Communist regime really tolerate people who praise democracy in public? No, it is just that the dictatorship has become more intelligent. The brainwashing of the Maoist era has been discarded and dissenters are tolerated, provided that they do not organize themselves. The Communist Party judged Madam Feng incapable of starting a popular uprising, though hundreds of millions of Chinese share her aspiration for freedom. There was her age also: she was 85.

She started reminiscing. In the Sixties, had she spoken as she did, the Party would not have hesitated to send a couple of Red Guards, boys no more than fifteen or sixteen years old, to torture her and force a confession of heresy out of her. She would have been beaten till she declared her love for the Party; she would have had to confess that she had been against progress, against history, against China, and an American agent in the bargain. Now communists no longer attack old people; the executioners of yesterday have become the businessmen of today. And they want at all costs to bury the past.

Feng said the Chinese had no memory at all; the under-forty generation knew little about the past unless someone decided to pursue the complex search for the truth. The current dictators being the direct descendants of yesterday's dictators, the Party does its best to see that history is not handed down from one generation to the next. Textbooks are silent about the horrors of the Revolution and the spate of calamities that followed, or else the past is idealized: the famines of '64 organized by the Party are forgotten, and the Cultural Revolution reduced to a mere outburst of secondary school pupils. Even in death, Mao continues to rule over China: the president of China, said Feng, ought to be called Mao III or Mao IV. Parents have no desire to tell their children much: the humiliations that they suffered were not the kind that they wished to share with anyone, not even their own children.

This old lady, upright, dignified, and fully alert, who had seen and lived through everything, also remembered everything—but her generation is fading away. Feng had been one of the key figures in the history of Communist China; as early as 1940, she had been by Mao's side when she was only twenty. She said that she had been a "professional revolutionary." Believing in the Revolution, she had obeyed the three Maoist dictates: every intellectual was an instrument of the Party; Mao's personality was sacrosanct; the human condition was the product of the class struggle. The Maoist ideology was a systematic reversal of Confucian philosophy. Confucius said human nature existed, filial piety was a man's foremost duty, and the learned man was obliged to point out to the emperor his error if he acted against morality. Mao Zedong negated human nature, subjugated the educated, made children spy on their parents and couples betray each other. Feng emphasized Mao's negation of Confucianism because she knew that many courtiers of China in the West believed that the Party was the continuation of the Empire and Maoism a new form of Chinese culture; this was putting it on a pedestal and so precluding any criticism. Feng said in truth that the communists had completely devastated Chinese thought and in the process destroyed the country's historical legacy; even today, they were busy wiping out all traces of classical China. The architects of Beijing had pleaded with Mao Zedong to preserve the old city; he had it razed to the ground. He ordered that factory chimneys replace pagodas, and his orders were carried out. Other cities met with the same fate: first ravaged in the name of the Revolution, they were now being wrecked in the name of modernization. Nowhere was the cry of the *Internationale,* "Let us make a blank slate of the past," better heard than in China. The task was all the more simple given that—as even Mao acknowledged—there was not a single well-read revolutionary.

Many years after these events, Feng was still trying to understand why she had believed in the Revolution. She confessed, "The youth believed in it because it was fashionable. . . . The Revolution seemed necessary to rid the country of its bureaucracy, corruption, and foreign colonization." No one had thought of the Japanese way of modernization. Japan concentrated on economic reconstruction while preserving its imperial regime; the Chinese were obsessed by the French and Russian Revolutions. "We were revolutionaries first and Marxists later; when the communists came, we rallied around them because they spoke the language of revolution." Fifty years later, she tried to justify her actions: "Like all Chinese, I, too, was looking for freedom."

Was it really freedom that every Chinese was aspiring for? The West had a different conception of China. Feng was infuriated by the Western indifference toward all those brave Chinese men and women fighting for democracy, many of whom had laid down their lives during their century-old struggle. Wherever the Chinese still had the right to demonstrate, they clamored for only one thing. In Hong Kong, 250,000 people gathered in December 2005, demanding that the Beijing government let them elect their leaders through universal suffrage. As for the supposed preference for enlightened despotism, Feng Lanrui pointed out that the Chinese had known of democratic ideas for over a hundred years. In 1912, Sun Yat-sen's republican government held elections on the basis of universal suffrage; a quarter of China's adult population took part. Women were excluded, as in Europe, but so were opium smokers and Buddhist monks. The republican Kuomintang Party got the majority, and China seemed no different from any Western democracy. The trouble was, Feng said, that the educated class in China delighted in everything new and Western. The Republic did not seem efficient enough to modernize the economy and act as bulwark against the Japanese. So on May 4, 1919, students took to the streets in Beijing, calling for a new revolution in favor of science and democracy. How this laudable objective gave rise to such a totalitarian, unscientific, and undemocratic regime was something everyone tried to explain in his own way.

The idea of cultural continuity finds favor in the West. So Mao was viewed as another chapter of the Empire, the founder of a new dynasty, ostensibly Marxist but actually in continuity with the celestial bureaucracy. To see in these peasants and workers bent on destroying old China the inheritors of the mandarins was really stretching the imagination, to say the least.

Feng provided a more reasonable explanation: the communists took advantage of their superior military organization, and the logistical support provided by the Soviet Union proved decisive. It was not Marxism but the Red Army that triumphed in Beijing in 1949, just as it had won the day in Moscow in 1917. What many described as a vast popular movement was, in point of fact, a coup d'état. That Chinese and Western intellectuals let themselves be taken in tells us more about their romanticism than the nature of the Revolution. Feng finally saw through the charade. In the early Eighties, a period of unparalleled intellectual freedom, Feng Lanrui published a series of economic works of liberal inspiration that marked her break with communism; they came to be considered as the textbooks of reformism, the nonrevolutionary way to democracy. In the spring of 1989, when the Beijing students began their uprising, she was, like many other liberal intellectuals at the time, skeptical, wary of their zeal for slogans, romantic gestures, and utopian dreams. She thought that they were ill informed about the history of their country and far too similar to the previous generation, even if they said the opposite in their slogans. The tragic end proved Feng Lanrui right: the students had failed to understand the nature of the Party.

If revolution was not the way, then how was democracy to arrive? "From the top," said Feng. Like most Chinese intellectuals, she was looking for subtle variations in the discourse of the Politburo, hoping for a Gorbachev or a Yeltsin to destroy the system from within. Some would call this attitude excessively cautious; others would see it as growing out of the overriding Chinese fear of another civil war.

People unfamiliar with the repression in China in the time of Mao Zedong and his immediate successors will not be able to appreciate the extraordinary nature of my conversation with Feng Lanrui in Beijing. Never before in contemporary history had an entire nation been put under constant surveillance: the Chinese not only had to speak alike; they had to think alike. Other authoritarian regimes allowed their subjects some private space provided that they kept quiet. Maoism practiced thought control: people had to "think correctly" in all earnestness. Every aspect of private life was regulated by the Party: the bedroom, marriage, and sexual practices. In the Seventies, any form of feeling was anesthetized; like parrots, the Chinese had to repeat the slogan of the day. One of Mao's quotations always prefaced any "personal conversation." A few second-rate books were the only reading material allowed, and eight revolutionary operas provided the sole entertainment. Placed all over—in city squares, railway stations, trains, offices, and factories—loudspeakers blared out martial music from dawn to dusk, making it physically impossible for people to speak, listen, or think. The basic distinction between Maoism and Stalinism was this: the Soviet leaders knew that they were lying, the people knew that communism was a sham, and though the lie was passed off as truth, few were taken in. Maoist leaders went further. It was not enough mechanically to regurgitate the official line. The brainwashing had to be so thorough that the Chinese internalized the lie, believing it to be the truth. The Maoist effort had more in common with the Catholic Inquisition than with atheist Stalinism. None of this has been spoken about in China because no attempt has been made to de-Maoize the country. At the behest of Deng Xiaoping in 1983, the Central Committee of the Party decided once and for all that Mao Zedong was 70 percent right and 30 percent wrong. Mao had used the same formula to describe Stalin. Why 70 percent right? There are any number of reasons for the 30 percent wrong: the mass elimination of landowners at the time of the liberation, the 20 million deaths during the Great Leap Forward from 1959 to 1962, the 30 million dead on account of the Cultural Revolution between 1966 and 1976 ... the 30 percent wrong was enough to charge Mao with crimes against humanity.

That Feng survived and the Chinese retained their sanity was testimony to the people's resistance to totalitarian savagery. Mao could no more create a *homo sinicus* than Stalin a *homo sovieticus*. Shorn of slogans and martial music, the pretense disintegrated; in its place, one found a vibrant, living people. My meeting with Madam Feng Lanrui in January 2005 was a turning point; it convinced me that I had to spend the Year of the Rooster in China, listening to its democrats; this was the least I could do.

The new generation: between Jesus and Tocqueville

Yu Jie is thirty; he could well be Feng's grandson. In Beijing, he has taken over her struggle. He refuses exile. He says, "It is here that the Party's cruel dictatorship is crushing the people, it is here that it has to be fought."

His generation, the third in the movement of democratic resistance since the 1949 Revolution, runs less of a risk than the previous one. Yu Jie has so far not suffered anything worse than interrogation in a police station, a relatively mild form of intimidation. With his writer's pince-nez and baby face, the authorities don't take him seriously: he is a lone intellectual with no organization. His only weapon is his pen, his army his readers: students, young graduates, girls and boys of his own age. This has spared him the Party's wrath: the scrupulousness of a writer poses no threat; an organization does. But the Party disapproves of too large a readership. Yu Jie's publishers are under constant pressure to reject his manuscripts or to limit the number of copies; sometimes, they are obliged to close shop.

Yu Jie is neither a fighter like Wei Jingsheng nor a commander like Wuer Kaixi. His writing, full of sensitivity, appeals to the soul of China, the subject of his books. He invites us to read again the literary works of the twentieth century so that we can revive the humanity and individuality of authors and their characters. The contrast will bring out the extent to which the Communist Party has dehumanized a society—a society that has enslaved its people, denying them their very identity and truth. Yu Jie discovered Alexis de Tocqueville, well-known to "rightist"—in other words, non-Marxist—intellectuals, and translated him into Chinese. Tocqueville's analysis of the French Revolution seemed to apply to the history of China. Yu Jie wrote an essay on this parallel.

In *The Old Regime and the French Revolution*, Tocqueville showed how the French Revolution was the outcome of the *ancien régime*'s inability to reform itself. Yu Jie says the same holds true for China. First in 1898, when the Empress Dowager rejected the rule of law that her reformist ministers were pressing for: that may well have preserved the Chinese empire by transforming it into a constitutional monarchy, as in Japan. Then in 1989, when Deng Xiaoping rejected the democratic reforms proposed by the students. In the long run, this second rejection could prove to be the Communist regime's undoing. Tocqueville's observation on France holds true for China as well: revolutions destroy the elite. The educated class, once the nobility of China, could not survive the 1949 Revolution, and it has never managed to reconstitute itself. There are scholars, but they are maintained by the Party; the institutions employing them severely curtail their freedom to think, express themselves, or even come up with the new ideas that China so badly needs. To ensure their submission, the government pays them generously, a reversal of the situation that prevailed before Tiananmen. Until 1989, economic hardship led academics to support the idea of revolt. Given a relative degree of material comfort, they tend to become conservative, favoring, at most, slow change.

Yu Jie does not lead the youth of China; he represents it. Political struggle holds no appeal for him; taking on the Party machinery is suicidal. Wei Jingsheng's time is over. The old combatant belonged to the bygone era of the Cultural Revolution, when good and evil were clearly defined and choices easy to make. China has changed, and so has the Communist Party, no less cruel but now more subtle. The democratic revolution that Feng and Wei had hoped for will not take place. The police and army successfully nip in the bud any protest movement. The urban population knows little of the struggles raging in factories and villages. Cities are cut off from the countryside; information is tightly controlled. Local uprisings remain restricted and will never amount to a revolution. Even the Internet is censored. So is China doomed to remain permanently under the control of the Communist Party? No: change will come, and human rights will triumph but not through a revolution or a change of heart of the Party. "The Party will never change. It will do everything possible to cling to power, including calling out the army; change will come through moral redemption."

In this Year of the Rooster, conversations turn quickly to morality, religion, and the spiritual void and how to fill it. The Chinese, true, have always been religious (mystical, superstitious, as you like); they have never lived far from temples or gods. The Communist Party destroyed the altars and exterminated religious orders, but Mao Zedong was quick to provide the people with another altar at which to worship: that of his divinized persona. So instead of the sacred texts, the Chinese were given the *Little Red Book*, which they had to repeat the way Daoists repeated their prayers and the Buddhists their mantras. The regime also supplied substitute saints, the martyrs of the Revolution celebrated by the clergy of the apparatchiks. Under Mao, every single Chinese had to confess his or her sins against the regime. Maoist monotheism, the cause of so much suffering, held the people in a vise-like grip. When Mao died, veneration of him stopped, and Marxism, existent only because Mao personified it, faded away. The Chinese were left without religion or ideology; the only agenda they had was the "get rich" program of Deng Xiaoping. But consumerism cannot give meaning to life, and only a minority currently reap its material benefits. Will the Chinese return to their traditional faiths?

Yu Jie rules out the old religions. Corrupted by centuries of political power, Daoism and Buddhism are not in a position to lay down a new moral order. As practiced by the Chinese, both these religions are more instrumental than spiritual, more immanent than transcendent: people invoke Buddha or the Immortal to get concrete benefits, not to renew mankind. Fresh inspiration will come from Christianity, whose universalism is obvious. The Catholic Church, though, is a bureaucracy, with a hierarchy similar in a way to that of the Communist Party. Because of its bureaucratic nature, the Roman Catholic Church has met with little success in China—no more than 10 million believers after a century of missionaries. Yu Jie thinks that evangelical Protestantism is the most suitable form of Christianity for China: no pastor, only reading the Bible and direct communion with God.

How was Yu Jie converted? His wife, a beautiful young woman, answers in his place: "God chose me." She converted five years ago at the University of Beijing. The numerous Protestants and English teachers from the United States discreetly help in this campus evangelization. The yearning for morality that Yu Jie talks about is perhaps one reason for the movement's popularity. Another is that intellectuals are taking a close look at why China lags behind other nations. What explains the superiority of the West? Science and democracy, said the students in May 1989, just as they did on May 4, 1919. But was not Christianity the bedrock of Western civilization? Many Chinese think so, making them lean toward this form of

Christianity. Is this similar to the traditional quest for elixirs to prolong life? Is Christ an elixir—or a revelation? So closely interlinked are these elements that no one—neither we nor the new faithful—can make a clear distinction between them.

Two years after Yu Jie's wife was chosen, Christ elected him. The young couple—both barely thirty—belong to Bible prayer and study groups. People gather twice a week in an apartment rented for the purpose. Is it a secret temple? Sometimes a pastor comes and helps out inconspicuously. He belongs to Wenzhou, the Chinese Jerusalem and a high spot in the history of evangelical missions. Who congregates? There are students, academics, and professionals. Is evangelical Protestantism the religion of the new elite, confined to posh localities? The movement is, in fact, widespread: some 40 million home evangelists congregate in these *house churches,* unfettered by any control. In addition, there are the 20 million "official" Protestants of the patriotic communities recognized by the Party. Yu Jie says that these 60 million Protestants and 10 million Catholics are enough to form the critical mass that will tilt the balance in favor of human rights. We need to remember that Christians played a major role in the democratization of Asia: Sun Yat-sen and Kim Dae Jung, the first democratic president of South Korea, were Catholics; democratic leaders are often Protestant in Taiwan and Catholic in Hong Kong. Yu Jie dreams of a new Martin Luther King emerging from the evangelization of China, showing a radically new way for his countrymen, far removed from ordinary Chinese practices, riots, and revolutions.

This evangelical religion is spreading across the world, gaining more adepts than any other religion. Though it originated in the United States, its Americanness is not so certain. Chinese rebels accept being attracted to American civilization; becoming evangelists gives them the feeling of participating in the American dream of an individualistic and democratic society. The personalized nature of this religion, in which each individual becomes his own temple, adds greatly to its appeal. Beyond Party control, the personal temple gives one the strength to confront it. Yu Jie says, "Without Christ, I could never have withstood the ten to fifteen hours of grilling I am often subjected to." The police keep interrogating him to divert him from his mission.

But with Christ by his side, he lives without fear "in the light of the truth," pushing back constantly the limits of censorship. In August of the Year of the Rooster, as the government celebrated the 1945 victory of the Communist Party over Japanese fascism, Yu Jie published in Hong Kong a text recalling that Japanese fascists had killed far fewer Chinese than had Mao Zedong. "As long as the body of that assassin lies in the center of Beijing, it is unthinkable that the civilized Olympic Games will be held there."

Look at Yu Jie, says the Party. He can say what he wants. What more proof do you need of freedom of speech in China? But Yu Jie cannot get his work published in China because of censorship. Had it not been for his fame, especially in the United States, he would be behind bars. Until the Olympic Games in 2008, this young writer will be able to express his views in relative safety, for the Party fears that, if they arrest him, American human rights organizations will boycott the games.

The Party is scared of mice

The length to which the Party goes to keep a watch on a few isolated democrats is amazing. These people have no army, no organization; their only links with the outside world are their computers. The mighty Chinese government is so afraid of what Miss Liu Di thinks and writes that she wound up in jail for a year, once more without trial.

Liu Di is a student in Beijing; she is in her twenties. Petite and nearsighted, she has taken on the cyber *nom de plume* of "stainless steel mouse." She translates into Chinese the texts of dissident writers from the former Communist Europe, including those of Václav Havel and the Polish journalist Adam Michnik, and posts them on a website called "Liberty and Democracy." The Security Department had deemed her dangerously subversive. Her site is blocked, inaccessible to Internet users. Freed after protests by human rights lawyers, she remains under surveillance. I had to make several attempts to meet her. The police tap her telephone, and each time we set an appointment, they stopped her from leaving the house. Those classified as "enemies of China" are kept under house arrest at the discretion of the Security Department. Some cyber-dissidents are less fortunate: in 2003, He Depu was sentenced to eight years of prison for suggesting the creation of a democratic party on his website.

Bewildered by all the attention the Party was giving her, Liu Di concluded that it was not as invincible as it appeared and had no backbone: "Sometimes, even high-ups are scared of mice."

I got the feeling that this stainless steel mouse was unaware of the risk she was running. What the Party really dreads is a mouse turning into a Václav Havel. The Soviet experience panicked the Party and had it scrambling to study the circumstances that led to the collapse of communism in the Soviet Union, Eastern Europe, and more recently, Ukraine and Georgia. In each case, they found a single fatal error that the Party had to avoid at all costs.

In the Soviet Union, the error was introducing political reforms before economic reforms. There had been nothing fundamentally wrong with the country, in this view; it was only Gorbachev's inept handling of the situation, his conceding the establishment of political pluralism, that proved ruinous. This convenient analysis sidestepped the real reasons for the Soviet Union's disintegration.

As for Poland, had the Communist Party banned unions and muzzled the Catholic Church, the country would have remained communist. This is the uniform opinion of the Chinese press and what is told to the cadres in the Party schools, which train those cadres to think identically. So the Communist Party keeps a close watch on religions, especially the Catholics who obey an external authority, and clamps down on unions to prevent a Chinese Solidarity from emerging.

In the Czech Republic, the Party had been foolish enough to let liberal intellectuals spout their pernicious philosophy unchecked. The Chinese Communist Party knew better.

Georgia is the latest victim to fall to democracy.

The Party dispatched a few experts from the Beijing Academy of Social Sciences, who concluded that nongovernmental organizations, some supported by American foundations, were the real culprits.

This was the view of the Communist Party in the Year of the Rooster. Consequently, all forms of association and the merest outline of civil society come under scrutiny. NGOs, even environmental ones or those fighting against AIDS, were banned. The paranoia extends to preventing Beijing and Shanghai apartment block co-owners from holding their assemblies. This could lead to associative autonomy, the Party believed; it must be controlled by the Party or else eliminated.

Obviously, such a superficial analysis of the downfall of communism in Europe fails to take into account local complexities. It avoids all discussion on the nature of totalitarian regimes—another taboo subject in China. By ascribing the failure of communism to mere ineptness, the Party deludes itself into thinking that it will last forever. Instead of devising strategies to stop the rot, it chases mice. Mice may be unable to overthrow the Party. But Liu Di and He Depu clearly show where the future lies.

CHAPTER TWO

Wild Grass

Until the age of sixty-five, Gao Yaojie worked as a doctor at the hospital in Zhengzhou, the capital of Henan. Hers was a well-ordered existence. Then, one day in 1994, her life overturned completely when two peasant women from the Shangcai district came to her clinic. Gao was surprised to see them. Henan is one of the poorest provinces in China, and peasants from the region hardly ever consult a doctor. They don't have the means to do so; there is no hospital, no clinic, not even a doctor in the countryside. And the Zhengzhou hospital where Dr. Gao headed the gynecology department meant a 200-mile journey for both women.

Ten years later, she still remembers vividly every detail of that visit; it changed her life in ways she could never have imagined. She found her life's mission, one that continues to guide her and will do so until the end of her days: she works single-mindedly to save China from an AIDS epidemic, hoping that it is not already too late. Despite her age, a weak heart, and frail legs, her energy is boundless. So deep is her commitment that she has written many books and posted innumerable articles on the web about unfortunate AIDS victims left to die in the villages of Henan. For her efforts, Gao has incurred the wrath of the Party and become what in political parlance is called "wild grass."

"Weed out the wild grass!" Mao Zedong issued this directive to Communist Party workers in 1959 after a brief moment of intellectual and artistic freedom. "Let a hundred flowers bloom," Mao had said. They did—and a petrified Mao slammed the lid on them. In fact, the "hundred flowers" period turned out to be a deadly ploy to hound out intellectuals and artists who had been most vocal in criticizing the regime. Mao decreed that 10 percent of them had to be "weeded out" of society; they were to be sent to labor camps or executed. Terms such as "bad elements" and "purging society," other legacies of the Cultural Revolution, are still used today. "Bad elements" and "wild grass" are counterrevolutionaries who cannot be reformed. When the Party wants to send out a strong message, it eliminates them; when it wishes to appear more moderate, as in the Year of Rooster, it isolates them. They are put under house arrest, frequently taken into custody or imprisoned without trial so that they do not proliferate and contaminate the healthy body of society. The problem is that you can never quite get rid of wild grass; it grows back as soon as it is weeded out.

Gao against the "blood heads"

The two Shangcai peasant women had made up their minds to go to a hospital only because their fever was unlike anything experienced in the villages of Henan. Hepatitis, dysentery, and tuberculosis were common, but this kind of fever and extreme fatigue did not correspond to any of the known pathologies. Dr. Gao was quick to make her diagnosis: both women had AIDS. Dr. Gao was hard put to understand it. Of course, she had heard of AIDS, but this was the first time she had actually seen a case, and she found it difficult to believe that the disease could exist in Henan.

In the early Eighties, when AIDS was first detected in the United States and later in Europe, the Chinese Ministry of Health declared it proof of capitalist dissoluteness. China, said the Ministry, was immune to such a disease. When some cases were detected in China, they were quickly put down to drug addiction (especially in Yunnan, where heroin is injected frequently) and homosexuality (in the large cosmopolitan cities like Shanghai and Beijing). Gao was a puritan and the wife of a Party dignitary; so she had accepted the official version unquestioningly. As they never stop saying in China, AIDS is "a dirty disease."

The case of the two peasant women was perplexing. On examining them, Gao noticed that needle pricks covered their arms. They said that they had been selling their blood regularly, twice a week on average, for the last ten years. This was their main source of income, as was the case in all the other villages of the Shangcai district. Gao began to piece together their story. She happened to chance upon one of the many scams going on in China. Hundreds of thousands of people had been contaminated in selling their blood. Gao undertook to find out how the epidemic began and how it spread. What she learned made her fear that AIDS would affect the entire country by 2005.

Gao immediately alerted the health authorities in Henan. She was told to keep her mouth shut: in 1994, AIDS was a state secret. The handful of doctors who had stumbled on it and the rare journalists who had dared to talk of it were safely behind bars. Gao found herself under police surveillance; she still is. Party cadres told her that if the presence of AIDS was confirmed, Henan would lose face. Henan was not the only province affected; there were others, too, so why should Henan be the first to admit it? If the fact became public, no one would buy Henan's agricultural produce, no Guangzhou factory would recruit its inhabitants, and none of its children would be able to join the army. What the cadres failed to tell Gao was that from the early Eighties on, the blood trade had been a lucrative business. The "blood heads" (the press uses the term "serpent heads" to refer to the organizers of the immigrant worker trade) more often than not had links with Party bosses in Henan and had made their fortune by selling blood. Many have escaped to the United States.

An argument often heard is that the victims were in it for the money, too, and they got what was coming to them. But Shangcai is one of the poorest districts in Henan. Selling one's blood became the main source of income for those who couldn't immigrate to the east. What they were paid, one dollar for forty centiliters, was just about enough to subsist in the village and pay the taxes that drain Chinese peasants.

Several victims told me that they used blood money to pay the fines slapped on them by the family-planning department when they had more than two children. Family-planning officials are more rapacious than taxmen. They keep a close watch on expectant mothers and ask them to abort the child even in the sixth month. They confiscate the property of couples if they have a third child. They can be bought over with blood money. Is there anyone who is not corrupt in Henan? The novelist Zhang Yu, author of a famous thriller series set in Zhengzhou, created a comical character, a policeman who had no future because he was honest. Not being corrupt, Zhang said, was to be suspect. His hero, a kind of Inspector Maigret of Henan, could spot a thief just by looking at him. Yet instead of being feared, he had become the laughingstock of the area, all because he refused to take bribes.

Gao decided to go to the Shangcai district to locate donors who were infected and find out how blood was taken. It transpired that a single syringe was used to collect the blood, which was centrifuged on the spot with equipment transported in a tractor. Only the plasma was conserved, with the globules and platelets then being injected back into the donors, who also had to pay for the operation. They were told that it would restore their strength and that they could sell their blood twice a week or even more often. Donors had to give back half of what they had earned for this transfusion.

When did the "blood heads" and the authorities in Henan realize they were spreading AIDS? Its mode of transmission was known in the West since 1986; the Chinese leadership must have been apprised of the reality no later than 1990. Yet the blood trade was so lucrative that six years passed before it was finally stopped in 1996. The ban was not the result of any introspection on the Party's part but of a sustained campaign by Gao, who finally found the right lever to manipulate: the international press. The *New York Times* and the French *Libération* investigated the matter; it was their reporting that compelled leaders in Beijing to order a total ban on the sale and purchase of blood.

Apart from the horror, the story is also illustrative of the Party's methods. Any wrongdoing is necessarily foreign; if exposed, it has to be stoutly denied. The bearers of bad tidings must be silenced; wild grass must be weeded out. But under no circumstances should one lose face in front of Westerners, who hold the key to economic development.

Dr. Gao had an uphill task ahead of her: helping the victims to cope. The Party decided that the simplest course was to isolate AIDS-affected villages and let the sick die. The police barred entry to these villages. New maps of Henan appeared without showing the contaminated districts: it was as if entire villages and their inhabitants had vanished! Neither Dr. Gao nor the foreign journalists let themselves be intimidated. AIDS was spreading at an alarming rate all over the country. In 2000, the Chinese government finally admitted the existence of the disease, less out of genuine concern than from the fear of driving away foreign investors. While introducing tritherapy, public information was kept to a bare minimum. On New Year's Day in 2005, the prime minister visited an AIDS-affected village in the Shangcai district and shook hands with several victims in front of television cameras. He said the district was a wonderful example of how to prevent and treat the disease—a "model" Chinese village. The hand of the Propaganda Department was evident: a horror story, slickly presented in a positive, humane light. The media played along, showing cheering images of people restored to health by tritherapy; a spanking-new dispensary set up in Shangcai also flashed frequently on the television screens. Every village in the district received a water tower; peasants now had access to running water even though it was not fit for drinking. Still, running water is a luxury in this poverty-stricken region where, if you don't have AIDS, you have dysentery and hepatitis. Each water tower bears the clearly visible inscription in blood-red pictograms: "With water, the government is bringing you happiness." Sadly, the people in the neighboring areas see these monuments to the glory of the Party as an AIDS border behind which are modern-day leper houses where the healthy dare not venture. The foreign press, of course, moved on to other stories. But Dr. Gao carried on undaunted.

I went with her to the Shangcai district. An asphalted path provided easy access to the first village. Wenlou was a model village with a model dispensary, a model doctor, and model social workers. These "model" workers sent from the capital built themselves palatial houses, easily recognizable by their bizarre Grecian porticos, a sign of Westernization, perhaps. They never stirred from their houses. Even for the educated, those who suffered from AIDS were not normal.

It was here that the former American president Bill Clinton came in the summer of 2005. Supposedly active against AIDS, he was all smiles as cameras clicked away, taking pictures of him with carefully selected AIDS orphans. Clinton's visit was part of the pact between Western leaders and the Communist authorities. The anti-AIDS foundation that he heads was allowed to work in Henan, provided that he did not go to the worst-hit areas. Because of the photo session with Clinton, the foundation could donate medicines to the local health authorities but could not monitor their distribution. The authorities made a mess of things, and many HIV-positive children died in the weeks that followed. The world got to see a smiling Clinton but will never get to see the victims.

Leaving behind the farce of Wenlou, we moved on to Nandawu. The path was no longer fit for vehicles. There was a police checkpoint at the entrance, but foreigners could get past it easily by hiding under a tarpaulin on a tractor trailer. You had to set out at dawn, though: policemen in China are not known to rise early. Once inside the village, there was no danger. The police were too frightened of AIDS to go in. Out of 3,500 inhabitants, 300 had died already, 600 were infected, and probably more, as screening was haphazard and many were too afraid to admit their symptoms. Gao talked to them at length, trying to rid them of their anxiety. Previously, she would come armed with medicines, but Party workers spread the rumor that they were poisoned. The simple, gullible peasants believed them. So now she only distributes clothes. The people lived in abject poverty: the sale of blood was banned, and the neighboring markets refused to buy their vegetables. Migrating to the city was the only way out, but this required getting fake identity papers, for no employer would ever recruit anyone from Henan. In the village, a few pigs and the kitchen garden provided the sole sustenance. Though small, these gardens, enriched with human excreta, yielded a good crop thanks to the skill of Chinese gardeners. In the village center stood a large modern house, protected by high brick walls and a wrought-iron gate. I wondered who owned it—a rich peasant or an official? The villagers laughed. They told me it belonged to a peasant like them who went to Guangzhou and made his fortune begging. He was looking for a bride in the village but couldn't find one because begging was looked down upon. Social hierarchy had to be maintained, epidemic or no epidemic: better to die in poverty than to lose face.

Did the victims receive any compensation? The Beijing government said they did, a claim backed by the media. Every patient supposedly received 120 yuan, or the equivalent of twelve dollars a month. This was a fair amount, but in truth, the villagers only got ten yuan, or one dollar. What happened to the rest? It went into the pockets of Party cadres who are not entitled to any official remuneration. This is common practice in China.

Eighty percent of the families were struck by AIDS; in every house, every hovel, a bedridden invalid lay dying. A Nazi death camp was my first reaction: real faces superimposed on memories of old photographs. Most of the sufferers did not have any medicine to give them relief. As for tritherapy, it requires constant monitoring, unthinkable in the village. A woman was putting a drip on her husband, bedridden for two years and covered with bedsores. She was clumsy and hurt him. What did the bottle contain? She did not know. The label said glucose. Why was she doing this? Because she felt she had to do something: "I saw in the hospital and on television that sick people had to be put on the drip."

Was there no doctor to come to see her husband? Yes, but he was very busy. What about the "village doctor"? Dr. Gao shrugged her shoulders. Just then, he appeared. He was one of the few the disease had spared. He said: "I'm a Christian, and the Bible forbids the sale of blood." Of Christianity he knew little more. How did he become a

Christian? "It's in the family," he replied. His knowledge of medicine was as limited as his knowledge of the Gospel. He had done a three-week course at the Zhengzhou hospital and produced a certificate to prove his medical credentials. He was not a fool, though, and joked about the progress of Chinese medicine. In Mao's time, his training had lasted only three days, after which the rank of barefoot doctor had been conferred on him. From three days to three weeks, China had moved forward. He said his main task was to be with the dying and console the survivors. Soon, only orphans would be left. They wouldn't go to school; no parent would survive to pay for their studies—free in principle—and no school would take them in. Teachers and families who remained unscathed refused to accept these children. A charitable organization run by a young Beijing democrat, Li Dan, tried to open a school for AIDS orphans, but the authorities closed it down. Li Dan said the orphans were a painful reminder of a story that the Party was doing its best to erase from public memory.

Yet AIDS cannot be wished away. It will continue to spread through the blood sold by the villagers. Gao single-handedly carries on her work of detecting new cases outside the officially declared contaminated zone. The Henan government decided that thirty-seven villages were affected and had to be quarantined. It arbitrarily fixed the number of victims at 25,000, whereas the number of people afflicted in the province itself had risen to at least 250,000. The central government acted in much the same way, declaring that China had no more than a million AIDS victims, an absurd figure considering that each year hospitals register an additional million new patients. To compound matters, a large number of villagers migrate from Henan to Beijing and Guangzhou, spreading the virus. Then there are all those who have received Henan blood transfusions. The trade continued unabated several years after its ban and persists even today. In 1998, two years after the ban, Gao identified stocks of contaminated blood collected from Henan. A hospital in Xian had rejected the blood, but another in Shanghai bought it cheap and used it. As the media refused to publish these well-established facts, Gao posted them on the Internet. She did this to save lives, she said; she had no wish to politicize her struggle. But there are others, "wild grass," who are ready to do battle.

The moral generation is taking over

Despite the horror of the blood trade and the countless victims abandoned by society, not much solidarity was generated in Henan. The dogma of individual enrichment has no place for compassion. In Beijing, however, some students, learning of the tragedy, decided to give up their studies and careers to work with Gao and her patients. Two of them, Li Dan and Hu Jia, sacrificed a lot more than their vacations. The two young men became disciples of Dr. Gao, who treats them like her children. She constantly fusses over them and tells them to take care of their health. Henan has a difficult climate and almost no hygiene. The frequent night journeys by train and the police harassment, detention, and threats all take their toll. In 2004, when he was twenty-four, Li Dan dropped out of Beijing University, where he was studying astronomy, to set up an NGO to look after AIDS orphans. Though legal, there were hardly any NGOs in China when he started out. Hardly much older, thirty-one-year-old Hu Jia also heads an association for the sick in the villages. So far, he has not managed to register his association as an NGO. In the eyes of the law, his is a capitalist company liable to taxation, even though it makes no profit. The authorities like dealing with companies; the company is a clear-cut entity, unlike the nebulous NGO—especially one with suspiciously pro-democratic leanings.

Having converted to Buddhism and become a disciple of the Dalai Lama, Hu Jia is deeply compassionate, a quality sadly lacking in China. He had the courage to link the Henan tragedy to the nature of the political regime. Despite his youth, Hu Jia has been a democratic activist for many years. On June 4, 1990, when he was only fifteen, he celebrated alone the first anniversary of the Tiananmen massacre, wearing a black suit borrowed from his father with a white flower in the button hole. On June 4, 2004, the fifteenth anniversary of Tiananmen, he went alone once again to the square, to be met by thousands of policemen and arrested immediately. Hu Jia comes down heavily on the Henan leaders for first encouraging the blood trade and later denying its horrendous consequences, a denial they persist in even today. He wonders why no one has been accused or prosecuted. The few attempts to get compensation from the Henan courts have been thrown out by the magistrates for lack of proof on the orders of the Party. Li Changchun, the governor of Henan in the Nineties when the blood trade was at its peak, is doing very well for himself and has reached the top of the Party ladder. In 2004, he was made a member of the Politburo, becoming number eight in the supreme hierarchy of China. He is presently in charge of propaganda.

The temptation to see the blood trade as a metaphor for the real nature of Chinese communism is powerful. How is it that the Party has not eliminated Hu Jia, the only one to have raised his voice against this terrifying fact? Why has this wild grass not been weeded out? His fame in the West acts as a protective shield. Arresting him on the eve of the Beijing Olympics would range the entire American media against the Chinese government.* We have to save Hu Jia, Li Dan, and Madam Gao. They are three wisps of straw struggling to stay afloat on a sea of blood. They are China's honor, perhaps its future.

Yan: a lone journalist fighting the censors

Yan offers a novel explanation for the corruption of the Chinese leaders: they are the only ones who know what is really happening in the country, and have come to the conclusion that the days of the Communist Party are numbered. They are trying to get rich as quickly as possible and stash away their money abroad, preferably in the United States. In fact, they now own entire Chinese localities in San Francisco, Hawaii, and Vancouver.

Yan ought to know: he is a seasoned, well-informed journalist. He also leads a dual existence. He is a columnist for a provincial

---

*Hu Jia was arrested on December 27, 2007.

daily and edits an internal reference publication for the Communist Party. The internal reference publication is a curious feature of Chinese journalism. In China, there are two kinds of newspapers, the first meant for public consumption and the other for Party cadres. One, intended for the masses, publishes only propaganda. Communist cadres know that whatever is published is pure fabrication because they have written the stories. But they do want to know the truth. For them, Yan selects reports from Chinese and foreign agencies, articles that cannot be published in China, extracts from the foreign press, and information from the Internet. All this is put together, photocopied, and circulated among the upper echelons of the administration. Cadres in China, depending on their rank and locality, receive copies of these internal reference publications. The main subjects deal with peasant uprisings, workers' revolts, assaults on cadres and policemen, factory managers killed by the workers, Falun Gong demonstrations in the United States, Chinese banks on the verge of bankruptcy, ecological disasters, and imminent epidemics. Had the press been free, Party cadres would have been able to put things in perspective and become inured to criticism. Since the press is anything but free, the divergence between the official version and reality is so sharp that leaders tend to lose their balance. Anticipating the future, the apparatchiks, say Yan, see the true facts as their death knell.

The contrast between the internal publication and public information is indeed striking. The public is presented with a rosy picture: dynamism, vitality, and enthusiasm are the keywords. Whenever a scandal is unearthed, it is used to exercise a salutary effect on society and prove the determination of the Party to root out corruption. The Propaganda Department orchestrates the entire show. Every ten days, it sends a note to news editors with a list of subjects to be taken up, the manner in which they are to be dealt with, and a list of subjects that are taboo. It also contains the names of heroes to be lauded, both past and present. This note is usually displayed prominently in newspaper offices. To keep their jobs, journalists have no choice but to yield. The most daring among them look for ways and means of circumventing these directives. Small news items revealing the cruelty of Chinese society find a place in the papers. Of course, there is no attempt to look at the deeper causes of the underlying malaise. Nonetheless, thanks to these intrepid reporters, the local press, the nearest to investigative field journalism, manages to publish a collection of reports of deception, trafficking, and extortion, providing an impressionistic sketch of a violent society that shows no mercy for the meek.

Such journalism, at the outer edge of the permissible, involves great risks. A notable case in September 2005 was that of Shi Tao, a Hunan journalist sentenced to ten years of prison for divulging state secrets. All he had done was publish the Propaganda Department's directives on the Internet. The purpose of this was to restore order and remind journalists that they could only practice their profession under the watchful eye of the Party. It also brought to light the collusion between the Chinese police and Yahoo, which had turned informer: Shi Tao had used his Yahoo address to send his message. When the CEO of Yahoo, of Chinese origin, was attacked by the American media for disclosing the name of the journalist, he offered the following justification: "We respect the customs of the countries where we do business." Which customs was he talking about? In acting the way it did, Yahoo was not complying with any law or even a written order of the police; all it did was use the same methods of censorship and turning informant as the Party. As a token of gratitude for this respect of Chinese customs, Yahoo was allowed to repurchase the portal Ali Baba, a very un-Chinese name. Whom did Yahoo invite to celebrate the occasion? Bill Clinton! And he was careful not to mention Shi Tao's name. Not to be outdone, Google removed the word "democracy" from its search engine and showed Taiwan as part of China. This is symptomatic of the unholy alliance that exists between the multinationals and the Party, one that has the blessings of a former U.S. president.

Yan says: "China is a threat to the West not because it sells cheap textiles and goods but because it is undermining the very principles on which Western society is founded: the respect for human rights, keeping one's word, and abiding by contracts." Clinton's praise of an American company that turned informer when it was convenient to do so was not merely straying from sound business practice in the face of fierce competition; it also dealt a blow to the American spirit. It was a tactical error as well. Making concessions for communist, not Chinese, customs is colluding with a regime that the Chinese despise. Yan is taken aback by the West's pusillanimity. He asks us to show more courage and not to give the Party the legitimacy that the Chinese deny it.

The day this interview took place, forty-two Chinese journalists in addition to Shi Tao went to prison for "divulging State secrets." The only crime of two of the journalists was to have revealed a new case of atypical pneumonia (SARS) in Guangzhou just a few hours before the municipal authorities officially acknowledged it. Another was guilty of procuring a copy of the president's speech to Party cadres, in which he expressed concern about the threat from democrats and men of religion.

The following month, Yan conceded that I was on the side of the Chinese democrats, an unusual position for a Frenchman. So he told me of his third identity. He posts on the Internet the results of field studies not considered worthy for internal publication. He reports life as it is lived every day in China. Some of his stories are edifying, others tragic. These vignettes, while considered too inconsequential for the internal publication, are considered too disturbing for public consumption. Why does he run such a risk? It is here alone that he can be true to his calling as a journalist. Who are his readers? He does not really know, but the website was sufficiently embarrassing for the Propaganda Department to block it. So Yan created another one. It is a constant race with the authorities. They keep blocking websites and e-mails they do not like; they spread viruses in message boxes and filter out what is forbidden. The mere mention of Taiwan is enough for a site to be destroyed. Mails containing the name of the Chinese head of state—worse still, that of the Taiwanese president or the word "democracy"—will never reach the people they are sent to. The Internet is a battlefield on which the authorities and democrats fight it out, honing their technical and semantic skills in the bargain. After browsing on the Internet, however, I note that it does appear that the 10,000 censors whom the Propaganda Department employs especially for this purpose are being outwitted by the ingenuity and sheer number of troublemakers.

The Internet has become the main source of information for the Chinese, with Internet users outnumbering the readers of the written press. People are generally well-informed, Yan says; they may not know the details but they have the general picture. What do those not connected on the Internet do? Even in the villages, there are teachers and Party cadres who surf the web and share gossip. For the discerning ones who can decipher the official press, there is much to be gleaned from it: the varying shades of censorship are so many signals to decode.

Yan feared that he may have said too much. He asked me if I would quote him. It was obvious, though, that Yan was yet another pseudonym.

Pan against sexual hypocrisy

Surprisingly, Pan Xiuming was not under police surveillance. This was rare for the people I had spoken with in Beijing. His particular field of study did not come under any of the categories that were anathema to the Party. Pan Xiuming is China's first sexologist. He pokes fun at the regime in a way the censors can't understand. He was the man who translated into Chinese the Kinsey report on American sexual practices. He is trying to use the same objective method in China.

Few know about Pan. He does not use the Internet; it is hard to trace him. This "bad element" is hidden in a corner of the People's University. His laboratory is located at the end of the corridor on the top floor of one the most run-down buildings on campus. The stench of dirty floor mops and slop pails are reminiscent of Mao's China, as filthy as it was chaste. The second-rate treatment doesn't bother Pan Xiuming. Like all academics of his generation, this sixty-year-old has suffered worse humiliations, of which his students have no idea. To make sure his discourse is not construed as salacious, he meets people in his office only in the presence of his wife and two Ph.D students, one of each sex. While he talks, his wife cooks dinner on a hot plate. This small team is studying the latest revolution to rock Chinese society: the sexual revolution.

Pan maintained that the Communist Party was not content to control people's minds; since 1949, it wanted to subjugate the body as well. The Revolution denied the Chinese all pleasures of the flesh; eroticism, public or private, was banned. The "liberation" of 1949 was certainly not a sexual one. For Mao Zedong, the true revolutionary had to be clean, free of material or carnal desire; unlike the rapacious Japanese and nationalist Kuomintang soldiers, Mao's fighters respected or feigned respect for other men's wives. After 1949, Mao's China became a sexual desert, at least officially; prostitution was eradicated, a success story that the communists boasted about constantly during the Sixties. Strangely enough, venereal disease did not disappear: it appears that the bestial instincts of Chinese revolutionaries had not been fully curbed. Pan said, "At the time, a sexual escapade led straight to a concentration camp. Homosexuality was liable to capital punishment." A totalitarian regime has never been able to accept any apolitical form of pleasure because it is viewed as a rival. Since 1980, the single-child policy was yet another reason to deny the Chinese their sexuality. Men were sent off to work in places far from their wives. A couple could only meet for twelve days a year, during the New Year vacations. In 1990, an extramarital sexual relationship was a bourgeois crime that could lead to prison. Until 1985, all erotic passages, even the slightest hint at sexuality, were expunged from Chinese literary classics. Readers who wanted to read the classics in their full form had to smuggle them in from Hong Kong, where they appeared unabridged.

Enforced chastity has not completely disappeared: in the army, conscripts must be spotless. Any form of sexual activity faces severe reprimand. The energy of the young must first and foremost be canalized for fighting. In the academies of fine arts, the study and representation of the nude form are strictly supervised. At the Hangzhou Academy, the most reputable fine arts academy in China, I am told that the distinction between eroticism and pornography does not exist in the Chinese language; it is up to teachers to guide their students so that they do not shock public morality. Mao Zedong, of course, was the notable exception to the puritanical rule. The memoirs of his private doctor tell us that Mao was the despoiler of many young virgins. The Great Helmsman was a cult figure and thus could do no wrong. He also made sure that no one else could enjoy his secret recipe for eternal youth.

Pan was the only scholar who explained the Revolution in terms of sexual repression and who sought to build up sexology as a social science. His desire for greater sexual freedom is not indicative of libertine propensities but is prompted by a felt need for a return to normalcy and a more humane face for post-totalitarian China. A case of freedom *post coitum,* perhaps.

He carries out his fieldwork with his students, investigates, and quantifies; his team started their inquiry at the university campus, and then moved on to the seediest quarters of Guangzhou and shelters of migrant workers. In his study, Pan concludes that the Chinese want to broaden their experience and try out different sexual positions. The under-forty age group believe that everything is worth trying: premarital, marital, and extramarital sex. Men have a greater tendency to abuse this newfound freedom than women—for the moment. Pan went into details that embarrassed the interpreter; modesty prevented her from translating. Even though she may have understood what was being talked about, she did not know the words in either Chinese or French. Pan helped her out, as many terms were universal. Both students nodded their heads sagaciously. It is not as if such terms are unknown in China. At the time of the Chinese Empire, there was a body of erotic literature and much-sought-after etchings that delighted Western collectors. According to Matteo Ricci, who lived in Beijing in the early seventeenth century, the city then had about 40,000 prostitutes and a considerable number of transvestites. Pan explained that this was before the eighteenth century.

The emperor Kangxi, who ruled from 1661 on, was a prude and had all traces of erotic practice destroyed; the only documents to have survived belonged to foreign amateurs. There were also some manuals (a ploy to get past the censors) in circulation, intended for young couples, which could be quite salacious. Kangxi's successors were just as repressive and imposed upon themselves, their entourage, and their people a regime of chastity that could be broken only to fulfill the needs of procreation. Did the emperor exercise his control over people's bedrooms? In ancient China, proximity and constant social control did not permit any form of indiscretion; indulgence meant being declared an outlaw. There were pleasure spots for the affluent and sailors at ports. For the most part, though, people had lost the taste for the pleasures of the flesh. Eroticism, it seems, is not so much a natural physical drive as a conditioned social response.

The Chinese are catching up quickly, says Pan. The single-child policy justified separation; today, it legitimizes eroticism by completely dissociating sexuality from reproduction. One of the students intervened, "Men are taking more advantage of sexual freedom than women; in comparison with the West, Chinese women are modest." The interpreter, who had found an accomplice, approved: sexual freedom is still relatively unknown for most Chinese women. Under Mao Zedong, Chinese women were conditioned to be workers, and forced to do the same physical jobs as men; in today's China, they are reduced to objects of desire. This is evident in the advertisements of new China, which makes a fetish of them. Life is not easy for a man in China, but it is even harder for a woman. In conclusion, Pan said, the sexual revolution was by no means complete. New habits are a reaction to the deprivation of the past, and not liberation. Total liberation will come only with the Westernization he hankers for: not only to enjoy amorous postures and practices but to restore the balance of the man-woman relationship. This relationship remains far from balanced in China. Except in the artistic milieu, terms such as feminism and homosexuality are barely mentioned, if at all. For about ten years, homosexuality has not been considered an offense or a psychiatric disease. But in Beijing and Shanghai, it is still considered an aberration.

Though prostitution is banned legally, it is proliferating and rampant in the large cities. Is this also part of the process of normalization in Chinese society? Pan interprets its mass development as one of the perversions of the Communist regime: prostitution is only banned in order to facilitate its management—and corruption—by the Party and the police. In Guangzhou, there are hotels with special floors comanaged by the trade and the police. The Party holds that prostitution is useful in attracting and taking advantage of foreign investors. The fines prostitutes must pay are not high: just enough to keep them under control without deterring them. A study Pan carried out in Guangzhou reveals how courtesans are selected and directed to serve the market: second wives for Taiwanese entrepreneurs; opulent courtesans for European, Japanese, and American businessmen; peasants and unemployed women for migrant workers who are without means but required to work on construction sites and in factories. The Communist Party has steered Chinese society to cater to the imperatives of economic development. As a result, prostitution is not just entertainment. In China, sex workers are seen as part of a national strategy. A Beijing student who occasionally works as a prostitute jokingly justified her job using the Party's vocabulary: "I am contributing to national development," she said, "without consuming gas, which is rare in China, and without causing pollution, another national problem."

A study by the Taipei Institute confirms Pan's findings: 90 percent of the Taiwanese who invest in Communist China keep a second wife who gets a monthly allowance and low rent. It has been clearly demonstrated that the abundant supply of such women constitutes a major incentive for the Taiwanese investor. Does it hold the same allure for Westerners? There is no independent study on the subject, but apparently the Communist Party carried out its own investigation and concluded that European and American entrepreneurs were just as susceptible.

Liu Xia, a Jew against fascism

"I'm a Jew," declares Liu Xia. She doesn't look like one. Her shaved head, fine features, and long black linen robe give her the appearance of a young Zen monk or a fashion model. Is she one of the last Chinese Jews described by Pearl S. Buck in her novel *Peony,* published in 1948? The American novelist dedicated the epilogue to the dying Jewish community of Kaifeng that melted in the process of intermingling. She wrote, "Wherever one sees a bolder face, a livelier look, a clearer voice, a skillfully traced line making the picture clearer, a more vigorous sculpture, Israel is there. Its spirit is reborn in each generation. It is no longer, but it lives forever."

Liu Xia is more circumspect; she feels no affinity for *Peony.* For her, being a Jew in China is like being a Jew in Nazi Germany in the midst of one's persecutors. The Communist regime is no different from Nazism or fascism, she believes. She reads everything on the subject published in the West; she compares and sees no difference. China's Jews are her dissidents, her free spirits, intellectuals, and artists, her trade-union leaders, peasant leaders, and independent priests. They are the wild grass the Communist Party is forever weeding out. Like the Jews in Nazi Germany, they are branded, categorized, watched, and eliminated.

What about the Cultural Revolution? Liu Xia says that nothing distinguishes it from Auschwitz. The Red Guards arrested and tortured anyone whose hands were clean, unsoiled by manual labor, or who had a university degree. Some 30 million people were slaughtered. The real difference is this: whereas Europe is trying to understand the reasons that led to Auschwitz in the hope of preventing it from ever happening again, such thinking is forbidden in China because the Party that ordered the Cultural Revolution is still in power. The current leaders were once Red Guards.

As in Nazi Germany, one becomes "Jewish" either by blood or by marriage, as is the case of Liu Xia. She herself is not involved in politics. She doesn't speak much, preferring to express herself through her photography and abstract painting, shown only to her close circle of friends. When her husband Liu Xiaobo was locked up, Liu Xia created an original, moving work, using photos of dolls with deformed faces as symbols of tortured prisoners. What threat could the Party see in that? But Liu Xiaobo is a "Jew"; he teaches literature. For his role as a student leader in 1989, he received ten years in prison. Liu Xiaobo refuses to live in exile, choosing to fight the regime where he is. His writing is his only weapon: on the Internet, he publishes a chronicle in defense of human rights in China. The Chinese constitution enshrines human rights but only to please foreigners, for they have no concrete legal effect. He also writes occasionally for the Hong Kong press, which, sadly, is losing its independence in relation to the Party. When Liu Xiaobo was imprisoned, Liu Xia automatically became a Jew and thus wild grass. It was then that she decided to shave her head to look like her prisoner husband. On leaving prison, his spirit of resistance as strong as ever, Liu Xiaobo let his hair grow back. Not so Liu Xia. She wanted to preserve her Jewishness until the end of fascism in China.

Is she being overly grim? She invites me to their tiny flat in a Beijing suburb. Four security men are posted in front of the building. As I reach it, a camera flashes. I am being photographed through the window of a car parked there. "In the morning," says Liu Xia, "when I draw open the curtains, the first thing I see are the security agents." The pressure never lets up. Sometimes, for no reason, Liu Xiaobo finds himself whisked away for questioning to the Security Department in an attempt to intimidate him. The "Jewish" couple is not in prison for the simple reason that their fame outside China is protecting them. Liu Xiaobo is a member of PEN, an international association of writers concerned about human rights, among other things. The fact that the security agents see them in the company of foreigners acts as a further shield. For the moment, they are safe. But the regime could choose at any time to eliminate this wild grass. A judge could accuse them, as so many others have been accused, of selling state secrets and plotting to overthrow the government. This is the standard charge leveled against all Chinese "Jews."

Tell me, asks Liu Xia, what is the difference between European fascism and Chinese communism? I keep quiet. Xia continues, "From the Thirties until 1950, French intellectuals had to visit Moscow. Romain Rolland, Louis Aragon, André Malraux—all heaped praise on the Stalinist regime. The same people or those who followed them now venerate China." One thinks of Malraux, said to be enamored of Stalin and Mao. Malraux was also the first French writer to have had a Chinese hero, Chen, in his book *The Human Condition*. But Chen was a faceless being with no personality of his own; being Chinese was enough to define him. No other character of Malraux has been dealt with in this way. Could this be a subconscious reflection of a certain image of China, one not peopled by any identifiable characters? The only writer who preserved France's honor in the Thirties was André Gide, who condemned Soviet fascism in his *Return from the USSR*. When will there be another Gide to denounce Chinese communism?" asks Liu Xia. She says French intellectuals liked Mao and the Cultural Revolution because they never experienced the events from within. I offered another explanation: perhaps, they were attracted to a kind of vicarious, revolutionary violence. Sartre was no more a humanist than Mao. "They liked violence for its own sake," she replies.

The Propaganda Department has successfully implanted a preposterous idea in the Western media: certainly, the Party is not democratic, but it is preventing China from sliding into fascism, an inevitability if it disintegrates. Liu Xia knows this argument well; it is one used by the Chinese media as well, on Party orders. Such a worthless argument merits no reply.

It is with a heavy heart that I leave Liu Xia, the "Jew" who has won a reprieve. She remains a hostage of a fascist regime.

CHAPTER THREE

The Mystics

"There is only one God: Jesus." Old Li's theology may be shaky, but his faith is not. I met Li quite by chance at Baoji in Shaanxi Province, located in central China. Wherever I went, I kept bumping into Christians; they seemed to be everywhere. Are there really so many, or is it just that they are more visible?

For a country the size of China, Baoji is a medium-size town, with a population of 800,000. Like all Chinese cities, it is an ordinary town, with nothing left of the pre-Sixties. Spicy noodles are its sole claim to fame. People stop at wayside stalls to eat them out of huge bowls. Communism has destroyed traditional architecture but has not been able to touch the large variety of local food. I met Li at an old people's home, hardly the kind of place to figure on a traveler's itinerary. But in a country where children are duty-bound to look after their parents, the home is nothing short of a revolution. So much for filial piety! Traditions are fast dying out in this single-child society, enamored of materialism. The aged have increasingly been left to their fate; the only time their children come to see them is at the New Year festival. The Baoji old people's home is a plain building. Since it receives no public aid, it takes in only pensioners who can pay. All the inmates are former civil servants.

The lady in charge assured me, "None of the pensioners has had any political trouble." I did not quite understand what she meant. But discrimination, to a greater or lesser degree, is a characteristic of Chinese society as a whole. Though these right-thinking civil servants do pay for their upkeep, the money is not enough; volunteers come in every day to visit and take care of the kitchen garden that provides their meals.

Old Li is a volunteer, even if his emaciated body and ageless face give him the appearance of a resident. But his eyes shine with the dancing light of a mystic. He loves Jesus, who he says made him good and, as he says, "made him run." Li calls himself a "new Christian." He wants to distinguish himself from China's old Christians, who were Christians because their ancestors had converted. He is a new Christian because his conversion is recent and because in Chinese, "new religion" means our reformed churches. A "Christian" in Chinese is a Protestant, as opposed to a Roman Catholic. Orthodox Christians, who can be found in northern China under Russian influence, claim theirs is the "true religion."

Before becoming Christian, Li was a Maoist—but not a communist, he hastens to add. As a worker in a Baoji factory, he didn't have enough education to join the Party. He is full of praise for Mao Zedong. What does he think of Deng Xiaoping's "70 percent good, 30 percent wrong" analysis? He is incensed. "Mao was 100 percent good for China." Li's story is proof. He had steadily worked his way up the workers' hierarchy to reach the seventh echelon, the highest. At sixty, he settled into a comfortable retirement. His wife, a teacher, has also retired. She, too, is Christian. Their joint pension seems a pittance when converted to dollars, but life is not expensive in Baoji. Had he never been a victim of the extortions of the Red Guard? He didn't know what I was talking about. He hadn't seen anything of the Cultural Revolution. His "work unit" had paid him his wages, given him food and accommodation. He had heard of the misfortunes of some, but they were "black families," landowners and enemies of the people. No one he knew came from such families. He has vague memories of schools being closed for reasons he has forgotten and youngsters with nothing to do. People do "silly things" at that age. Fortunately, Mao Zedong restored order and sent everyone back to school. That was how Li, a worker of the seventh echelon and a member of the workers' aristocracy, had experienced Maoism. This is also what schoolchildren learn in their textbooks.

American-Chinese Christians

Soon after he retired, Li began to find it hard to swallow. He tried everything he could but got no relief. Then his wife heard of a bishop, a certain Wang. The bishop placed both his hands on old Li's head and called upon Jesus. Li was cured and converted. Both he and his wife started attending catechism. They read the Gospel, learned hymns, and joined the Christian community of the Living Source. They were baptized together. The community has 2,500 faithful in Baoji. On Sunday mornings, they congregate joyously in the newly built temple in the city center. Bishop Wang, ninety-seven years old, leads the prayer and delivers lengthy sermons. He takes care not to ask people to convert or make them go into a trance, as is the practice of Pentecostal celebrants. He carefully follows the code of conduct that the Party laid down for authorized pastors.

The bishop says Christians are "good and charitable, obedient children and good parents." For Bishop Wang, the Gospel is like the epistles of Confucius; there is no contradiction. "Jesus is as Chinese as he is European," he says. This was a lesson he had learned from an American pastor who converted him in 1942. At the time, he had been a young peasant in Shaanxi. His entire family had followed him on the path of Christianity. "Buddha was Indian, not Chinese, yet Buddhism is a Chinese religion. So Christianity is and will remain Chinese." What about the notion of original sin? It is a concept alien to every belief and tradition in China. Would the Chinese have to embrace it to become Christians, or the Christians abandon it to become Chinese? Bishop Wang once again states: "There is only one God." His disciple Li listens rapturously. He is stirred by the vitality of his bishop and does not profess the least interest in abstruse metaphysics.

The authorities have given a great deal of latitude to the large congregation assembled in this huge temple. "Christians only do good," Wang says, "so the local government cannot but encourage them." What he does not say is that the religion he belongs to has the Party's blessings and that he himself is paid by the Party. In exchange, he has agreed to respect "the three principles of autonomy" of the church in China: no foreign missions, no foreign subsidy, and no interference from foreign ecclesiastics. A Communist apparatchik vets his sermons. In addition, every Sunday he has to denounce the Falun Gong sect, a task he does not find distasteful. Wang shares the Party's views about Catholics, more tightly controlled than the Protestants. "They pray to the pope, not to God. The pope only recognizes Taiwan, not real China."

Hadn't Taiwanese Christians helped in building the Protestant temple of Baoji? Yes, but they were originally from Shaanxi. They had "strayed" to Taiwan. The church piano, too, had been donated by a Baoji immigrant in California. In fact, the church's entire look was American. Wang had cut out a photo of a Los Angeles temple from a magazine and asked local artisans to replicate it. Was it an evangelical, Baptist, or Pentecostal church, or something else? Wang said it was pointless to go into details. He did not make any distinction between these reformed sects. You had to know only one thing: "There are real Christians, and there are Catholics, who are heretics." Did he approve of the "Protestants of silence"? Yu Jie had spoken of them and their practice of meeting without a pastor to study the Bible. Both Wang and Li claimed not to have heard of them. That was probably true. The house churches recruit first and foremost intellectuals in big cities. Will the Protestants of silence and the patriotic Protestants together be able to constitute the critical spiritual and revolutionary mass that Yu Jie hopes for? It seems unlikely, for their motivations are not the same.

For his part, Li, still a Maoist and a patriot, rails against the conduct of the pontiff. The Catholics pray to the pope, not God, he charges. What kind of Christians does that make them? "Catholicism is all well and good for Shaanxi peasants. They're a credulous lot. Some of them have even joined the Falun Gong. It just shows how stupid they are and their inability to recognize the true God." Li and

Wang, because they are against the Vatican and the Falun Gong, are close to the Party line. This makes them appear more as objective allies of the Party than as dissidents.

But how far can the Protestants go, and how much influence will they have in the future? No one can tell. Like his fellow brethren, Li is not satisfied just believing. He feels that he must spread the faith. "Jesus makes me run," he says. It is a fact that Li is traveling across China. New Christians are zealous proselytizers, a factor that has contributed significantly to the growth of official Protestant churches. When he is not helping out at the old people's home, Li travels by train or bus to meet other Christians and convert new ones. He wants China to become "a large happy family, united by a single God." He seems to recall that this was what President Mao Zedong wanted.

Li's faith may well move mountains, but can it move the Communist Party? There is a curious link between Christianity and communism in China. In 1899, a Protestant pastor introduced the country to Communist thought through *The Global Magazine,* a review he published in Shanghai. It was there that Sun Yat-sen discovered *The Communist Manifesto.* Until today, the Chinese Party remains grateful to this unusual missionary. The present alliance between official Protestants and the Party is reminiscent of an older association between the Jesuits and the imperial court. Yesterday's Jesuits and today's evangelists both brought their God to China under the guise of modernity. But whereas the Jesuits failed to impose Catholicism as the official religion of the Empire, the Protestants may well succeed. American churches are at work behind the scenes, and their resources are immense.

The myth of an atheist China: a Jesuit invention

Why are we blind to the gods in China when they are so prolific? Peopled with Buddhas, saints, and immortals, the Chinese pantheon is no less impressive than the Indian one. There is a reason for our blindness. Our understanding of the Chinese civilization was shaped by the travel accounts of Italian and French Jesuits and all their

prejudices. The misconceptions we formed persisted for three centuries in our literature and philosophy. Take, for instance, Louis
Lecomte, the father of sinology, or of the French love of things
Chinese, to be more precise. When, in the footsteps of that other
great pioneer, the Italian Matteo Ricci, Father Lecomte visited China
from 1686 to 1691, he decided resolutely to ignore the temples and
faiths. In his *New Memoirs on the Present Situation in China,* he wrote
that the Chinese practiced the godless morality expounded by the
atheist philosopher Confucius. His writings contributed greatly to the
theories of the Enlightenment. Surely, our Jesuit concluded, with their
fine sense of morality the Chinese were living in the expectation of
the God of the Christians. They were empty vessels waiting to be
filled. This was the argument that the Jesuits supported since the time
of Matteo Ricci in their bid to win favor with the pope and the courts
of Europe.

Were Lecomte and all the missionaries sincere? How could they
not have seen the temples overflowing with people day and night, the
impressive ceremonies, the long funerals, the incense, the bells, the
Daoist masters and the Buddhist monks, the two main religions of old
China that owed nothing to Confucius? When Lecomte was in China,
there were more temples in Beijing than churches in any European city.
Beijing was a holy city. Yet he dismissed all this as "a bunch of superstitious practices of the Chinese," unworthy of being treated as religions. Until the twentieth century, no French travelers after Lecomte
took the slightest interest in Daoism, the source of these "superstitious
practices." Nor did they bother about Chinese Buddhism.

A Chinese traveler to Europe observing Europeans cross themselves in front of a crucifix or burn a candle in front of the icon of a
saint could just as easily have concluded that Europeans were a
superstitious people without religion.

There are none so blind as those who will not see. So it was for
our feckless explorers. The Jesuits only chose to mix with mandarins
who held both the popular religions in contempt and did their best
to repress them. The mandarins were disciples of Confucius, whom

they used to legitimize social order, hierarchy, stability, respect for elders, and veneration of the emperor by his subjects. What of Confucius the philosopher? The Confucians, said Matteo Ricci, constituted an academy of learned men to which Christians could easily subscribe. Confucius claimed to base his philosophy on the revelations of a mythical golden age. Was Confucianism a religion or a philosophy? If a philosophy, it was certainly not a secular one, with its temples, rituals, and sacrifices. Buffaloes were slaughtered, the Master of Heaven invoked, and ancestors worshiped. Was it, then, an atheist religion? The concept found favor with Leibniz, Montesquieu, and Voltaire. In his *Essay on Universal History*, Voltaire asserted that Chinese society was characterized by a high degree of morality even though it had no religion. An abstract god, the Master of Heaven, kept watch. Evidently, the Supreme Being of the French philosophers had Chinese origins. And atheist French intellectuals have always felt a great affinity for China and its supposedly godless society.

The accounts of the Dutch travelers were at variance with the French view of China. These travelers had come to trade, not to evangelize. Consequently, they had a very different perception of seventeenth-century China; they were more attentive to the popular religions than to the Confucianism of the court. Dealing mainly with bourgeois guilds, they had little to do with the celestial bureaucrats. Two centuries later, the situation remains the same. Northern Europe continues to trade with China without a very developed diplomatic relationship. Public opinion is sensitive to human rights violations in China. It is just the opposite in France. Ideology triumphs over pragmatism. Having inherited the Jesuit worldview and being partial to the idea of enlightened despotism, French leaders are happy to do business with "strong" Beijing regimes. Civil society and democrats do not count. The accommodating attitude toward the establishment is meant to protect our interests. It also stems from our ignorance of Daoism, the religion of the people, which is both individualistic and rebellious.

Daoism, the religion of subversion

In China, the elite have had one religion, the people another. The conflict persists; it has only assumed a new form. Confucianism was the ideology of the ruling class and its civil servants, the atheist religion at the top. Confucian cosmology established a hierarchy between man and nature. The world could be preserved only if man submitted to the higher order. Of course, the rules of such an order were known only to the princes and mandarins. Daoism and Buddhism were the religions of the ordinary people. In Europe, we are conversant with Buddhism but know little or nothing of Daoism. Lao-tzu, a contemporary of Confucius and Plato, said that in the beginning there was Tao, or the Way. Daoism is, in point of fact, the real great religion of China. All the sects in China, including Christianity and Buddhism, have been visibly influenced by it.

Daoism is the antithesis of Confucianism. In Daoist cosmology, man and nature merge. Our body is but a representation of nature. It is by taking care of the self that we can maintain the order of the world. In the image of the sages and immortals that people its pantheon, the Daoist aspires to longevity and prosperity for both the self and the immediate community but displays indifference to the Imperial State.

The Daoist and Confucian cosmologies gave rise to two distinct ideologies, the Confucians looking to the state and the Daoists to the individual. "A good prince," wrote Lao-tzu, "is one whose name no one knows." Hostile to the established order, Daoists remain free spirits to this day, refusing to be cowed by the state and its agents. In the golden age of Daoism, unlike the golden age of Confucianism, man lived in harmony with nature and at peace with his neighbors. That was "before the princes introduced turmoil because it was their will to decide everything in accordance with abstract principles," Master Bao Jingyan wrote in the third century A.D. His thoughts, truly anarchist, were translated into the French by Jean Lévi.

Daoism is a democratic creed. At the time of the Empire, the faithful elected their priests. The elected leaders of Daoist associations were aldermen responsible for law and order and well-being. In the nineteenth century, Daoist associations in overseas Chinese colonies, especially Borneo, transformed themselves into democratic republics. They were crushed by the Dutch, who had colonized Borneo. These Chinese Daoists were not passive nor did they conform to the stereotype in which the Confucians and Jesuits sought to enclose them. Daoist temples were havens of civil society that resisted the highhandedness of the administration. In overseas China, the Daoist temples were and remain places of economic solidarity and initiative. Many a Chinese venture has been financed by a Daoist association. This is still the case in Taiwan. Most of the 10,000 Chinese restaurants in the United States got started thanks to funds raised by Daoist associations. In 2005, the sinologist and philosopher François Jullien wrote, "It is impossible to understand contemporary China without understanding Confucianism." But can China be understood without any knowledge of Daoism?

Daoism practices tolerance, enabling the Chinese to amalgamate diverse practices and sinicize beliefs that came from elsewhere. In India, only monks who renounced the world could become Buddhists. Not so in China. Any lay person could do so as long as he revered the Buddha and followed his precepts. Like the Daoist immortals, the Chinese Buddha became an intercessor. In turn, Daoism derived a great deal from Buddhism, in particular its spirit of compassion. From the Confucians, the Chinese took geomancy and the cult of the ancestors. Kristofer Schipper, a sociologist of Daoism, notes that the various religions, including Islam and Christianity, coexisted peacefully, as if governed by a concordat. From time immemorial, the faithful mingled freely in the towns and villages of China. There was never any segregation.

Westerners often wonder if the Chinese know the meaning of individual freedom. Their religions provide the answer. There is a plethora of gods and cults, but all are based on the principle of inner freedom. Regardless of whether one is Daoist, Confucian, or Buddhist, one is answerable for one's acts, the individual merit of which is rewarded. The reward is here on earth for the Daoists and

Confucians, in the other world for the Buddhists. I hope this description demolishes the pseudo-cultural hypothesis that denies the Chinese free will and declares them unfit for democracy.

No, communism is not Confucian

Was communism not just another form of Confucianism, which was the religion of the state during the Empire? This is yet another hypothesis that the Party puts forth and that is currently in vogue in the West. It provides a certain mystique and allows the Party to mitigate its exactions. If the Party is part of a long tradition, it cannot be criticized for its misdemeanors. Tradition, after all, must be respected. The Party is also aware that Confucius retains a certain appeal in China, and even more so outside, whereas Karl Marx and Mao Zedong have lost their luster. It makes more strategic sense, then, to hide behind Confucius.

To give credence to this semblance of cultural continuity, the Party has recently had some "temples of Confucius" restored. Some are not temples at all but old examination halls where learned contenders competed to become mandarins. They are museums. The real places of worship, where the sacrifices and rituals were performed, have been destroyed. This is the Party's way of sanitizing Confucianism, presenting it as an abstract philosophy shorn of the divine. As part of the same firefighting exercise in the Year of the Rooster, the Party has rebuilt the walls of Qufu, the birthplace of Confucius in Shandong. It is thought that he was born there twenty-five centuries ago. All the inhabitants of the city are named Kong. Qufu has become an amusement park for Chinese and foreign tourists. In this way, an austere creed has been cleverly packaged and marketed, and Confucianism has become yet another commodity.

To further obfuscate the real nature of Confucianism, the Party is falling back on rhetoric that ostensibly borrows from Confucian vocabulary or anything that sounds like it. The new feature in the Year of the Rooster is the liberal use of words such as "harmony"and "frugality," vague terms that one can associate with any Oriental religion. Does one have to invoke Confucius and harmony to get children to respect their parents, students their teachers, and, most of all, subjects the Party?

The leaders, starting from the head of the state, have gone one step further in this phony Confucianism, advocating moral lessons to inculcate "values" in students. In his New Year speech, Hu Jintao said the youth must receive "ethical" (read: Confucian) education and "ideological" (read: Marxist) education, suggesting that Confucianism and Marxism were complementary. This spirit of syncretism has prompted a spate of lectures by Confucian philosophers in the Party schools where the cadres are trained. The leaders hope that this return to values will result in greater probity among the apparatchiks and a decline in corruption. Whether the leaders really believe that their discourse on values is enough to change the behavior of the Party is a debatable point. We are entering an arcane domain, one that the uninitiated cannot hope to penetrate. It is as if the members of a sect had been hypnotized by the constant repetition of their own rituals.

Such dubious discourse on values deserves to be trashed. The history of the relationship between the Party and Confucianism is proof of their total incompatibility. From the May 4 student movement of 1919 to the Cultural Revolution of 1966–76, every uprising in contemporary China has been against Confucianism. "Down with Master Kong!" was the slogan in 1919 and in 1966, two defining moments in China's "progressive" march forward. The Party destroyed Confucianism on the ground that it was reactionary, harking back to a golden age. The Party itself worships a golden age, but one still to come. As Confucians held the very idea of progress in aversion, it was natural that the communists would vilify them, offering instead their own version of Confucian philosophy. True Confucianism was based on a specific set of rites and rituals, celebrations and sacrifices. Its liturgy has been forgotten and its priests eliminated. No one reads the texts of Confucius; perhaps no one even knows how. What remains is the selective incantation of those Confucian values that suit the Party. Even if they do know them,

Chinese leaders are careful not to quote the writings of Confucius and Mencius against despotism. The power of the sovereign was limited, curtailed by the rights of his subjects. We must keep this in mind before giving any verdict on the cultural continuity of an eternal China and the reductionist view of communism as a continuation of the Empire in a new garb. Anticlericalism is, in point of fact, the only tradition the Party can claim to draw its inspiration from.

How anticlericalism ravaged China

Anticlericalism is not new to the Chinese. It is by no means a Communist invention. Close contact with the West convinced Chinese emperors of Europe's technical superiority. If China wanted to catch up, moral reform was required. The Japanese, however, chose to reform the state, a task they began in 1868. This is an important date. It was then that China and Japan embarked on separate paths; ever since, they have differed in their approaches. The Japanese emperor got rid of the old elite to build a new one. In China, the educated aristocracy of Beijing found nothing wrong with the country's institutions. It was traditions and superstitions that had caused the decline. So from 1898 onward, the state and the provinces took over Daoist, Buddhist, and Confucian temples. In principle, they were to be converted into schools. Many places of worship were desecrated and destroyed, monasteries dispersed, and Daoist masters were liquidated. There were hardly any schools, but some universities, including the first universities of Beijing and Fuzhou, continued to be housed in old temples and their gardens. The Cultural Revolution, generally associated with the destruction of religious edifices, was an extension of the progressives' iconoclastic outburst. The French Terror of 1793 and the 1917 Soviet Revolution are perhaps the only equivalents in history. In the immediate neighborhood, however, Korea and Japan successfully married religion and modernity.

This hatred for popular gods is specifically Chinese. Why did the political elite dislike them so much? The contempt of Confucian bureaucrats for popular, Daoist, and Buddhist "superstitions" smacked of the same anticlericalism before they, too, came to be objects of contempt. Another reason was the humiliation of the Chinese elite when confronted with Western "superiority." The ease with which Westerners subjugated the people with opium convinced the elite that all was not well with Chinese civilization. It had to be eradicated and replaced by something new. The obsession to destroy the old and build a modern Chinese individual rid of his superstitions and fears dates back to this period. We need to see the violence of the revolutions in this light. Anything old—temple, city, monument, archive—had to be destroyed. Foreigners look in vain for traces of old China. Beijing was leveled and rebuilt. The destruction of old China was a deliberate policy. Only the ashes remain, preserved as remembrances and not as places that once breathed life.

The self-hatred responsible for the complete annihilation of religion and a large part of their heritage can be found neither in India nor in Japan. Japan was never colonized, so it had no reason to reject tradition. India was colonized, but there was none of the humiliation that changed China into a nation of opium addicts. India boasts of as many religions as those of ancient China, yet no one in India suggests progress hinges on the extermination of religion.

Sadly, state anticlericalism led to the opposite of what the progressives had hoped for. Certainly, religions were greatly weakened, especially Confucianism, more dependent on rites than on inner conviction. Daoist and Buddhist churches suffered. They lost their places of worship, liturgical books were destroyed, the clerics and the faithful scattered. In the name of progress, a rich and ancient legacy was wrecked; the destruction was comparable to the obliteration of pre-Columbian civilization in America. A social disaster was waiting to happen. Charity and solidarity existed only in Daoist and Buddhist associations. There was no institution to replace them, leaving the poor, the old, the infirm, and the unemployed with no place to go to. In the Year of the Rooster, the Chinese government urged Buddhists to rebuild old people's homes and dispensaries. But perhaps it was too late. Economic disaster was to come as well. Daoist associations had acted as banks that financed enterprises in China and overseas.

Their elimination deprived mainland China of time-tested practices on which a flourishing trade had been built in the past.

Has all this led the Party to give up its policy of ridding China of its gods? No, it has only changed its methods. As in the case of the democrats, the repression is more subtle. People are free to believe, provided they do not organize themselves; if they do, it has to be under Party supervision. Religions are authorized only if they follow the instructions of the patriotic Daoist, Buddhist, Catholic, Protestant, and Muslim associations. Needless to say, these are branches of the Party in charge of organizational matters. They also meddle in theology when they think it is not sufficiently rational. The instruction booklet for monks brought out by the Daoist Association states: "Attaining immortality through inner refinement and alchemy is quite obviously impossible." This may be a scientific claim, but it questions the truth of a belief that lies at the very heart of Daoism.

Turning religions into museums is another way of doing away with them. Daoist temples were allowed to reopen in 1990 under the control of the tourist offices. What interests the Party is the tourist appeal of these picturesque temples and the income they rake in to the public coffers. Take the case of the famous Mount Wudang monastery in Hubei Province, which for five centuries welcomed hermits desirous of escaping the world. In the past, pilgrims had to cross the forest and climb thousands of stairs to reach the temple. Today, a cable car takes them up. The monks looking after the monastery sell postcards and religious trinkets. A few remaining pilgrims, recognizable by their yellow caps, try to pray to the gods, surrounded by hordes of noisy tourists armed with cameras. "Look, religion can once again be practiced freely in China!" Communist leaders tell us. Yet all that remains in Beijing of the 700 temples that existed before the Revolution is a single Daoist structure—the White Clouds temple—which has been sanctioned officially and is more like a museum than a place of worship. The government is doing exactly the same thing in Tibet: reducing places of national and religious importance to tourist spots. The lures of tourism are more likely to wipe out Tibetan Buddhism than the People's Army.

The gods are tired

I visited old temples and saw new churches coming up, but when I looked closely, none seemed real. They were more like centers of the Communist Party and committees for the retired. Perhaps I hadn't looked closely enough. There had to be a real Daoist monk somewhere, proof that the gods could stand up to anticlericalism and the attempts to ossify religion. A scholar advised me to head for the city of Fuzhou, where I was likely to find a monk who had mastered the cosmology and liturgy of Daoism, not just its magical signs.

For many years, Fuzhou was the largest port in China. In the early twentieth century, Paul Claudel had been France's counsel in "Fou-Tchéou," and he sent his dispatches from there.

The temple of the jade emperor is perched on top of a hill surrounded by graceless buildings in the city center. A monk in his thirties recited canonical texts for his own salvation and order in the world. Had I found the last of the Daoist monks? His long hair was in a bun tied at the top of his head, proof of his dedication. A Daoist monk never cuts his hair, in contrast to Buddhist monks, who shave their heads because the length of the hair measures the passage of time. Should a superior cut the hair of a Daoist monk, it is a sign that he has committed a very serious error.

The monk in front of me did not attract any attention: new China does not set much store by material renunciation, asceticism, retreats in caves, sitting in meditative postures, studying paradoxical and cryptic texts, mastering complex liturgy, and the vegetarian diet. The psalms, chants in classical Chinese, evening recitation, and gong and drum did not draw the faithful. It was if they could not see or hear the long-haired man in the blue tunic. They moved around him to get close to the incense holder, pray hurriedly to the jade emperor, and light a stick of incense in the hope that their wish—for money, health, or love—would be gratified immediately. Daoists do not see anything wrong in this, because Daoism is a personal affair. I found that the devotees were either very young—they came to pray for love or success in exams—or very old: they obviously came to pray for good health. The generation in the middle, educated during the Cultural Revolution, has little or no interest in religion.

The monk himself did not seem to care whether he had any disciples. It was as if he, too, was not looking at the crowds around him. Absorbed in his personal alchemy, he must have been praying for a long life and the immortality of the soul and the body. Who knows— at the end of his days he may even turn into a bird. In China, past and present, Daoist monks like him are perceived as a threat to the state, not because of what they do, but because they do nothing. Their inaction is an existential denial of what the state and the Party expect from their subjects.

What are we to make of the monk in Fuzhou? His manner of renouncing the world to live in a monastery is more reflective of "new China" than "ancient China." After his marathon three-hour chanting, he explained to me that, while watching television with his family, he saw a monk and thought it was his own reflection. That was the day he found his true vocation. We might interpret his example either as the renaissance of Daoism or proof that Daoism survives only as an archaeological vestige. The same can be said for popular traditions. In the New Year, effigies of the god of prosperity, common to both Buddhism and Daoism, decorate the doors. The god appears in a modern light, brandishing hundred-yuan notes. During the Festival of Light, it is customary for families to gather around tombs. Do they come to pray for the peace of the departed souls, or simply to enjoy an outing in the countryside?

If they aren't already dead, the gods of ancient China seem to me exhausted by their century-long struggle against anticlericalism and communism. The recent profusion of Protestant churches is perhaps the outcome. As we shall see later, Daoism is still going strong in Taiwan, the other China, ample proof that religion does not necessarily have to take a backseat to modernization; Taiwan is more modern than Communist China. It was anticlericalism that swept away the temples on the mainland. In Taiwan, the feeling was not so strong: even though the Kuomintang leaders, refugees from the

mainland, had no love for Daoism, they did not set out to exterminate it as systematically as the communists did.

The grand return of the sects

Exterminate ancient gods, and new ones will appear. In all probability, the traditional faiths will not give rise to a religious renaissance;
that will come from what the Party calls the sects. This is not a new
phenomenon: in the history of China, every time the state has
repressed religions, underground sects and secret societies have pros-
pered. In 1898, anticlericalism gave rise to the sect of the Unique
and Truthful Way, which counted millions of followers, even from
within the Communist Party. During the last ten years, 50 million
Chinese have reportedly converted to the Falun Gong, the wheel of
dharma. The real number is anybody's guess. The only way to gauge
its mass impact is by the number of followers who have been
arrested.

In Communist China, the Falun Gong is persecuted; its followers
wind up imprisoned, tortured, and die "accidentally" in custody.
Their only crime is to follow a religion and believe in the saintliness
of their guide, Li Hongzhi, who is a refugee in the United States. For
this reason alone, a democrat is duty-bound to hear what they have
to say and support their cause. Solidarity for these martyrs does not
come easy, though, as their discourse seems irrational, to say the
least. Both in and out of China, the Falun Gong recruits members
from among the educated. Its spokespersons are often academics
and lawyers who are relatively easy to meet. They begin their argument by cataloging the ills that members of the sect have had to suffer, and one commiserates with them. Then they explain their creed:
how each individual can master the karmic wheel that he carries at
the level of the navel, thereby removing all evil. They tell you that just
reading Li Hongzhi's book can cure cancer. They talk of a third eye
in the middle of the forehead. An economics professor at Taipei
University explained to me in perfect English (Falun Gong, like all

religions, enjoys freedom in Taiwan): "In the beginning, I had no belief except in ghosts, especially in the month of July." His words did give me a start, but then I remembered this was Taiwan, where everybody believes in ghosts. He continued, "My wife had an incurable cancer, but after joining the Falun Gong, she was cured." How? "She read Li Hongzhi's book and practiced the physical exercises prescribed by the Master." After his wife's recovery, the professor joined the sect, and now initiates new adherents to its mysteries.

In English, "sect" is not a pejorative term; it means a religious creed like any other. "Cult" is the pejorative word. For the communists, the Falun Gong is a cult.

The professor becomes passionate and tries to convert me for my own good. However, he doesn't press his case too far. As I get ready to leave, he gives me a voluminous set of documents. He tells me I can also consult the Falun Gong website.

I consulted the site and read the books. Li Hongzhi borrows from the teachings of Buddhism, condemning the appearances of the material world and calling for compassion. He adds Daoist precepts, especially the practice of *qigong,* said to lead to immortality. To top it all off, he throws in a bit of American science fiction. Followers are prepared for the end of the world. None of this is new. What is remarkable is the organization of the network. Members disseminate information through the Internet. To practice their exercises and meditate, the faithful assemble in private places, flats, or parks. Falun Gong is peaceful, claiming to derive its inspiration from nonviolence. One can leave it as easily as one can join. To date, it has not been involved in any major financial scandal—there is not much money in circulation. Followers must buy the master's book, a modest expenditure. Exiled to the United States, Li Hongzhi lives comfortably off his royalties. His public appearances are rare. He wants to preserve his mystique.

As must be the case with most non-believing Western democrats, I feel there is no valid reason for the Party to exterminate Falun Gong. It is a difficult conclusion for any rational defender of human rights to reach, for Falun Gong is not rational. Yet democracy requires that we support the right to difference, even when verging on the delirious. Why does the Party view Falun Gong as China's Number One enemy? How does Falun Gong generate so much enthusiasm among millions of Chinese? These are questions we need to examine.

Falun Gong, an antiparty

At the start, Li Hongzhi was a Party cadre and a Party-backed *qigong* master. In the Seventies and Eighties, its adherents projected *qigong* as the science of the body, a respectable discipline like traditional medicine and acupuncture. The communists called these "patriotic alternatives" to Western knowledge. In the Seventies, university laboratories invited *qigong* masters to displace distant objects by focusing their inner reserves of energy. By the Eighties, the whole of China was in the grip of a *qigong* fever. In parks, millions of Chinese practiced the slow movements of a gymnastic exercise that the Party believed "purged" all religious content. The cadres took part in these mass exercises. Exercise, however, was not the only reason that people came out. Many felt a latent nostalgia for Buddhism and Daoism. Some, remembering their childhood rituals, enjoyed this revival of ancient practices. Li Hongzhi combined Maoist methods with classical religion, collecting huge crowds in stadiums, making them repeat slogans, and calling them to come up on stage. The choreography was perfect, and the Master was always right. Most saw *qigong* as a pretext to meet, a way of overcoming loneliness in an atomized society. Li Hongzhi won people over easily. After fifty years of organized violence, informing on one another, and hatred, at last someone spoke the language of love and goodwill. *Qigong* practitioners started to rebuild trust and cooperation, both of which were anathema to Chinese communism.

Retired people constitute the bulk of Falun Gong members. This is natural. Retirees are the most isolated group in society. But civil servants, army officers, academics, and even Party members are among those who believe in Li Hongzhi's message. Their adherence is a source of great concern to the Party, stoking its fear of being destroyed from within. Even I was taken aback at the way communists, materialists, and atheists were flocking to join the Falun Gong fold. Some of them told me that Falun Gong had given them a sense of fraternity that they could never have in the Party, a throwback to the old secret societies that mixed rites and mutual aid. Now this is something the Party will not tolerate. Even if Falun Gong has no political ambitions, it is an antiparty.

On April 17, 1999, 10,000 Falun Gong followers gathered in silence in front of the Beijing government headquarters. They had consulted one another on the Internet and decided that this was how they would protest against an article in the press denigrating Li Hongzhi. The Party leadership was stunned. Falun Gong, they discovered, was an organized movement, capable of circumventing the regime through the Internet. The ability to associate outside the Party is what the Party fears the most. Anything unorganized is tolerated; anything organized is not. Ever since that day in 1999, Falun Gong followers have been hounded and imprisoned by the police, the usual method of repression. In keeping with the principle of nonviolence, its followers never offer resistance.

The government was clear: there were to be no more Falun Gong members in Beijing. From the capital to the heart of China, local committees would be held responsible. If the Party caught a follower in Beijing, the local boss in the follower's home city had to pay a fine and would lose his job. So the local bosses became vigilant, asking people to keep them informed. No one blamed them for using strong-arm tactics. Threats, internment without trial, prison, torture, execution—no questions were asked. Falun Gong members are in a majority in the "labor reeducation centers." The police have the power to send anyone they consider a threat to law and order to these centers for four years without any legal procedure or trial. There, the followers are kept along with petty thieves, prostitutes, drug addicts, and, until very recently, homosexuals. The Year of the Rooster also saw a sharp increase in the number of incarcerated Protestant pastors and unofficial Catholic priests. They, too, are deviants who merit no trial. They need lessons in morality and manual labor so that they can return to the straight and narrow path. Sadly, no one has bothered to investigate these centers, and little is known about the conditions in which people are being detained. Those who have managed to survive the ordeal speak of torture. The authorities are particularly harsh on followers of sects, forcing them to disavow their faith. In December 2005, the United Nations Commissioner for human rights, Manfred Nowak, confirmed the use of torture in these centers. The Chinese authorities could not refuse him access to at least some of them.

Some of the "nonviolent" methods that the Party adopted are comical, to say the least. A local apparatchik, for example, sees old people of the locality still meeting to practice *qigong*. They have been doing this for many years. They think *qigong* will keep them healthy, which it does. But how is one to distinguish between someone practicing *qigong* as a form of gymnastics and a Falun Gong member doing so out of devotion to the Master? The apparatchik is clever. He identifies the places where the *qigong* enthusiasts meet: parks, lakesides, riverbanks, and near temples. He installs gym equipment there and puts up posters urging the public to use these modern devices, rather than the outmoded *qigong*. Old men start exercising on a swing-like apparatus and other such contraptions. The Party also encourages people to waltz in these traditional meeting places. Loudspeakers blare out Western music, old couples begin to dance, and ancient China fades away. No harm is done, provided news does not reach the top. In this way, the Falun Gong, though no longer visible, has become a vast secret society with which the Party must contend. Its members speak in veiled terms; it recruits new followers through the Internet and text messages.

Falun Gong is a threat because it operates in the realm of beliefs and conscience, where the Party has no control. It is unflinching in its resistance, producing many a martyr. The history of China offers several instances of mystic revolts that led to the overthrow of imperial dynasties. The last such revolt was the famous Taiping rebellion, whose leaders believed that bullets would pass them by. The rebellion destabilized the last of the Manchu dynasty. Falun Gong is also

mystical, and, though history may not repeat itself, most liberal intellectuals in Beijing and those in exile accept that Falun Gong has
become their objective ally.

Quantifying Chinese faith

The large-scale reconstruction of Daoist and Buddhist temples and
the fervor of the new Christians are suggestive of a religious upsurge
in China. Most conversations veer toward moral or mystical speculation. Many causes underlie this quest for the transcendent: the
post-Maoist ideological void, crass materialism, widespread decadence, and memories of old practices. But these are just impressionistic sketches of the intangible. Or so I thought. The Communist
Party has even managed to quantify religious fervor.

The main function of the Institute of Religions in Beijing is to act
as a watchdog. Its scholars do not study theology; their job is to prevent excesses. I met with two acolytes, one experienced and authoritarian, and the other more modern. Their roles were clearly
delineated: the old face of the Party and the new face of the Party.

In case I had forgotten, the older man reminded me that China recognizes all patriotic religions. Since the 1949 Revolution, five religions—
Catholicism, Protestantism, Daoism, Buddhism, and Islam—have
received this status. Anything else is either not religious or a counterrevolutionary cult. "Patriotic religious organizations" manage places of
worship and also decide what practices should be followed or banned.
Is proselytizing allowed? Yes, provided the authorized religion is taught
by a member of a patriotic association and is Chinese. Catholic missionaries sent by the Vatican, Korean pastors, and Japanese Buddhists
are liable to expulsion. The younger apparatchik assured me with a
broad smile: "This isn't chauvinism. The Chinese want to be educated
by the Chinese." Is that so? How, then, did Buddhism, Islam, and
Christianity come to China in the first place, one wonders.

I told them of my experiences in the Chinese provinces. Could
one talk of a religious renaissance? The two men consulted each

other in low voices. The young apparatchik replied in a modern fashion: "We are," he began, "among scholars. I shall thus give you an honest and scientific answer." Before going any further, he thought it prudent to have tea served. A young peasant girl poured boiling water from a flask over the tea leaves. She was dressed in a five-star bellboy uniform not quite her size. Once the tea leaves had settled at the bottom of the cup, we drank, burning our lips in the bargain. One had to suck to swallow the herb tea without the leaves. It was a noisy exercise, requiring a great deal of concentration.

"No, we don't see any religious renaissance in China," continued the young apparatchik. The researchers at the institute had counted the members of the five patriotic religious associations. In 2005, the number stood at 100 million. The researchers exclude the possibility of believing without joining any group: that is not scientific. A hundred million is roughly the same figure as in 1950, when the first religious census was conducted. From 1966 to 1976, during the Cultural Revolution, the number of believers decreased significantly. With the restoration of religious freedom in 1985, the number went back up, stabilizing at about 100 million. But China's population has doubled since 1950, which means that in fifty years, the proportion of believers has come down by half. The apparatchiks were all smiles. They thought they had convinced me.

That only 300 million "have religion," out of a population of a billion, means that communism and economic progress provide a better alternative, supplanting religion. Both the commissars looked very pleased with this. I counterattacked: "It is obvious that the number of Protestants is increasing."

They replied: "They were very few in the past. They are just catching up with the Catholics. That's normal."

The truth is that Protestants outnumber Catholics ten to one. But the Party finds it easier to deal with scattered evangelical groups than with an organized Catholic Church that receives its orders from outside. Between the Vatican and Yankee Protestantism, the Communist Party prefers the Americans.

The two commissars showed me out courteously, advising me on how to proceed further with my inquiry. Subjective impressions were not reliable. The institute had a scientific answer to all my queries.

Perhaps like the Jesuits of the past, I, too, was a prisoner of my prejudices.

They had not seen any religion in China. I seemed to find it everywhere.

Many North American Protestant observers talk about a mass conversion of the Chinese to an evangelical religion. Through their fervor, they believe, the converts will overthrow the Communist Party and bring in democracy. Christianity, the way it is spreading in China, is more Chinese than Christian. And if the history of China teaches us anything at all, it is that no single religion has ever been able to dominate the others. It appears more likely that religions and sects will remain scattered. But this very plurality is a sign of hope in a China struggling to get rid of the think-alike syndrome.

CHAPTER FOUR

The Dispossessed

Moving westward from seafaring China is like journeying back in time to discover the secret of the Chinese economic miracle. The experience is overwhelming.

As I wait at the Beijing airport, more efficient than any in Europe, the whole country seems brand-new. I recall the giant statue of Mao Zedong that once welcomed visitors. It was removed; no one knows when. But Mao's statues have not disappeared altogether. They can be seen in most large cities except Beijing and Shanghai. Two hours later, I reach Xian. We are still in new China. Everything works, and everything is oversize. The huge airports and highways are often empty. They were built to unify the Chinese provinces and create a single market. Until only a few years ago, China had as many markets as provinces. Each market was a closed entity, running its agriculture and industry like an autarchy. Custom duties and all kinds of physical and administrative barriers protected local enterprise. That period is over. One can now talk of a single Chinese market, unprecedented in the country's history. Highways abound, and some of the Party's cadres have made their fortunes. How are they financed? The exorbitant toll tax is out of the reach of the poor and most travelers. Political leaders are the main, and sometimes the sole, highway users in central and western China. Their black Audis can be seen speeding down the highways. Where is the money going to come from?

73

The craze for highways

In the poorest regions, where highways and airports have little utility, they are financed by state-owned banks that have no choice but to bow down to the dictates of the local Communist Party. They know they will never recover their investment. Even in the more prosperous provinces, the toll tax is not enough to pay back the loan. Highway companies, public enterprises for the most part, acquire land dirt cheap on both sides of the road with the peasants receiving hardly any compensation. Real-estate speculation raises prices, making some of these ventures so profitable that Western banks invest in them with eyes closed.

Western travelers are impressed by the speed at which the network is developing. They don't see the conditions in which it is being built. The crews recruited from the countryside work eighty hours a week. They get makeshift accommodation, are poorly fed, and can't leave the site. "Labor camps," as they are called, is the most neutral term to describe these prisons. The liberal writer Wang Yi, a professor of law at Chengdu, points out that the Nazis, too, built splendid roadways in the Thirties, and Westerners were just as wonderstruck.

Giving preference to highways and private cars makes little sense in a country as vast and poor as China. The railways and public-urban transport are a thousand times more suited to carry the massive flows of people and goods over long distances. It would enable the western and central provinces to industrialize and send their goods to the ports. Yet the Chinese government has invested in only one rail line—the one through Tibet, inaugurated in 2006. It has hardly any economic utility, but China will be able to colonize this rebellious province more easily and send in the army, if need be. The Tibetans understand as much.

Highways are a lucrative business for the Party cadres, and they can be constructed quickly. That is why the government is so keen on them. The leaders are impatient. They are looking for quick gains, both for themselves and for China. There is no long-term strategy. No one wants to think ahead. Perhaps no one believes in the long term. Capital is for infrastructure alone; education and health get short shrift, because Chinese development is not based on developing human resources. In Japan and Korea, it was just the opposite. Sometimes in the course of their speeches, the leaders in Beijing admit these errors. Things will be different in the future, they promise: the poorest provinces will have schools, hospitals, factories, and trains. For the moment, though, these remain empty slogans. The immediate reality, as we will see, is quite different.

East to West: a journey in time

Moving west of Xian, we take the highway on which work is going on day and night, held back only on account of a shortage of concrete. We are still in the developed world, but overloaded trucks from bygone days pass us from the opposite direction. It is as if the history of China is unfurling before us. New factories are coming up; those of the Maoist period are crumbling. The new ones are private; the old ones were public. The principle of creative destruction, so dear to free-market economists, is at work here as never before or elsewhere. The Catholic and Protestant churches in the villages we drive by indicate a religious awakening. We are in Shaanxi Province, where the first Christian church was built in the seventh century by a Nestorian sect from Persia that was later dissolved. From the very beginning, Christianity in China has had to strike a delicate balance between being Chinese enough not to appear alien, yet not so Chinese as to lose its identity and merge into the religions of the country.

From the road, we can see steles atop funeral mounds that lie scattered over the corn and wheat fields. The steles are arranged in accordance with the principles of geomancy. In early spring, during the Festival of the Dead, also known as the Festival of Light or the Cold Meal Festival (people eat food prepared the evening before), people weed the burial mounds, an homage of the living to their ancestors. Families come to burn incense and paper money, things the dead take with them to purgatory. Families separated by the Revolution reunite at these tombs. The Festival of Light is about re-creating civil society and keeping memories alive. Each tomb is a small victory over the authorities. If the Party had its way, people would have to cremate their dead en masse to free cultivable land. The peasants resist. They keep sowing and harvesting around the mounds.

After the first 100 miles or so, the highway begins to shrink. The tarmac deteriorates rapidly until there is nothing left of the road. Trucks get stuck in potholes, and some fall into ravines. We have crossed the Shaanxi border to enter Gansu. A *tofu* road, I am told. The local officials embezzled the money. A few were jailed, but the Party cadres were not bothered. All the world over, public works are a good source of funding for political parties. China is no exception. When corruption is too flagrant, the Party punishes the underlings, without touching the system itself that is so profitable.

The *tofu* road comes to an end. A stony path takes it place, winding its way up the mountains. A few toll bridges slow us down further. Uniformed inspectors tell us we can either pay the tax or make a donation. We give the money; otherwise, they'll slap a huge fine on us. It is the same story on all Chinese roads. Officials in fancy uniforms extort money from travelers on the pretext of collecting wholly unjustified taxes. According to Chinese government estimates, 40 percent of taxes taken from the peasants have no legal basis and never go into the public coffers.

The construction boom has not reached the village. With their adobe walls and curved tiled roofs, the farmhouses have remained unchanged for centuries. Our adventure has finally come to an end. We have reached the commune of the Pagoda of the Phoenix. Twelve thousand people live in its ten villages with picturesque names like the Ducks' Pond and Mao's Family Hamlet. As I am a guest of the Party's local secretary, I can stay here without having to explain my visit to the police. I met the secretary at the Baoji hospital where his daughter was being treated. Chance friendships are the best introductions in China.

From afar, the Chinese countryside appears deceptively calm and idyllic. In truth, it is neither. It is an understatement to say that the

Shaanxi and Gansu villages are poor. It fails to describe the complete destitution of the area. The houses are bare. The only furniture consists of a minimum of bedding, a gas stove, and a few stools. The adobe walls provide little protection against the scorching heat and the bitter cold. A brick brazier, a *kang*, provides the only heating. The brazier is lit with harvest waste and twigs from the mountainside, used very sparingly. Hygiene is unheard of, running water scarce. The villages have no public square where people can meet. In fact, there is no social life at all. Old clan feuds spoil good neighborly relations, each family keeping to itself. Some things have changed. The commune does have electricity and television. The public channel, the only one, parrots government sermons, indifferent to what is happening in the world. A few variety shows are thrown in to provide some entertainment and break the isolation.

Where have all the young men gone? In the narrow streets, one sees children of school age and withered old men, pensively drawing on their pipes. The large number of children suggests that parents are careless about practicing family planning. In any case, the single-child norm of the more populated regions is relaxed in Shaanxi Province, where couples are allowed two children. But on average, they have three, either not declaring the third child or paying an enormous fine.

My first trip took place in the spring of the Year of the Rooster. During my second visit, in the autumn, the young were working in the fields, handpicking the cornstalks and tilling the land with wooden rakes to sow the wheat. Each family cultivates two-and-a-half acres located on terraces perilously clinging onto the mountainsides, eroded by the river, which often floods. With no tools and only human manure, you need the patience of a gardener to survive on this poor soil. Fortunately, the peasants can sell the harvests from some apple and walnut trees, their only source of income. Even this is depleted by intermediaries, who drive up in trucks and take advantage of the peasants' lack of organization.

There are no men and hardly any young women, who see migration to the cities, the sites, and factories of eastern China as the only hope they have. Already, the countryside is poor, and policies are designed to choke it even further, making it impossible for the peasants to improve their lot in the village. This is the major difference between China and other developing countries. India, Brazil, and Indonesia are also rural economies with an equally dense population. But in these countries, peasants can raise their voices and sometimes be heard. The Chinese peasants have no voice. So it is hard for them to show enterprise, learn, and look after themselves.

Eight hundred million condemned to lifelong poverty

A common argument is this: there are just too many Chinese living on scarce and barren land; they are thus condemned to live in poverty. But with each passing year, the peasants are getting poorer and poorer—something the government admits—and are left with no option but to leave for the city. In the Sixties, the introduction of new seeds and technology increased yields considerably, wiping out famine and food shortages. In the Seventies, the clumsily executed experiment of setting up factories in the villages showed that it was not impossible to develop local agriculture and food processing with the help of the worker-peasants. Other countries—India and Bangladesh, for instance—use innovative methods such as the cultivation of cash crops, private cooperatives, and micro-credit to help farmers improve their lot without uprooting them. China made no such attempt because the peasants have no voice. They cannot invest in the future. They cannot obtain credit, and, as the land belongs to the state and not to them, they have no collateral to offer. In a poor country, unequal access to credit is like a sentence of lifelong poverty. The Party is aware of this. Yet it is not willing to give peasants full ownership instead of the right to cultivate. Property would create a middle class, which would not be dependent on the Party for its survival.

The administration's allocation of plots by family does not permit the consolidation of land holdings, necessary for more productive mechanized farming. Significantly, national rice and wheat production has stagnated at the same level for the past fifteen years. From my brief conversations with the villagers—it is not easy talking to them, for the Party secretary is never far off—it appears that they would like to come together to sell their apples and even build a fruit-juice factory. The Party is in no mood to oblige. It would mean abandoning the policy of land fragmentation, giving credit to the peasants, eliminating intermediaries, and connecting the village with a proper road. We may think that these are steps in the right direction, but it would be a "headache" for the Party secretary. He would have to account to his district bosses for all these transgressions against the dominant ideology. So he prefers the status quo.

What about schools? The peasants pin all their hopes on their children, believing that education will enable them to escape from poverty. Parents are willing to spend what little they have on their children's education. The Pagoda of the Phoenix has a quite respectable-looking school that lends itself well to official functions. In principle, the commune's 2,000-odd children are supposed to get nine years of compulsory education. But a quarter of them can be seen loitering about in the streets or working in the fields. The principal of the school says, "They are handicapped children. We are not equipped to take them in." I have a feeling that the real handicap is their parents' poverty and inability to pay the fees.

Isn't education free? In the cities, schools can be free or dependent on public enterprises, but not so in the villages. Parents have to contribute toward the school's supplies, including the purchase of chalk, heating, the canteen, and anything else the principal thinks necessary. Teachers don't mind receiving gifts from time to time. The children of obliging parents get greater personal attention, and their promotion is assured; eventually, they may be able to enroll in high school. Of course, it is true that teachers earn a pittance, with a monthly salary of eighty yuan. Their accommodations consist of a single unheated room equipped with nothing more than a mean bed and a stove. No teacher trained in the city is willing to work here. The village teachers are often peasants who have completed a two-week training course. Between classes, they attend to their fields. Few of these semi-teachers are truly devoted to their jobs. They know just enough to teach the children how to read, write, and count. The nine years of compulsory education trumpeted by the Party turns out to be yet another fabrication. In truth, a quarter of the Chinese population is illiterate, more girls than boys.

For a peasant, the worst thing that can happen is falling ill. The nearest doctor is at Baoji, a five-hour bus journey on a bumpy road. Hospitalization is prohibitively expensive and beyond the means of most peasants. No matter what the emergency, all hospitals in China ask for an 800-yuan deposit before admitting any patient. The deposit is supposed to cover various medical procedures, whose prices are listed. Most modern hospitals display the price list above the cash counter. Payment must be made in advance. Doctors sell medicines separately, at exorbitant prices. For most families, going to hospital means being in debt for many years. And even after paying exorbitantly, the treatment is at times worse than the disease. Injections and drips are a must for every patient; the district hospitals claim that they have both therapeutic and magical properties. Syringes are commonly reused and medicines dispensed long after their expiry date. Many patients get hepatitis, which becomes cancerous. Widows in the village are legion. Who cares?

Atypical pneumonia and bird flu figure high on the list of concerns of the Chinese government and the international community, even though the number of victims is small. Tuberculosis, malaria, hepatitis, cholera, and dysentery, however, afflict tens if not hundreds of millions of Chinese—but the government is not bothered, because these are traditional diseases that kill only local people in remote areas. Preventing bird flu is a complex, expensive, and perhaps futile business. But teaching people a few elementary precautions could save many lives. No one knows about hygiene in the villages. People never wash their hands. They live in close proximity to animals, a key source of infection. The Party does not care. Spending on health care brings neither instant glory nor quick profit. Consequently, life expectancy in China's rural West is on average ten years less than in the eastern cities. Life expectancy is actually going down in the villages.

As the majority simply can't afford medical care, they turn toward magical practices, the opium of the people, according to Marx. Master Zhao is the village doctor.

Zhao claims to be a Daoist priest. As proof, he produces a certificate stamped by the Daoist Patriotic Association, a religious wing of the Communist Party. Getting such a certificate does not require much knowledge of theology. Good relations with the association and a discreet bribe will do the trick. In China, everything has become commercialized, even the priesthood. Master Zhao has a long beard and smooth manners. "Thanks to the Party," he was able to restore the Pagoda of the Phoenix, which was destroyed during the Cultural Revolution. The Pagoda looks as it did before, only more gleaming. Zhao wants me to know that he is not in politics. His principal duty is to preside over funerals and help souls find deliverance so that they don't return to trouble the living. He is also the local doctor. People come to him with all kinds of ailments: headaches, cancers, depressions. Zhao gives them incense sticks. He makes potions from bark and herbs. He puts his hands on the patient's head while mumbling ancient prayers. He has a treatment for everything, but nothing is free. Sometimes, his therapy can be dangerous. Chinese medicine has never been tested scientifically, and its efficacy is doubtful. The toxic mixtures he prescribes can cost a patient his life.

Wasn't hygiene better before the liberal reforms, when there was "real communism"? The village did have a dispensary in Mao's time. Its ruins still remain. The elders remember the barefoot doctor, a young woman from the city posted to the village during the Cultural Revolution. Master Zhao, they feel, is more skilled.

Similar conditions prevail elsewhere. But perhaps I am painting an unduly grim picture. Evidently, things have improved since the Sixties, when peasants were reduced to eating grass and bark after the Party took away their harvests. Even if they remain in their villages, Chinese peasants survive, an improvement over the period of collectivization and the other such great leaps forward from the Fifties up until 1978. The return to private cultivation (not to be confused with private property), known as the 1979 Reform, saved the peasantry from famine. Yet 100 million still don't get three square meals a day. That is not a small number, even in China.

Are we to praise the Party's wisdom for this meager progress? Certainly, the Party doesn't stop blowing its own trumpet. Yet all it has done is to return to the peasant the rice bowl it had snatched from him. The 1979 Reform was the brainchild of Deng Xiaoping. It is not so much a testimony to his genius as to the rationality of the Chinese peasant. He works when the Party lets him. When his land and harvest are confiscated, he and millions like him perish. The Party's self-satisfaction is absurd. And why this constant comparison between the China of today and the China of the past to reassure ourselves that it is making progress under the Party's tutelage? Should China not instead be compared with other countries that face similar challenges? Would that not be more worthwhile, seeing what China was and what it could become, given the hardworking nature of its people and the hunger for education of its peasantry? This seems the fairest yardstick. The Party doesn't think so. Developing agriculture and improving the lot of 800 million peasants are not high on its list of priorities.

How the young are forced to leave their villages

Even before I ask anything, Lu tells me: "The Party doesn't command any more, and it doesn't even manage: it only advises." Lu is the Party secretary of the Pagoda of the Phoenix. His superiors must have dressed him down when they learned that a foreigner was venturing into their territory without prior authorization. Lu seems sincere. He is a local peasant, not an apparatchik sent arbitrarily by the Party. In many villages, the Party secretary is a tyrant, but there are few complaints against young Lu. No doubt, the villagers have to pay for his and his wife's upkeep. They have built the couple a modern house covered with white tiles, and they pay all Lu's petty expenses such as cigarettes and bus fare when he goes to the city. In every village, the Party lives off the poor peasants. When the local bosses invite their family and friends to visit, the villagers must look after them—an unofficial tax, and a heavy one. Often the Party secretary appropriates a plot of land to build his house. Either the peasants submit or they file a petition, sometimes taking their fight all the way to Beijing. En route, the police beat them and throw the ringleaders behind bars. When petitioners are too numerous in the capital, the police round them up and keep them in a stadium until they can be sent back to their villages. If a petitioner happens to win his case, the press lauds the fairness of the national leaders and laments the negligence of the local cadres. That's how things work. Apparatchiks can do anything, provided the top doesn't have to hear about it.

Lu, however, is not too greedy. "He can read and write," villagers tell me. He's been to high school; he understands official correspondence, which he translates into vernacular for the villagers. Lu is proud of having been elected by the twenty-nine members of his cell. Isn't that a small number in a village of 2,000 people? The Party should recruit more actively, he agrees, but few are willing to "devote themselves to the people." How many women are in the Party? Taken aback by the question, Lu makes a mental count and admits that there are none. After giving the matter some thought, he concedes that it would be good to have one or two.

Lu reverts to the slogans that he has been instructed to repeat for my benefit: "The Party has only one mission: the development of China." His task is to explain this to the villagers. The country comes first, then the village. This means ensuring an inexhaustible supply of cheap, obedient labor for the factories. As soon as girls and boys turn sixteen, Lu urges them to leave the Pagoda of the Phoenix and sell their labor elsewhere. The district Party has set for him an annual quota of emigrants in accordance with age, sex, and qualifications. The quotas are based on the needs of the industry and service sectors in the cities and the distant East. If Lu fails to meet his quota, the Party will punish him with a fine or a demotion. However, as the young leave the village even before they are asked to, Lu doesn't have a problem.

Parents, too, are eager for their children to go. Teenagers who remain in the village are deemed good for nothing. If they emigrate, the families hope they will send back a portion of their earnings. Some do; others disappear without a trace. Very few children come back to take care of their parents. The market economy has supplanted filial piety, once a cardinal Chinese virtue. The number of orphans increases by the day. Fathers go to work in far-off places and never return. Unable to raise their children alone, mothers emigrate in turn, or commit suicide by swallowing pesticide, a cheap poison freely available in the villages. Who is to pay for the education of the abandoned children? As soon as these children can, they, too, will join the 100 million—or is it 200 million?—migrants in search of work.

The Communist regime has been consistent, if nothing else. When in 1958 Mao Zedong ordered industry's Great Leap Forward, local Party cadres received the same instructions: 20 million had to be sent to the factories. Three years later, the Great Leap failed, as could have been predicted. Widespread famine resulted, and the 20 million were sent back to their villages. Mao marveled at this feat. What other party in the world could displace 20 million people by simply snapping its fingers? he asked.

It was from old Wang that I got stray bits of information about the school, life as a farmer, the suicides, and the people who left, never to return. He is the village chief, duly elected through universal suffrage. He also heads the strongest clan in the village, so powerful that he doesn't need to buy votes. Who is the real leader: the village chief or the Party secretary? Old Wang's primary task is to settle quarrels between feuding families. He is also hoping to pool together the village apples to set up a fruit-juice factory, but Lu opposes the idea. Who decides? Lu, admits old Wang. Everywhere in China—city, village, factory, and university—the power structure is the same, patterned on the central model. The Party decides, the administration executes, and the army and the police keep watch. Submitting to the Party dictates, old Wang, too, encourages the young to leave, advising the "girls to join the service sector and the boys to look for manual work." His own daughter works as a waitress in a Xian restaurant. Does he have any news of her? Wang doesn't answer. To speak of his sorrows with a foreigner would be to lose face. This inherent feature of Chinese civilization makes it difficult to probe. Censorship can be skirted but not social attitudes. One must not lose face.

The migrant, a second-zone citizen

The children of the Pagoda of the Phoenix are forever roaming, like characters in an epic, moving from site to site, factory to factory. Sometimes they get paid, sometimes they don't. At the start of the Year of the Rooster, unpaid wages, according to official estimates, amounted to 360 billion yuan. The government has told employers to settle the workers' dues before the end of the year. The migrants will suffer from cold and hunger. Other migrants will attack them, bandits will rob them, and the police will fine them heavily. Yet, in comparison to the brutality of the past, they are still better off.

During the last fifty years, peasants needed prior authorization to travel by train or in the city. Until 1984, they had to get a ration ticket for their food, valid only in the local market. They could not work in the city without a permit. These domestic passports were abolished only recently, and more in theory than in practice, at least for the moment. The kind of corruption they lead to is not difficult to imagine.

The free movement of peasants has allowed construction activity to proceed at a feverish pace. Peasants are working on sites, constructing factories, putting up buildings, making roads—in short, serving the town dwellers. The differences between a peasant and someone from the city stand out. Every detail tells them apart: their clothes, their behavior, their manners, the very language they speak. In the cities, people talk in Mandarin or one of the major provincial languages, or both. The peasants use a dialect. Racism against peasants is common in cities like Beijing and Shanghai, akin to the contempt in which Europeans hold African migrants. One reader wrote to the Shandong daily advocating separate transport systems for migrants, because they stink. Yet they are all Chinese, or supposedly so.

In addition to geographic and economic biases, legal discrimination exists as well, a legacy of the Communist revolution little known outside China. In the Fifties, Mao Zedong's government decided to divide China into two categories: agricultural and nonagricultural, the official nomenclature used to this day. Each Chinese is issued at birth a family booklet, or *hukou*, which indicates the category to which one belongs and the family's place of origin. Children inherit their mother's place of origin, and there is little they can do to change it. One's fate is determined to a large extent by one's *hukou*, because individual rights vary according to one's place of origin. The *hukou* sticks to an individual's skin his entire life, as with the castes in India. The American Fei-Ling Wang—the only sociologist to have studied in depth this extremely delicate subject, shrouded in secrecy—was imprisoned during his research trip in 2004 and sent back to the United States. In November 2005, the Party announced the "phased" abolition of the *hukou*, but this attempt at national reunification is not likely to deter the municipal authorities from setting up fresh legal barriers against the integration of the rural population, as they are already doing.

Out-of-bounds for villagers

Farm migrants do not have access to most of the public services that city dwellers do. Rural workers are denied public housing, primary education, and health care, all subsidized by the city or the firm, on the grounds that they are not taxpayers or that they do not pay for such services. One had an inkling of their condition in 2005, when the mayor of Beijing announced the establishment of special schools for the children of the city's 3 million migrants. All the existing schools had refused to take them in. The Shanghai municipality has its own way of ensuring that rural workers can't integrate, as we shall see.

One-third of Shanghai's 17 million inhabitants are migrants, yet it is virtually impossible for them to become citizens with their identity cards, which in principle give them access to public services. In Shanghai, as in all other Chinese cities, there is a sort of local nationality by blood. With the winds of reform blowing over the city in the Year of the Rooster, the municipality has decided to issue local identity cards on the basis of marriage, but the conditions are so restrictive that they appear ridiculous. A non-Shanghai woman married to a Shanghai man can get nationality after fifteen years of her marriage, which means the couple's children will automatically become citizens of Shanghai, as nationality is handed down by the mother. The authors of this daring innovation told me, though, that a man from Shanghai would have to be very "poor or handicapped" to marry a "foreigner." What happens if a non-Shanghai man marries a Shanghai woman? I asked. The new law has not provided for such an eventuality, they told me at the mayor's office, because it was unthinkable that a Shanghai woman would marry an "outsider."

Town-hall officials said that if all immigrants were granted citizenship, by marriage or otherwise, they would flood schools and hospitals and demand public housing. The city's infrastructure wouldn't be able to take the load. Were the news to spread to the countryside, millions would flock to Shanghai, creating huge ghettos around the city. The art of "good governance" is to attract just enough migrants to meet the city's need for laborers, garbage collectors, and waiters without letting them integrate or proliferate. Even in distant villages, people are aware of the low wages and the shabby way that workers are treated; this puts a damper on their fascination for Shanghai. Yet there is always a way to circumvent a ban in China. Fake papers can be obtained, and phone numbers are scribbled all over the city's walls, offering such services. But it entails a heavy expenditure that few migrant workers can afford.

So like all large cities, Shanghai and Beijing have their nonurban areas. One-third of the people live at the edges, citizens of the second zone, who can never integrate because they are constantly on the move. Educating one's children or finding a decent place to live is impossible. Jobs are insecure. The weakest go elsewhere, only to be replaced by a fresh influx of bonded labor. Madam Han Qiui, one of the rare Beijing sociologists to take an interest in the subject, says that "migrants pay dearly for China's development." Her studies show that the few migrants who manage to urbanize legally are university-degree holders and wealthy traders. You can change your *hukou* if you have a doctorate or make a large investment. The rest must go back to their villages or move from city to city.

Few children have succeeded in changing their peasant status through education. Village schools, as we have seen, are substandard. Even if one passes the national examination, university education is very expensive. The limited social mobility is limited further because urban elites are self-perpetuating. Their children monopolize the best schools and universities and often go abroad for higher studies. Children from a rural background account for no more than 20 percent of the total number of students in Beijing's universities, whereas the peasantry constitutes 80 percent of the total population. Their proportion keeps declining, and other students treat them as second-class citizens. Essentially, China's economic development is based on the urban population's exploitation of the rural population, with the Party providing the legal framework for doing so.

Mao Zedong: the Great Helmsman still

How could a Communist government create two peoples, almost two races, within a single nation? Our incredulity stems from our ignorance of the Party's true nature. Mao Zedong had proclaimed his was a peasant-led revolution but, as the historian Lucien Bianco pointed out, peasants merely constituted the "rank and file" of the Communist army. They fought without getting anything in return. Li Lulu, a Beijing sociologist, says, "It was like France of 1789. Peasants burned down the castles of French aristocrats, and lawyers came to power." In China, pen pushers, army officers, and a worker avant-garde took control. Workers, not peasants, were the privileged ones. Mao himself did not dream of any bucolic utopia. He wanted to establish China as an industrial and military power. In 1959, at the height of the famine caused by the Great Leap Forward, his government exported food grains to build nuclear weapons and distilled grain into alcohol to launch rockets. We would do well to remember this.

The foreign-currency reserves accumulated in Mao's time were intended to finance military spending. Can things be very different under his direct descendants?

Maoist development failed because it based itself on nationalized enterprises, a planned economy, and closed borders. But the industrial project Mao cherished was clear. Deng Xiaoping's move to liberalize the economy was not so much a change in strategy as the abandoning of an inefficient technique for a time-tested method. During Mao's rule and afterward, during the Revolution and after the 1949 liberation, however, the peasants were never more than the proletariat of the industrial project. They still are. No more than 200,000 villagers manage each year to escape from their plight and join the category of legal citizens.

In the Year of the Rooster, the peasants are no longer passive. The villages simmer with discontent.

The time of mutinies and repression

In May 2005, at Shengyou in Hebei Province, a militia squad of the local government expelled a hundred peasant families who had refused to give up their land without compensation for the construction of a power plant. Armed with pitchforks, the peasants resisted. Twelve were killed. Work on the power plant commenced.

It would have been just another peasant revolt had a Beijing journalist not been alerted by a distress text message from a villager. By the time the journalist reached the site, it was all over; the police had surrounded the village. No mention appeared in the press, and the journalist was arrested. But the rumors spread, the incident was discussed on the Internet, and the government in Beijing took notice. Local cadres, it emerged, had siphoned off most of the compensation money that the government had set aside, leaving only crumbs for the peasants. The villagers had filed petition after petition and demonstrated outside the Party headquarters, but to no avail. So they decided to squat on their land in a day-and-night vigil. It was then that the Party-hired goons moved in. The only extraordinary thing about this incident is that it came to light. Such revolts are an everyday occurrence all over the Chinese countryside. But there are usually no witnesses, and when there are, they are unwilling to talk.

In September 2005, at Dongyang in Zhejiang Province, 1,000 peasants clashed with the police for several hours. The authorities had tried to remove the barricade put up by the villagers to block access to five polluting chemical factories. The factories had been built on agricultural land without permission. Saturated with toxic effluents, the surrounding land had become uncultivable. The peasants contracted skin diseases, some of them cancerous. In June 2005, the local government had promised to close down these factories. In September, they were still running. The local officials had been bought off. Tensions reached a flashpoint, and the villagers revolted. A Hong Kong journalist who managed to reach Dongyang with the help of the rebel leaders filmed the clash and posted his film on the Internet. The press was told to ignore the story, but papers in Hong Kong, and eventually America, took it up. A similar skirmish took place in Dongzhou, close to the Hong Kong border, on December 6. The villagers whose land had been taken to build a power plant received hardly any compensation. During a clash with the police, a number of them—anywhere from three to thirty—were shot down. This was the first time since the Tiananmen massacre in 1989 that the police had fired on a crowd. It was also the first time that the news spread outside China, thanks, once again, to the Hong Kong press, alerted by a villager. The Hong Kong press is relaying news of revolts in increasingly far-flung areas, but the news remains only a trickle. The regions are remote, witnesses' accounts are rare, there are no photos, and Hong Kong is becoming vulnerable to pressure from the Beijing government.

Are these sporadic episodes, to be expected in so vast a country, or part of a general uprising of the rural population? The Party is not sure. During a secret government meeting in July 2005, the Minister of Security admitted that in 2004, China had witnessed 74,000 mass incidents, in which 3.76 million people had taken part, and that the number was fast increasing. The precise nature of the statistics leads one to believe that the actual figure is higher, with many incidents going unreported. Local information is selectively relayed to the central government. This "secret" information is leaked to the press so that it can turn it to good account. On the Party's orders, the press exhorts peasants to "respect the law" and go through "proper channels" to get grievances redressed. In other words, peasants are told to direct their complaints to the petitions office. The editors did not, however, deny the legitimacy of the grievances. What the Party was saying was: the peasants had reason to protest. The Party was their ally. The real culprits were corrupt local cadres, real-estate speculators, and unscrupulous entrepreneurs.

For a long time, the Party sought to minimize the peasant revolts, describing them as the unavoidable fallout of urban and industrial development. Until the Year of the Rooster, the uprisings seemed dispersed and localized, with no apparent link. Yet they are part of a long historical tradition. From time immemorial, peasants have been prompt to take up their pitchforks to bring erring mandarins, tax inspectors—and now Party cadres—into line. Only during Mao's time was the peasantry quiet. It was a period of terror. Since the Nineties, the repression has been less severe and information more easily available, explaining perhaps the increasing number of open rebellions. But will the Internet and mobile phones enable the peasants to organize themselves sufficiently so that they can start a full-fledged revolution?

Peasant leaders do arise from time to time in the prosperous eastern countryside. They are often migrants who have returned from the city or ex-army men. They have the capacity to organize and coordinate. The Party is not afraid of stray rebellions, but it does fear coordinated action. When the number of protests was acknowledged officially in 2005, the Party devised a new strategy to contain peasant discontent. Not surprisingly, its premises were based on ideological considerations rather than realities on the ground. It issued directives aimed at strengthening the Party's hold. There was no attempt to give the peasants a voice.

The Party is always right

I meet Dang Guoying, director of the Institute for Rural Development in Beijing. He is also an advisor to the central government. His job is to inculcate new right-thinking in Party cadres. He says there are "five reasons for the peasant protests." The Communist Party has abandoned its revolutionaries and taken on experts, whose job it is to find the middle path. Analysis and quantification are their way of resolving conflicts.

Taxes are the first reason. In addition to the national tax, fixed at 8.48 percent of income, local cadres impose a further burden on the peasants, levying multiple taxes to finance village infrastructure. A few villagers, however, outraged at Party cadres buying cars and building houses with tax proceeds, took the law into their own hands and settled scores with the tax collectors, sometimes even murdering them. The central government, believing that the peasant anger had some justification, announced the abolition of all taxes on peasants at the beginning of the Year of the Rooster. The main cause of discontent has thus been removed, concludes Dang, thanks to the alliance between the Communist Party and the peasantry. Whom is he trying to fool? Or has the government gotten carried away by its own rhetoric? Taxes may well have been abolished officially, but the local cadres continue to bleed the peasants, making them pay an endless number of fees and fines. This is the real cause of anger.

The second reason for the peasant protests, Dang says, is birth control. The peasants hate family-planning inspectors even more than tax inspectors: their inspection visits often culminate in skirmishes. But the birth-control program has been an unqualified success, says Dang. So the anger will soon subside. What is one to believe? The Chinese population is growing at double the rate of the one-child-per-family goal. Has the Party given up on its plan? Or in the absence of any reliable data on population, has it assumed that reality and discourse are one and the same?

Reason number three: the peasants overestimate the profits of the village enterprises because "they don't have any knowledge of accounting." These collective enterprises, numerous in the country-side, provide the peasants with additional employment, and the redistributed profits improve their quality of life. But the cadres alone know what the real profits are, if there are any at all. Feeling cheated, the peasants protest. Privatization is the Party's answer. Dang Guoying thinks that this should resolve all conflicts. How? Privatization in urban China is a strategy to let Communist cadres become the private owners of the enterprises they oversee. There is no reason for things to be different in the countryside. In theory, the conflict will be resolved. Socialist enterprises will become capitalistic ventures, with owners and workers instead of cadres and citizens. They will not be the Party's responsibility any more.

Reason number four: property. Peasants whose lands are expropriated by real-estate builders and industrial entrepreneurs receive barely any compensation. Often, it is simply an affair of land-grabbing. In the future, the central government will ensure that the peasants receive compensation reflecting the real value of the land. The problem, however, according to Dang, is the peasants' profligacy. "They waste the money they get on banquets, gambling, and women, and end up bankrupt without any work." There may be some truth to that.

The fifth and last reason, and the most decisive, says Dang Guoying, which encompasses the other four, is that cadres do not carry out central directives with enough devotion and efficiency. The center is just and fair to all peasants, but its local representatives need to mend their ways. The Party schools are working at sensitizing Party officials to the condition of the peasants. A greater awareness on their part will remove the reasons for revolt.

That peasants are capable of having their own opinions, expressing themselves, being represented, and communicating with Communist cadres has not been considered. In the Party-State, there is no room for dialogue and consensus building. The center knows what is good for the periphery, the top order for the bottom order. Good officials of a good party make for a good government.

I mention the rumors I hear: there are peasant organizations in Zhejiang whose leaders are ready to talk with Party representatives.

Dang Guoying is dismissive. "We know about the existence of these plots," he says. Any form of organization outside the Party is a plot.

Dang Guoying's approach will not put an end to the mutinies. But will the mutinies amount to a revolution? It is difficult to say. With the police, militia, and army at its command, the Party can break up the riots at any time. In doing so, however, it may well revive the taste for violence among both those who revolt and those who repress it. From a cynical point of view, the mutinies serve the Party's purpose, strengthening the central state and reinforcing the Party as the sole guarantor of order.

Will the communists become socialists?

Early October, and it is autumn in Beijing, the time of the national day, holidays, and a "golden week." The light is softer, the weather milder, there is less dust and smoke, and the pollution no longer hides the mountains that shield the capital from the northerly winds. It is also the time for good resolutions. This year, in a sudden about-face, the country's leaders seem to have taken note of the terrible injustices creating rural-urban disparities, with a prosperous urban China and an impoverished peasantry. For a moment, it seemed as if a social-democratic revolution was in the offing, at least on paper.

It all began on the national day, with the head of state paying warm tribute to "the migrants without whom China could never have developed." At last, the nameless, dispossessed migrant worker was being given a human face. A new five-year plan for 2006–11 was released, the eleventh since the constitution of the People's Republic. There has been a change in vocabulary, though. It is no longer called a plan, but a "program." The "program" emphasizes the primary role of the market economy, with public intervention playing a secondary role. It fixes a new goal for China: harmony, a vaguely Confucian term for restoring parity between cities and villages, peasants and town dwellers, rural and industrial provinces, the center and the west. After the humiliation of the past twenty-five years of "reform," the peasants will, within five years, have access to schools, health, and prosperity. An ambitious program indeed! How does the government intend to achieve these goals? The program states that it will act "scientifically." Official commentators like using this word. What is a *scientific* program? It suggests the opposite of revolution, a desire to break with the past. This is the explanation given to those who hanker for the state-controlled economy and other great leaps forward of the past. But how is a scientific economy going to address the concerns of the poor when the market is free and the state is curtailing its own role? Once again, the solution is scientific: the New Harmony will flow from democracy.

Democracy: has one heard correctly?

In the same month of October, a decidedly revolutionary one, the Communist Party also brought out a lengthy white paper on democracy in China. It was an emotional moment for me when I began reading it. At last, I thought, the government had shown the courage to denounce its own tyranny, to support free speech and pluralism. What followed was a complete letdown, which I should have expected.

The white paper was released in English at the same time as the Chinese version, proof that it was intended as much for Western consumption as for the Chinese people, who paid scant attention to the event. Written in official language, the white paper is merely a catalog of all the Party's achievements since 1949. There is not the slightest trace of remorse. China does not need any lessons in democracy from the world, it states. Democracy exists in several forms: bi-party, multiparty, and single party. China has a higher form of democracy because a democratic party, the Communist Party, is at the helm of affairs. The Party is democratic because free discussion is encouraged within it (though not outside of it). China is a democracy because the people chose the Party of their own free will . . . in 1949, and because the Party wields power only to serve the people. At no point does the white paper consider the possibility of curbing the Communist Party's monopoly. It does promise that local elections will give greater power to village and area chiefs to implement Party policies.

The celebration of migrants, a promise of social harmony and scientific economics, and the rhetoric of democracy were all part of the customary autumn ritual. Was there nothing new under the Beijing sun? Liberal activists in China didn't bother to hide their skepticism. Yet the Western community in China—the press and company strategists—has more faith in the Party than the Chinese do. In order to justify their continued presence in the country, most segments of the Western community are always ready to be cheerleaders and hail the Party: after all, it has conceded the existence of social injustice, peasant revolts, and the popular demand for democracy. The economic reforms begun in 1979 would necessarily lead to "political reforms." The Chinese president and his prime minister were genuine reformers, well-informed and courteous, and resisted, alas, by Party old-timers. The very same analysis was applied to the "favorable" developments in the Soviet Union before it crumbled. But, unlike the Soviet Union, the Chinese Communist Party is at the peak of a prosperity curve. So why should it undertake reforms that would weaken it? Had it been part of a democracy, the Party would have built schools and dispensaries to achieve its mandate. But since it does not have to face elections, there is no incentive to divert profitable industrial investment to social infrastructure, where the returns are slow. And the Party is not in the habit of altruism. So how can one believe the neo-Confucian, Marxist ideology spouted by leaders who have advanced themselves through sheer cruelty and cunning? Ding Yfan, a political commentator close to the establishment, attempts to provide a more compelling reason. His job is to woo skeptical Westerners visiting China. He says the Party will implement its social agenda because, shaken by the peasant revolts, it fears losing power. But the Party is not known to act out of enlightened self-interest, and fear is not a wise counselor. Economic considerations far outweigh any concern for social harmony. More than Confucius and Machiavelli, Marx provides a better explanation for why the Party will not change its line.

The impossibility of reforming the Party

The nascent national power of China is based on its high growth rate, achieved through the exploitation of rural labor by firms geared for the world market. Any change in this system would require at least partial reconversion to the domestic market. The government would have to invest in rural education, health-care, and transport services, investments that have a long gestation period. As a result, the growth rate would go down mechanically. Now the Communist Party has no popular base. It derives its support from a class of civil servants and army officers. Would they accept a drop in income in the name of social harmony? This seems unlikely. The Party is a prisoner of its base, of the political and economic system it has created. Any change would be suicidal.

The so-called social-democratic revolution of October 2005 ended in a typically Chinese way. At the same time as the announcement of the scientific program for harmony and the release of the white paper on democracy, a Chinese rocket carried two astronauts into space. The Chinese president monopolized the television screen, congratulating the astronauts at the time of takeoff, during their flight, and upon their return to Earth. "The whole world marvels at China's success," trumpeted the headlines of Chinese dailies. Yet for the price of one rocket, hundreds of schools and hospitals could have been built. There would have been greater harmony, but the world might not have been as impressed.

During the same month of October, near Guangzhou in the small southern town of Taishi, 2,000 inhabitants demanded the resignation of the notoriously corrupt village chief. They had signed a petition, the legal method for registering protest. The chief reacted by sending militia, hired by the Party, to pummel the signatories until they withdrew their petition. In December, in the same province, the most prosperous in China, the Dongzhou shoot-out occurred.

Looking ahead, what does the future hold for China? Do the growing number of petitions and demonstrations indicate the beginnings of a civil society? The appearance of new militias, brown or red shirts, the police's lack of hesitation to fire on crowds—are these ominous signs? As long as the Party wants to keep the dispossessed as they are, it will need the police, the army, and the militias. And the exploitation of the proletariat will continue to be the bedrock of the Chinese economy.

CHAPTER FIVE

The Downtrodden

"**W**orkers of the province, welcome!" This is the message on the banner, displayed prominently in bold letters on the façade of the Man Sum textile factory at Zhongshan in Guangdong Province. Guangzhou, the migrants' El Dorado, their ultimate destination! Of the province's 100 million inhabitants, one-third are migrant workers. The lucky ones, from the Pagoda of the Phoenix, get a job here. Man Sum is a model factory in which employees are relatively well treated. Another banner says, "We will hire you, keep you on our payrolls, and pay steady wages."

In early 2005, as mentioned, the Chinese government had, in all earnestness, asked employers to pay what they owed their workers in arrears by the end of the year. Some public- and private-sector firms had not paid their workers for two years. Kept on probation, these workers live in constant fear of being replaced by other migrants ready to take their place. The import of the Man Sum banners was to allay these fears, which is why the local authorities chose to take me there as part of their conducted tour.

Numerous banners read "Jobs Available," a reflection of the concerns of the day. Guangdong is developing so rapidly that, in spite of the steady flow of migrants, there are still plenty of vacancies. Companies try hard to lure employees away from their competitors. Employees move from one company to the next, hoping to increase their modest wages or improve their working conditions. Migrants categorize employers as "good" or "bad." Employers from mainland China are the worst, followed by those from Taiwan, Hong Kong, South Korea, and Japan. European firms offer better working conditions than even the American ones. The competition is cutthroat, especially among Chinese firms. Sometimes, companies adopt violent means to copy goods of other firms and produce them at half the price to eliminate their rivals. It's a no-holds-barred market economy.

Guangdong Province alone accounts for one-third of all foreign investment and exports. Currently, it is facing stiff competition from other provinces that have set up the same global workshops. Gao, the man who founded the Man Sum enterprise and authored the banners, is sensitive to the ethical concerns of his European, and particularly American, clients. They buy their stock from him at the lowest possible price and sell it in domestic supermarkets. Of course, as a condition for purchase, the Westerners stipulate that Gao mustn't "overexploit" his workers. Representatives from Wal-Mart come regularly to inspect his factory. Eighty percent of the goods sold in America's largest chain store are made in China. The inspectors check whether the factory conditions are fair to workers while also maintaining quality.

Export companies in China are geared wholly to cater to the tastes of Western, primarily American, consumers. American consumers drive the Chinese economy. The country's prosperity depends on them. Non-Americans do not play such a decisive role. Wal-Mart alone buys more from China than do Australia and Canada put together. Before they start their visit, Gao takes the inspectors to see the staff quarters, canteens, dispensaries, and kitchen gardens. Besides free accommodations—four workers to a room—workers earn about 100 dollars a month. The figure varies, because Gao pays the workers on a piecemeal basis and deducts money when a piece is badly executed or material is wasted.

Gao shows us around his factories in a Hummer, the most expensive American car on the market. The Cantonese do not think material success indecent. The source of Gao's wealth is there for all to see. The word "devotion" appears frequently on the banners displayed in the workshops. (Thirty years ago, it was "revolution.") As reward for this devotion to the factory, the blessings of the gods are sought. In every workshop, there is an altar before which incense sticks burn. The little shrines are dedicated to the god of prosperity, a reminder of the deep link between Daoism and the spirit of enterprise, contrary to what the Asia experts have been drumming into us for the past forty years. The French, like Léon Vandermeersch, and the Americans, like Hermann Kahn, have always attributed the economic success of Japan, Korea, and, more recently China, to the Confucian spirit. It was Confucianism, they maintained, that was responsible for the discipline in these countries' factories. The fact is, however, that Confucianism idealizes authority, and it looks down on trade. A disciple of Confucius aspires only to public office; he will never stoop to sell cloth. The management in Korea and Japan was no more authoritarian than the political regime. In China, a dictatorial government enforces discipline, denies its workers any rights, and frowns on trade unions. The role of Confucianism, it seems, has been much overrated. And yet, without entrepreneurs, there can be no companies. Gao, the founder of Man Sum, is Daoist, like most Chinese entrepreneurs, and is open to the world. Gao worships the god of prosperity, not the somber Master Kong.

The real authors of the success story

Factories like Man Sum can be found in Bangladesh, the Philippines, and Mexico. In the past, they existed in Europe, the United States, and, until quite recently, in Japan, Korea, and Taiwan. The success of these factories lies in the quality of their workers, who labor for long hours at low wages. Workers usually put in forty-five hours per week plus overtime; they also work extra time to compensate for the frequent electricity breakdowns. The equipment consists of fifty-year-old, secondhand Japanese machines that have been overhauled. The workers' skill more than compensates for the occasional shortcomings of the machinery. Unlike in Europe, capital is scarce and manpower abundant. If a worker slows down, he is at once fired and promptly replaced.

Does that mean that China's economy is based on the exploitation of cheap labor drawn from an inexhaustible supply of rural workers? Other countries also have vast manpower reserves, yet they have been unable to derive any advantage. Low wages are certainly one of the reasons for Gao's success on the international market, but more important is his capacity to use them. Without Gao's entrepreneurial skills, and those of hundreds and thousands of employers like him from the coastal provinces, there would have been no Chinese economic miracle. Gao knows how to organize and direct his army of workers; he also knows how to attract major international buyers and get them to place giant orders (he manufactures a million T-shirts, for example). He keeps his word, maintains quality, and sticks to his prices and deadlines. Such rigor is hard to find in the industrialized world.

People like Gao do not appear out of the blue. They belong to a long tradition. Guangdong Province had always been a major trading center for adventurous merchants, until the Communist Revolution prohibited them from doing business. Many sought refuge in Hong Kong, where they flourished under liberal British rule. Overseas Chinese have played a major role in reviving commerce on the mainland. Had it not been for the 200-million-strong Chinese diaspora in Hong Kong, Taiwan, and Singapore, and farther off in the United States, France, Australia, and Canada, the Chinese economy could have never taken off at such a sustained pace. The capital for Man Sum came from Hong Kong: 60 percent of "foreign" investment in China is actually of Chinese origin. The owner of this typical export firm is Chinese, hailing from Hong Kong, and overseas Chinese manage the marketing network. The free Chinese have restored their not-so-free brethren to the ranks of the employed.

To give the devil his due, the Party has contributed to Guangdong's industrial prosperity by allying with entrepreneurs (a third of province Party bosses are big industrialists) and submitting to the dictates of the market economy. It has provided the necessary infrastructure. Roads, ports, and airports are built with foreign investors, local factories, and exports in mind. Though the electricity supply is still erratic, companies have started building captive thermal-power plants. They accept pollution as one of the necessary evils of growth. The Party ensures a steady supply of obedient workers. Little has been done, though, in the area of health care, and there are few hospitals. So the affluent go to Hong Kong for treatment. As for the poor workers, they are dispensable and easily replaced.

The precedent of the Industrial Revolution

Whenever the brutality of its methods is criticized, the Chinese leadership is quick to point out that all developed countries went through a stage of massive rural migration to urban industry. After all, the Europeans did the same thing not so long ago. With economic growth, the situation will automatically return to normal in China. This is what took place in the past in Europe. China is going through a phase of *transition*. In the long run, development will resolve all the uncertainties resulting from change. Wasn't this a golden rule accepted first by the liberal economists of the eighteenth century and later by Karl Marx in the nineteenth? The question we need to ask is whether there can be any meaningful comparison between twenty-first century China and nineteenth-century Europe.

It is true that whenever the traditional farmer has moved away from the land to work in a factory, quick growth has followed. A man with a machine is more productive than a man working with a sickle in his field. The so-called Chinese miracle is the automatic result of the migration from rural to urban areas. Chinese growth is higher than what it was in Europe at a comparable stage, because China has particularly low agricultural productivity, whereas her factories have benefited from Western technology. Like Korea, Japan, and Taiwan fifty years ago, China has taken advantage of technologies developed elsewhere and shortened its economic takeoff by 100 years. The last to join the growth bandwagon reaps the fruits of what came before. Thus economic growth in China is the product of its massive rural exodus and its late takeoff. The idea here is not to detract from its success but to put it into perspective.

Pursuing further the comparison between Europe of the Industrial Revolution and today's China, growth in China has been far more brutal than the European example and has exacted a much higher price in human terms. Both Christians and socialists condemned the human suffering caused by the Industrial Revolution in France and Great Britain, preparing the ground for Marx's work. Is China, with its hundreds of millions of workers hovering at the outskirts of its cities, only different in terms of sheer numbers? The Party spokesmen tell us that everything is happening as it did in Europe but on a much larger scale and much faster. There is really nothing to worry about. Yet even a passing reference to issues such as pollution and poor working conditions is enough to brand one an enemy of Great China, jealous of its success. It needs to be stressed: the difference between China and Europe is not merely a question of numbers and speed.

During Europe's Industrial Revolution, there were social cushions—now forgotten or denigrated, such as the Church—and charitable organizations before public welfare institutions were put into place. China has no such buffer because the Revolution destroyed traditional support institutions, which are forbidden to this day. A few charitable organizations, trying to provide succor to the helpless, are islands of solidarity in an ocean of distress. They take their inspiration from the West and are financed by Westerners. The Communist authorities have started to take note of them. In the Sixties, the communists exterminated Buddhist associations. Now the very same communists are encouraging them to set up hospitals and old people's homes. In Shanghai, the Catholic diocese has regained some influence. It provides medical assistance to the poor, many of whom are Christian, often peasants or fishermen, and helps in the education of their children.

Yet institutional solidarity remains negligible. When all is said and done, the Chinese peasant who moves out of his village to work in a factory is at the mercy of the market in a way that the French and

British worker never was. Were Engels alive today, he would see clearly what he only glimpsed in the England of his time. For the first time in the history of mankind, the Party has created a labor market not tempered by law, dissent, or collective bargaining. Economists had imagined such a scenario only on paper. Chinese leaders have shown that the classical economists were right: the less hampered the labor market, the greater the growth will be. But no economist ever had the kind of unlimited power that the leaders of China enjoy.

Optimistic supporters of the transition theory feel that, while Chinese capitalism is savage at the moment, it will ultimately become civilized and embrace the rule of law. Indeed, the Chinese government promulgates many laws, not unlike those in force in Western countries. There are laws covering the right to property, contracts, accounting, safety, and protecting the rights of employees, but they exist only on paper, and their chief purpose is to help employers with political clout or eliminate foreign competitors. Eventually, under pressure from foreign investors, Chinese markets may start functioning according to a conventional set of laws. In Europe, the law preceded capitalism; in China, the opposite is true. From the very outset, the Industrial Revolution observed existing law, property rights, and contracts. In China, profit came first. Respect for property and contractual obligations has yet to follow. This is an unknown path that, though very desirable, is fraught with uncertainty.

A competitor hardly to be feared as yet

Is there any reason for us in Europe and the United States to fear the "Chinese workshop"? Should Chinese goods be rejected out of hand? I see no reason for such hysteria. China is adding to our prosperity. The West is not compelled to buy clothes, shoes, toys, sporting goods, and electronic equipment from China. It does so because Chinese prices are consistently lower, which enhances Western purchasing power. Since the beginning of the Industrial Revolution in the early eighteenth century, economic development has hinged on the international division of labor. Yet any relocation of production to a more conducive environment has always given rise to heated debate, anguish, and the tendency to look inward. Until now, the most efficient solution has been to accept such division of labor and create new comparative advantages. Take the case of textiles. Even the most efficient Cantonese factory takes three months to send a new product to Europe, whereas some factories in France and Italy can do so in three days. But producing garments in Europe would not make much economic sense. Where could we get 10,000 workers at one's beck and call? And why pay a hundred times more just for the "Made in Europe" tag? Ultimately, the real loser will be the Western consumer.

As the Chinese purchase more goods from the West, the economic benefit we derive from China's success will become clearer. Already the Chinese are buying our machines, airplanes, and cosmetics. It is in our interest that they prosper further, for we will become richer. Of course, observation is not going to matter much to a worker who has lost his job because labor in China is cheaper. The international division of labor is edging him out, he feels. Indeed, this may be the fate of countries unable to restructure their economies and give up the old for the new. But the issue is more complex than competition. Often it brings to the fore a process of decay that had set in much earlier.

The enemies of the free market in Europe and the United States condemn economics as immoral. Of course, the definition of morality is related to geographical location. If we assume that the Chinese have as much of a right to development as anyone else, then economics merits being called a social science. But won't such altruistic humanism and compassion be suicidal for the West? Aren't we running the risk of being overtaken by China?

This is hardly likely to happen. At present, China is an economic midget. Its per-capita income is twenty times lower than that of Europe, its GDP no more than that of Italy. Before the midget turns into a giant that can take on Europe, Japan, and America, it has to overcome several internal contradictions: unpredictable political institutions, the absence of the rule of law, mass poverty, an insufficient energy supply, banks on the verge of ruin, the flight of national capital, and the risk of epidemics. These are just a few of the imponderables that could derail the Chinese economy. We in the West can only be threatened if we choose to sit back and do nothing.

No innovation, only imitation

Given the low degree of innovation in China, the Chinese threat recedes even further. Chinese firms merely assemble or copy goods designed abroad. There were times in the past when China enjoyed a clear superiority—the "invasion" of Chinese silk 2,000 years ago, or porcelain in the eighteenth century. Chinese factories had mastered technologies the West did not have. Today, however, China has not created any brand, innovation, or manufacturing process of world standard. According to official figures, high-tech goods account for 50 percent of the country's exports. This is wishful thinking on the part of the government: included in this category are household appliances and anything else with a bit of electronics. These, too, are rarely designed in China.

Whether it's electronics, garments, consumer durables, or cars, Chinese firms are content to assemble, subcontract, or recopy. At times, they respect intellectual property, though generally it is ignored. Piracy is the norm. Enter any shop in China and you can get the imitation of any Western luxury or electronic good at half the price. It is easy to visit a T-shirt factory, not so one producing pirated DVDs, imitation drugs, and refined chemicals. They are under the protection of gangs—the Triads. How much the Chinese counterfeit industry earns is anyone's guess, but it is certainly substantial. The list of counterfeit goods includes pirated software sold via the Internet around the world. This has become a source of great concern for Western firms. Because this illegal trade is virtual, there is no way of controlling it. The ingenuity of Chinese piracy knows no bounds. In the summer of 2005, the bookstores of mainland China were selling the seventh volume of the Harry Potter series even before it had been written by its British author. In defense of the Chinese counterfeiter, imitation is part of a long tradition. As far back as the 1660s, the Spanish missionary Navarrete had observed that the Cantonese artisans were "past masters in the art of counterfeiting, selling in China as the genuine article the fakes they had copied from the West."

These days, to show the world that it means business, the government occasionally arrests copyright violators. As the adage goes, it "kills a chicken to frighten the monkeys." Since piracy forms one of the main planks of the economic system, however, it cannot be eliminated. The concept of intellectual property has no meaning for Chinese producers, who see it as yet another form of Western protectionism. There is a School of Intellectual Property at the University of Shanghai. Its director, responsible for educating future Chinese entrepreneurs, says: "International brands are far too expensive. Their high price excludes most of mankind from the benefits of the world economy." In other words, intellectual property is theft, and pirates are philanthropists.

Now that "Made in China" goods are flooding the world, we need to understand what the label means. Most exported goods are only assembled in China, not designed there. To take up the Man Sum example once again, the Guangdong factory buys its cloth from the Philippines and accessories from Korea to reproduce models designed by its American and European clients. The international division of labor is a common feature of industry around the world, but industrial production in China is particularly dependent on decisions taken elsewhere and on capital and goods from abroad. In most Chinese firms, labor, not creativity, constitutes the local value added, which is not a winning formula in the long run.

Some may argue that Korea and Japan experienced a similar phase before they managed to set up systems and produce brands of international repute. China, too, may replicate the same virtuous cycle. Such a development does not seem likely in the near future, however. China lacks innovation not because it is a new economy but because its institutions do not foster the innovative spirit.

Clearly, the government's economic strategy is to make quick money through the exploitation of the labor force. Wages remain low because the Party has curbed all forms of unionism and strengthened its nexus with firms, both domestic and foreign, to keep workers suppressed. In Korea and Japan, the reverse was true: trade-union demands and the end of the rural exodus forced entrepreneurs to mechanize and innovate. Nothing of the kind is happening in China: the Party's labor pump is capable of drawing reserves for a long time to come. Firms will continue to reap the benefits of cheap labor without any impetus to innovate. Why innovate when there is no talk of sustained development? The emphasis is on getting rich fast. The complete indifference to the environment and public health reflects this preference for the short term. The government's efforts to reduce pollution in Beijing are not motivated by any comprehensive policy on environment but rather to facilitate holding the Olympic Games in the city. Protecting the environment, as we all know, does not yield immediate returns.

Furthermore, the regime, by its very nature, is incapable of long-term thinking. A precarious legal system, shaky intellectual property rights, unpredictable taxation, and the Party's own capriciousness have created a climate of instability where everyone is out to make a fast buck and invest the proceeds abroad. It is pointless investing in research, for there are no immediate profits. Similarly, why respect trademarks when a cheaper solution is available? Researchers sent to the U.S. come back with innovations on which quick returns can be obtained. Whether this is legal hardly matters. It is also helpful to make the purchase of foreign goods contingent on the transfer of technology, as in the case of the Airbus. Such strategies are efficient if a country is content to imitate. In the long run, however, it means condemning China to follow rather than to lead.

Once again, the Communist regime is being consistent. In the Sixties, Mao Zedong, in a hurry to acquire nuclear weapons, preferred copying Russian, American, and French technology, instead of promoting Chinese research. The country had good spies, and China was able to conduct its first nuclear test in 1964. Has China changed? The official statistics show a constant increase in the number of engineers. So much the better! It is heartening to learn that their ranks are swelling. What their training is worth is another matter altogether. Chinese universities do not encourage independent thinking: students are required to remain passive. Discussion is circumscribed by political taboos, and the best students go abroad to enhance their qualifications. Most of them stay on and become Americans. The few who return are lauded for their heroism.

These are many reasons to minimize the supposed threat of a prosperous China. I am convinced that we are barking up the wrong tree. Semi-developed countries pose a far more serious challenge to the world order than nations content with their level of prosperity. And can one use the term "development" at all in the Chinese context? Instead of working toward national development, the Party is building a political and military power. To satisfy this ambition, 80 percent of the rural population is being exploited by 20 percent of the urban population. Some parts of Chinese society are getting rich. Yet the vast majority is being excluded from the development process.

Shanghai: a failure in comparison with Hong Kong

It is undeniable that some 200 million Chinese have become affluent. But will China gain the supremacy that its leaders are dreaming of, not just in Asia but across the world? If Shanghai is any indication, that prospect seems improbable.

Shanghai, a failed city? Isn't this flamboyant metropolis, with its elevated roadways and high-rise buildings, the symbol of China's technological breakthrough? First and foremost, Shanghai is China's display window to the rest of the world. The Shanghai and Beijing leadership designed the city to be attractive to foreign capital and, if possible, to motivate Hong Kong to reinvest in the mainland.

In the Nineties, while the Shanghai of rusty factories and decadent European palaces slept, the Shanghai plan's stated objectives were to make the city a worthy competitor to Hong Kong and eventually supplant it. Hong Kong has always been the yardstick of success. Fifteen years later, Shanghai has lost out, and the question of competition does not even arise.

Shanghai, the financial capital of Asia? Hardly. The stock market is weak and has ruined millions of small investors. Large Chinese firms prefer to have their shares listed on the Hong Kong stock exchange. Shanghai fares no better in the service sector. As in the rest of China, the service culture is conspicuously absent, whether the business is hotels, retailing, or something else. Town planning leaves much to be desired. There are a few achievements thanks mainly to foreign architects, but otherwise the city is unlivable. In their hurry to build, the local authorities completely neglected public health and communications. Half of the city's 17 million inhabitants—the population of a fairly large European country—have no proper sanitation, as the color of the River Huangpu makes plain. What about art, fashion, design, and advertising? The few art galleries are meant to reassure us that the new generation of visual artists has not lost its creativity. Yet despite all the hype in the Western media about Shanghai giving rise to a new civilization, the city hardly creates anything. In support of their stories, foreign journalists actively promote a handful of stars, whose photographs are reproduced ad nauseam. As for cinema and music, the Shanghai opera, whose building was designed by a French architect and ignored for a long time, can only make ends meet by staging imported Broadway musicals.

The leaders of Shanghai thought that all they had to do to become another Hong Kong was to copy Hong Kong's high-rise architecture. But, as the chairman of the Hong Kong and Shanghai Banking Corporation (HSBC) said, "Hong Kong is both a city and a culture." Hong Kong is more "comfortable" than Shanghai because the rule of law prevails and the judiciary and the press are free. Unable to shake off the legacy of communist China, Shanghai is still very much an urban jungle. The market economy, many believed, followed the principle of the survival of the fittest, and bankers were a law unto themselves. The fact is, however, that bankers prefer Hong Kong's rule of law to the Shanghai jungle. So except for the façade, nothing has changed. Shanghai is as it was before 1990—the industrial township of Mao Zedong's dreams.

After the 1949 Revolution, the communists decided to punish the citizens of Shanghai, which had been a cosmopolitan financial center, by pushing them into heavy industry. Even today, one has only to move away from the wharf at the Bund, the European face of city, miraculously preserved, to see a few cable lengths from the river the drab world of factories: immense industrial zones for building steel, communications equipment, chemicals, and automobiles, the four pillars of the Shanghai economy. This is the real Shanghai. The city directly manages these industries, none of which has been privatized. They employ half the working population and account for most of the city's finances. Shanghai lives off its industries, not its services. Employment and the budget are the prime concerns of the local government, which pays scant attention to so-called creative sectors such as fashion and the service industries.

It is said that the state-owned industries in Shanghai are well managed, affording much satisfaction to the advocates of socialism while casting the liberals in a state of disarray. Are they really that well managed? Since the Nineties, the Shanghai government has called in foreign consultants to improve production technology. Yet these enterprises have no say in the number of people they employ and are generally overstaffed. The local government makes such decisions because employment guarantees social stability in Shanghai, a factor that one cannot measure in economic terms alone. Furthermore, the state-owned industries enjoy monopoly status, with the local authorities making sure, for a variety of reasons, that no Chinese or foreign competitor disturbs them. The relative efficiency of Shanghai industry is thus all the more difficult to verify.

Shanghai and Hong Kong are worlds apart. The assembly lines, textiles, and electronics that made Hong Kong affluent have relocated to China and other Asian countries since the Eighties. What remains in Hong Kong are consulting, marketing, and financial services, which employ more people with a higher level of skills and a greater earning capacity.

Is it just a question of a delayed start for Shanghai? The city's future is an open question. China is certainly large enough to accommodate two financial cities, Hong Kong and Shanghai, just as Frankfurt and London coexist in Europe. What Shanghai lacks, though, is a stable legal and business climate, the comfort factor identified by the HSBC chairman. And there is no indication that things are about to change in the near future.

In fact, change seems less likely in Shanghai than in other Chinese cities because it is even more closely watched by security agents and the Propaganda Department. In Beijing and Guangzhou, some journalists, writers, and lawyers manage to get past the police net and have their say, but in Shanghai, the merest hint of dissident behavior is enough to put one behind bars. Shanghai is the most repressive city in China. Several student and worker movements, some democratic, others not, started here. It was here that the Communist Party took root in 1925. For this reason, the current leaders do not permit any freedom of expression. Of all the cities I visited in the Year of the Rooster, Shanghai was the only one where I could not meet a single dissident. No sooner had I telephoned people whose names I knew, than security agents monitoring the Internet and telephonic communication would place them under house arrest. Shanghai has lost out to Hong Kong, because the government persists in its preference for heavy industry and clamps down on all forms of freedom. Shanghai is nothing but a façade of modernity erected by the Party, which pursues its vision of what the China of tomorrow should look like. Foreigners on a hurried visit tend to lose their critical faculties the moment they land in China. They gaze, wonderstruck, at the façade erected for their benefit.

Investing in China?

Attracting capital from the West is absolutely vital for the Chinese economy. Without the massive inflows of foreign capital, China cannot develop. The question is whether foreign firms are getting good returns on their investments in China. So far, whenever they are asked about the profitability of their China ventures, which is often, CEOs or their bankers maintain a studious silence. Accounting procedures offer one good reason for this reticence. Products manufactured in China by multinationals are part of an international production chain: designed in the West or Japan, they are assembled in China, packaged elsewhere, and sold somewhere else. In these circumstances, it is hard to isolate the Chinese contribution.

Actually, the main cause for the discomfiture of foreign investors in China is that their ventures are not really making a profit. They feel that they must have a presence in China, if not for immediate gain, then for future returns. And so one has to be in China for the sake of being in China. According to an HSBC manager, when a businessman enters the Chinese market, he tends to lose all sense of discrimination. He thinks the country is an exception in which the rules of sound financial management do not apply. It is also true that his Chinese counterparts try to get around the rules. Honesty has not been factored into the Chinese economic model: accounts are fudged, contracts are not binding, justice is linked to status, corruption is the norm, and there is scant respect for intellectual property. As if to prove that it was not immune to this madness, HSBC, too, decided to throw caution to the wind. In 2005, it went ahead with the first Western acquisition of holdings in the notoriously badly managed Chinese banks, sinking under the weight of bad debts. A spate of acquisitions followed. They all say the same thing: China is too vast a market to ignore. Companies must position themselves strategically if they want to sell to the burgeoning Chinese middle class, which will soon adopt Western consumer habits. What will happen if the Chinese gamble does not pay off? Insurance companies will reimburse some Western firms. Other firms that put their China operations in the "politically risky investment" category will simply pass the burden on to the taxpayers of their own countries. But, of course, these scenarios will never come to pass, we are told. It will not be long before the vast Chinese market starts playing by the rules, and the Communist government becomes a normal state.

Every investment contains an element of uncertainty. But the craze for the Chinese market defies all logic. Rational considerations are abandoned altogether. China watchers are of two kinds: the believers and the nonbelievers. Though both depend on the same unreliable sources of information, the believer will tell you that things are getting better with each passing day, while the nonbeliever will say that nothing has changed at all. So you either have a rosy picture or a gloomy one; there are no shades of gray. The passion for China is absolute, and when one believes, one doesn't question.

The European economic press is just as mesmerized, overawed by the size and the promise of the Chinese market. It does not analyze the successes and failures to date. Why are Italian exporters more successful in China than the French? Do the Italians work more effectively, or do their Chinese partners play a role? Do the French and Italians follow different methods? Finding answers to these questions will tell us something not just about the behavior of Europeans in China but also about the Chinese themselves. Until then, China will remain terra incognita.

Are the bankers and Western businessmen, who are investing their shareholders' money in China abusing the trust placed in them? Western shareholders, swayed by what they read in the press, want to be trendy and have a presence in China. The moment a company starts doing business with China, its share price goes up. And firms with no presence in China become marginalized. The prudent investor—and there are a few—is not likely to be among the delegation accompanying a European head of state on a visit to China.

CHAPTER SIX

Skewed Development

Mao Yushi is one of China's most lucid economists. This is reason enough for the public security militia to keep him under permanent surveillance. He worries not about himself but about the waste of public money. Four men, and sometimes two cars, are stationed in front of the building where he lives. Then there are the men who tail him whenever he goes out. It all seems so silly. He is nearly eighty and not about to run away.

Like all independent intellectuals in China—they are a dying breed—Mao Yushi leads a simple life. He lives in a run-down building in Beijing, a rambling edifice built in the Sixties, freezing in winter and sweltering in summer. The tiny apartment that he shares with his wife overflows with books, souvenirs, and plastic tubs to collect the rainwater that seeps through the roof. He could live far more comfortably if he worked for the Party. The government is happy to buy off intellectuals, a much cheaper way of neutralizing them than round-the-clock surveillance. It is also effective. Most of the old rebels have become "experts" who stick to their discipline. Perhaps the word "intellectual" in the sense that we understand it is a misnomer. Comparing China with the West, the novelist A Cheng, who lived for several years in the United States before returning to Beijing, says that there are many literates in his country but few intellectuals.

In fragile health and a little hard of hearing, Mao Yushi has no illusions about his inability to overthrow the Communist Party.

When he intervenes publicly, he is neither aggressive nor revolutionary. His is a gentle brand of sarcasm. In 2004, around the fifteenth anniversary of the Tiananmen repression, he wrote a letter to the head of state suggesting that those responsible for the massacre acknowledge their role and ask forgiveness from the Chinese people. This would be the best way to put behind them a painful episode and move ahead, he proposed; any delay would only exacerbate hatred. Cosigned by other liberal intellectuals, Mao Yushi's letter circulated on the Internet and was taken up by the foreign press, but to no avail. The leaders of mighty China were not in the habit of being told what to do, no matter how gently. In 2005, he offended the authorities again, publishing a collection of his articles under the title *Give Freedom to Ones You Love*. The censors were not amused, and the publisher had to withdraw the book from circulation. Mao filed a case against the publisher, because filing a case against the Propaganda Department itself is impossible. The publisher lost. Is the rule of law gaining ground in China or is it just illusion? Winning the case was meaningless, as Mao Yushi's book is not available anywhere. Books no longer burn in China; they just vanish.

What economic miracle?

Mao Yushi is even more provocative when he says that economic development in China is not a miracle but an illusion.

Isn't he happy with the country's 9 to 10 percent annual growth rate? He would be, if he were sure that the figure were accurate. But since statistics are the sole prerogative of the government, there is no way of ascertaining their veracity. And since the government has never been known for its truthfulness, any information that it gives must be taken with a grain of salt. Between 1960 and 1980, it abandoned data collection altogether. When the exercise was taken up again in 1980, there were many incongruities. In 1990, for example, the authorities said that 95 million hectares were under cultivation—in other words, 0.08 hectares per capita, a figure even lower than Bangladesh's. This raised the specter of famine, for it appeared impossible that China could feed its people with that little land. Satellite pictures revealed the error, and in 2000 the figure was raised to 130 million hectares. In fact, it is 150 million. The Party had deliberately underestimated the amount of land under cultivation to suggest that China had achieved spectacular gains in agricultural productivity. This is just one of the countless instances of manipulated figures.

So Mao Yushi did his own calculations, spotting discrepancies and missing figures along the way. (When numbers get uncomfortable, official statisticians simply omit them.) To get a true picture, Mao went over the fudged statistics year by year and arrived at a growth rate of about 8 percent per annum. This is a healthy rate, due principally to the mechanical shift of the unproductive or idle peasant population to industry. It is comparable with the growth rates of Japan and Korea during their takeoff phases. But it can hardly be called a miracle; further, when seen in isolation, it has no meaning. First, one would need to subtract all the negative effects of Chinese development: widespread damage to the environment, soil depletion, pollution and its resultant epidemics, and the collective, individual, and social crisis caused by mass migration. Mao Yushi, considered by economists to be a pioneer in the field, reckons the annual amount of environmental destruction to be about 10 percent of the total production. As experts outside China do not dispute, this should logically be deducted from China's wealth.

Mao Yushi acknowledges that no development can take place without a large-scale rural-urban shift and that a certain amount of damage to the natural environment is inevitable. But he questions the government's savagery, and he thinks that the current growth is not sustainable. Natural bottlenecks—scarcity of energy, of raw materials, of water—will interfere. Raw materials and energy can be imported, but not water, which is now a rare commodity in China—and there is no attempt at water management. Because water is free, it is wasted and polluted, and goes untreated. The Chinese government does not view purification plants as useful investments. As a result, hundreds of millions of Chinese have no access to drinking water, and many die.

In addition to recalculating the growth rate and deducting its negative impact, Mao Yushi has questioned the nature of Chinese growth. Many of the goods produced in China are worthless, either because there is no market for them or because they are substandard. This is particularly true of public companies. About 100,000 such enterprises continue to run in the old Maoist style, producing because they have to justify their existence and achieve the targets set by the Party. Once an enterprise meets or exceeds its target, its responsibility is over. It doesn't matter what happens to the goods that it has produced. The public firms' objective is simply to provide employment to those whom the Party cannot dismiss or redeploy to other activities.

I ask Mao how such companies can survive in a market economy. But China is not a market economy, Mao retorts. Most public-sector companies have no real accounting system, so there is no way of ascertaining their profitability. In any case, the banks will bail them out. The Party gives the banks a list of people to whom loans are to go for political or personal reasons, with instructions that they are not to ask for repayment.

All this will change, I'm told, when I'm in Beijing. Banks will function strictly along commercial lines. But so far, it has not happened. Political considerations take priority over everything else, explaining the large number of buildings, both residential and business, that are more often empty than not, and the roads and airports that serve little or no purpose. The profits of growth, especially export earnings, are squandered on such unproductive investments, which in the long run generate neither wealth nor employment. The fact that investment decisions are based on political considerations, not the market, constitutes the central flaw of the Chinese economy, and, according to Mao Yushi, it is partly responsible for the high unemployment rate. The Party maintains a discreet silence, preferring to emphasize the high growth rate.

Twenty percent unemployed

Unemployment has been limited to 3.5 percent. At least that's the official figure, announced at the beginning of each year. The real figure is incalculable. The hundred-million-strong floating population—migrants who travel from place to place, going wherever they can find work or returning to their villages—are neither employed nor unemployed. The same holds true for millions of idle peasants who are either wholly or mostly landless. If they had the freedom to work in the city, they would. So are 20 percent of the Chinese unemployed? It seems plausible. Unemployment affects not just the poor. Two-thirds of China's engineers, university degree holders, cannot find work commensurate with their qualifications even three years after they finish their studies. Their unemployment has to do with the nature of China's development, which is based on the massive deployment of unskilled labor rather than the development of research and the service sector, which require more educated manpower. Is it any wonder, then, that so many engineers and technically qualified people leave for the United States and Canada?

As a result, despite of a high growth rate, there is still a dearth of jobs because profits are invested in unproductive ventures. Foreign investment does not generate much employment, either, since overseas companies prefer to set up high-productivity units requiring little labor. And export firms in the textile and IT sectors recruit mostly untrained girls on short-term contracts. There are no jobs for poor peasants, students, or workers laid off by the public factories.

What does Mao Yushi suggest? Nothing original; only that China follow the path of Japan, Taiwan, Singapore, Hong Kong, and Korea—all countries that managed to make good. If export earnings are well spent, employment will follow growth. Developing medium-size towns makes more sense than concentrating capital on the east coast and creating unmanageable agglomerations. In the final analysis, the solution is to invest in human resources, education, and health care, which would reduce social tension and enable China to move from primitive capitalism to sustained development. The first Asian "tigers" based their economies on the quality of their human resources; the Chinese government believes in exploiting labor. Is anyone ready to take up Mao Yushi's ideas? No, because economic organization is only a reflection of political organization. An urban class dominates the country, bureaucrats run the Party, the peasants have no say, and hence the interests of the establishment dictate economic choices.

Chinese banks: ticking time bombs

What does Mao Yushi think is in the cards for China's economy? Bankruptcy, he says, because banks keep making loans that will never be paid back. The banks are in no immediate danger, because the money coming in far exceeds the money being lent out. A healthy cash position acts as a buffer. In the recent past, though, there have been some scares—especially in Guangzhou in 2002, when depositors learned that the manager of their bank had run away with the cash box. But the Central Bank stepped in immediately, supplying fresh money to allay fears. On the whole, the Chinese show a surprising degree of confidence in their banks, admits Mao Yushi, which is how they can go on granting loans on the Party's instructions without worrying about the risks.

When will the bubble burst? Not as long as the world market supports Chinese growth, foreign investors remain attracted to China, and the Chinese continue to keep their savings in banks and post offices. Savings nationwide constitute a huge amount, stable because people have little choice. After ruining many an investor, the Shanghai stock exchange is no longer an option; the export of capital is prohibited by law; investment opportunities outside the bank are almost nonexistent; real estate, the only alternative, requires a very high level of investment. So Chinese investors either put their money in the bank or invest in the soaring real-estate market, which, with millions of apartments and offices still lying vacant, could go bust at any moment. If, by some chance, a war or epidemic turned the world away from China or if the Chinese became nervous about their savings, the ensuing panic would wipe out the banks, plunging the country into disaster. The Chinese, says Mao Yushi, can accept losing some or all of their freedom, but if they lose their savings, they will never forgive the Communist Party. The Party knows this and is doing its best to stave off bankruptcy.

In 2005, Chinese banks began a series of reforms to bring their practices gradually into line with Western standards. Foreign banks willingly invested in the modernization plan, hoping to use Chinese banking networks to sell a whole range of new products, including credit cards and attractive investment schemes, to a 100 million prosperous Chinese. The question is whether Chinese banks are reformable. The subject may appear technical, but it lies at the heart of the Communist system.

The central government needs better-managed banks that can finance rational activities, because if the banks went bankrupt and the investors lost their money, the Party would collapse. But if banks functioned rationally, they would no longer be at the beck and call of the local Party bosses to whom no bank can currently refuse a loan. The loans prop up unproductive local firms that provide jobs and perks. Without the loans, the cadres would lose their influence and public-sector jobs would dry up. Students would suffer, too: banks would stop giving them loans, knowing that they would never return the money. As things stand, they dare not ask these future cadres to honor their debts. Reforming the banking system is thus fraught with danger. There could be a student revolt, thousands of loss-making enterprises could close down, and the local bosses could become toothless.

How will the Party reconcile these conflicting pulls and pressures? Will it be able to avoid bankruptcy by adopting more rational policies, and at the same time guarantee social stability by maintaining the local chiefs' power to grant loans? Who will be hit first: local cadres, students, the new unemployed, or the financial system? Chinese leaders and foreign investors keep their fingers crossed. If capital keeps flowing in, growth continues, and small investors remain compliant, the contradictions will disappear on their own because of a plentiful cash supply. Mao Yushi is right: the Party's future depends on the future of the banks.

The elusive middle class

Isn't China moving spontaneously toward democracy? Hasn't growth created an independent middle class that will clamor for greater political freedom?

Mao Yushi does not think so. What exists is a class of "parvenus" whose purchasing power depends on proximity to the Party rather than education or enterprise. They consist mainly of bureaucrats and high-ranking officials who, by virtue of their office, are entitled to all kinds of favors and perks. The fortunes of this pseudo–middle class are closely linked to the Party's. Except for a handful of genuine individual entrepreneurs, the parvenus work in public administration, the army (an economic power in itself), state enterprises, and firms de jure private but de facto owned by the Party, its legion of cadres, and the army. There are the apparatchiks and the "entrepreneurchiks"—entrepreneurs by the grace of the Party!

A variety of fringe benefits, legal and illegal, helps this new class maintain its lifestyle. The administration and public enterprises pick up the tabs for almost all the parvenus' imported luxury cars, two-thirds of their mobile phones, and three-fourths of their restaurant bills, as well as their entertainment, expense accounts, call girls, study trips abroad, and lavish spending at Macao and Las Vegas casinos. The absence of safe private property increases the parvenus' dependence on the Party. Most people have only occupation rights—on land, in an apartment, or in an enterprise. Property is a gray zone, leaving its occupants in a permanent state of uncertainty. For instance, apartment owners in a collective housing block have real ownership rights, but the building is constructed on a plot granted for a limited period to the contractor by the state, the army, or the local government. No one can say what will become of the apartment owners when the lease expires. Because ownership is so uncertain, the entrepreneurchiks are always looking for ways to become rich overnight and stash their money abroad. Foreign investors, however, are more disposed to take long-term risks, either because they are covered by insurance or because they feel less threatened by the government than do the Chinese.

Getting a loan and not repaying it is a specifically Chinese way of amassing wealth. Loans are easily available for those who have connections, which the Chinese call *guanxi*. A 5 percent commission, however, has to be paid to the people at the bank (it goes directly into their pockets) and 15 percent to the local Party cadres for getting the loan approved. In principle, the money is to be invested in real estate or industry. How it is actually used is a different matter altogether. Apart from an initial 20 percent, the debtors don't have to repay anything as long as they continue to enjoy the Party's patronage. The fact that the Party can withdraw these advantages at any time helps in curbing dissidence but raises doubts about the mechanistic theory that the Chinese economy is generating a middle class that will necessarily ask for democracy. This Korean scenario of one thing leading to another seems improbable in China. Parvenus do not form a civil society. Dependent as they are on the political establishment, they are hardly likely to press for the democratization of a regime that ensures their prosperity.

The dependency is not just material. My personal view is that the educational system is instrumental in fostering it. Students must never question the teacher. Theirs is not to think and argue but to listen and learn by rote. Discussion and originality receive no encouragement. This failure to develop critical thinking is as detrimental to the cause of democracy as material dependence on the Party.

Transition: a convenient explanation

"Your criticism is valid, but we are in a transitional phase"—the standard argument that the authorities put forward. They do not need a Mao Yushi or a Western observer to point out the flaws of Chinese development. They are fully aware of its weaknesses and conveniently lump them together under the general category of "transition."

Mass migrations and the human suffering that they cause—epidemics, prostitution, and bad investments—are supposedly symptoms of transition. Development, I am told time and time again, is the panacea for all evils; with development, things will sort themselves out. This is a convenient ploy to preclude embarrassing questions. Any attempt to delve further means being branded an enemy of China or an ignoramus, unaware of realities on the ground. It is impossible to have a reasonable discussion with cadres and officials; there seems to be a real ideological barrier. The current set of Chinese leaders is self-righteous and considers criticism either silly or prompted by ulterior motives. Those who support the market economy unconditionally share this "it will all work out" optimism, even in the face of everything going wrong.

Michael Bernstam, a well-known economist with the Hoover Institution at Stanford University, has studied the shift of old totalitarian regimes to a market economy and concluded that educational and health infrastructure was often well developed in the period of despotism. Cuba, the Soviet Union, and Mao's China invested heavily in these areas, the showcases of their regimes. Though society was like a prison, people were relatively healthy and educated, and life expectancy increased. No sooner had these countries embraced the market economy than nonproductive investments—schools and hospitals—began to suffer, sacrificed for industry. So health and education declined. We have to wait for the transition to end, Bernstam argues, before a new threshold of development can be reached, enabling governments to reinvest in health care and education. Already in China, the more fortunate are paying for their health care and education, and the schools and hospitals that they use are much better than the ones that the Communist regime used to provide free of charge.

Bernstam applies the same logic to the environment. In an authoritarian society and a stagnant economy, the environment remains stable. During the transitional phase, development causes destruction; once this phase is over, however, society and firms once again have the means to protect the environment, save water and energy, and reduce pollution through costlier techniques of production.

The American economist, an icon of unfettered markets, is in agreement with the Chinese strategists. In short, he is asking us to choose between stagnating in good health and developing at a risk. There are winners and losers in both cases, but they are not the same. Since there can't be only winners, someone must act as the referee. The question is who. In China, it is the Communist Party. In India, the only country currently comparable with China, arbitration is democratic.

China and India: a comparison

Why India? Comparing China and India is a recent phenomenon that began during the Year of the Rooster. These two neighboring countries have always been alien to each other. Fifteen centuries ago, for example, when Buddha's disciples went from India to China, the Chinese so transformed their message that it resembled Daoism more than Buddhism. In the Sixties, the Himalayan region saw a few military skirmishes, the sole purpose of which was to reassure the Communist army of its superiority. Other than that, there has been little contact, each country following its separate path. India chose conservatism, China revolution. Until the end of the twentieth century, zero growth and mass poverty were the result in both. The fall of the Soviet Union and the demonstration of the market economy's superiority served as a wakeup call for both countries almost simultaneously. Rajiv Gandhi converted his people to liberalism in 1989, Deng Xiaoping his in 1992. The Indians and the Chinese embraced globalization at the same time, with its constraints on the one hand and its efficiency on the other.

In their race to development, China appears to have taken the lead, recording an average growth rate of 9 percent as against India's 6 percent. In terms of per-capita income, too, the Chinese, who started at the same level as the Indians, have become twice as rich in the space of fifteen years: $1,200 per annum on average, compared with $600. But this is an overall figure. It fails to take into account the unequal distribution of incomes. Nor does it reflect noneconomic values, such as democracy, freedom of religion, and respect for life.

Chinese growth is fueled to a great extent by foreign investors (often Chinese). Why do they prefer China over India by a wide margin? China lets them get rich fast. The Communist Party speeds up formalities, makes available a compliant workforce, and does not care about social rights and the environment. This is the advantage of an authoritarian regime. India is a democracy where citizens have rights, which makes everything so much slower. In the long run, India is more predictable, but China offers quick profits.

The Chinese also have a formidable propaganda machine at their disposal. Large Western firms are vying with one another to take part in China's "great economic adventure." To express the slightest doubt about the Chinese market is to be dubbed a loser and an enemy of China even by certain sections of the Western press.

Until 2005, no Chinese economist expressed interest in India, and few Indians paid any attention to China. Awareness developed after the Indian economist and Nobel Prize winner Amartya Sen studied China. In exchange, Chinese delegations set out to discover India. Sen's study led him to conclude that China is ahead of India only if one uses inaccurate statistics. The Chinese found in India an alternative model of development.

China as seen from India

Can India and China be compared? Comparisons based on a single factor like growth rate, ignoring historical and civilizational differences, are meaningless. What is interesting, however, is the sudden need felt by both countries to look at each other afresh, and the new thinking to which this could give rise. Amartya Sen challenged China's much-vaunted growth rate. A growth rate that does not take into account the human factor, he told the Chinese, is skewed. Now, the average life expectancy in China has not increased; in fact, it is declining in the western provinces. Education, health, and the environment have been the casualties of a purely quantitative approach to growth. Conversely, people are living longer in India, regardless of which part of the country or strata of society they belong to, even though initially, life expectancy there was lower. In 1979, when China launched its economic reforms, the Chinese lived fourteen years longer than the Indians, on average. They had the benefit of a widespread basic health system, nonexistent in India. Twenty-five years later, life expectancy remains the same in China, whereas in India it has gone up from fifty-seven to sixty-four years. In some Indian states, especially Kerala, it has reached seventy-four, much higher than the average in China. Child mortality in Kerala is now 33 percent lower than in China, where there has been hardly any change.

The sex ratio is another important human indicator, because it indicates the extent of female infanticide and respect for human life. Here again, India is better placed than China: 107 females per 100 males in India, as against 94 in China. In Kerala, the ratio is the same as in Western Europe.

Amartya Sen's optimism needs to be qualified, however. Specific cases and averages are misleading in countries as diverse as India and China. One can argue, for instance, that Kerala is not representative of the whole of India. And the life expectancy in Shanghai and Beijing is higher than in Kerala. But the overall pattern is clear: the quality of life, as defined in terms of life expectancy, child mortality, and sex ratio, is improving faster in India, a democracy, than in China.

Certainly China is growing rich, but if we consider the human factor, is it really developing? And while India is developing slowly, will it not make *progress* faster?

It all depends on what we understand by the terms "development" and "progress." Amartya Sen believes that human indicators are a better way to measure progress than the growth rate. Isn't this a philosophical choice, more reflective of the ethos of a people? What shapes our conception of development: culture or democracy? Is it because debate is forbidden in China that health care and education have been sacrificed at the altar of the market economy? It is always the poor, the most numerous, who suffer. But whereas the poor in China have no voice, in India they vote and the media are ever vigilant. Indian politicians cannot afford to alienate them: they need their votes. Thus values like family, tradition, and religion are preserved. They may not be quantifiable, but they contribute to general well-being. Cultural and spiritual values find no place in China's march forward. A poor person in India with the same income as a poor person in China may be richer, in fact, because he still has his religion and his traditions. One has preserved what the other has been deprived of.

Indians are happy with the qualitative approach because it gives them an excuse for their indolence. But it also worries a few Chinese.

India as seen from China

Chen Xin, an economist at the Academy of Social Sciences in Beijing, is one of those who are worried. Ever since his visit to India, he looks at China differently.

Before 1989, the Academy was the "liberal" laboratory of the regime. It was here that the privatization of state-owned companies and the opening of the Chinese economy to the world market were conceived. After the student revolt, which academics had supported, old scholars were sidelined to make way for a new, more cautious, generation of researchers. Listening to what they have to say gives one a sense of the limits the Communist Party places on thinking.

Chen Xin is a symbol of the new wave; he speaks reasonable English and does not wear a tie, which for a Chinese intellectual is tantamount to dissidence. We are alone in his office. This, too, is unusual, since normally there is a third person on hand to keep an eye on things and take notes while serving tea. For a moment, I think this is an indication of greater freedom. Then I realize that I am being naïve. The note takers of the past, who transcribed even the most humdrum of conversations, have been replaced by cameras. The censors have acquired technical savvy.

Chen Xin visited India and concluded that India was developing at the same pace as China. It was not practically feasible, he felt, for the people of both countries, about 3 billion human beings, to achieve Western standards of living simultaneously. Let us suppose that growth in both countries rises, and each Indian and Chinese person acquires a car and other Western luxuries. This would lead to a practical and environmental impasse. Even if one could find ways and means to reduce energy and raw material consumption radically, there would still not be enough to satisfy the demand of both Asia and the West. The world would become a giant parking lot. At present, China has only one car for every seventy inhabitants, in comparison with America's one car for every two. Yet Beijing and Shanghai are already congested with traffic. Will it be possible to meet the needs of Chinese or Indian consumerism at the expense of the Western consumer? Chen Xin does not think so. He doubts Westerners will ever curtail their energy consumption and share resources with Chinese and Indian consumers. In any case, the United States currently dominates the world's raw-material and energy markets, and will not hesitate to put a brake on growth in China and India the moment it feels that they are lowering American standards of living.

Chen Xin says his intention is not to launch an anti-imperialist tirade; he is simply stating facts. What, then, are his conclusions? He thinks that, in contrast to the Western model of development, China must adopt a model based on the Eastern concept of harmony. His words are almost heresy. At present, the Communist Party will not hear of any alternative to consumerism and globalization. Chen Xin clarifies: the Chinese should be given the choice between two ways of life—the Western way, the course that has already been charted in the eastern provinces; and the Eastern way, which could prevail elsewhere. For this to be a real choice, the state must invest massively in education and health care for the peasants and direct them toward more remunerative activities in order to end migration. Chen Xin says such a harmonious China would have to enjoy greater political freedom and managerial autonomy. His naturalist vision veers between the genius of India and utopian socialism.

Chen Xin thinks he found what he was looking for in Kerala, the social paradise of those in search of alternatives. The state boasts widespread education, gender equality, interreligious harmony, and high life expectancy. Better still, Kerala is politically correct, governed by the local Communist Party. Life is all the more sweet, as people don't have to work very hard. Yet it is the remittances from workers in the Gulf and Great Britain that has made all this possible. Without them, the government would not be able to finance the education and health of its people. This is a point that people tend to overlook. And when these workers return, they are laden with all kinds of consumer goods, something the utopians chose to ignore. Indian harmony is not always based on asceticism.

The Kerala model, more mythical than real, is not easy to replicate. What makes it interesting is that a new generation of Chinese academics is turning to the state in their quest for harmony. Does this signal a shift in Chinese policy, or is it some new surprise? The economist's search for harmony is akin to the educated classes' desire for a value-based society and the religious fervor overcoming an increasing number of Chinese. But there is a red line that Chen Xin cannot cross: the dictatorship of the Party. The Chinese mind has been so conditioned by what is permissible and what is not that he thinks of harmony as independent from democracy. But without democracy, there can be no understanding of India.

Democracy makes all the difference

Democracy, and nothing else, inclines India toward harmony. And because it is not a democracy, China is driven by the quest for power. The Indian peasant has some hope of getting electricity, roads, schools, and dispensaries in his village. Villagers in China have no such hopes. The Indians vote, and the Chinese don't. Elected Indian legislators cannot afford to ignore the demands of their voters. By contrast, the job of a local Chinese Communist Party secretary is to send as many villagers as possible to the industrial zones. Political power flows from contradictory legitimacies, which leads to divergent economic strategies. No doubt market forces are at work in India just as much as in China, pushing people out of their villages, promoting consumerism and a more materialistic way of life. But while in India, democracy tempers the market and the people are relatively free to choose, the Party does not believe in giving the Chinese real choice.

Indian leaders are not obsessed with the idea of resurrecting an imperial power that they have never known. Whenever power goes to leaders' heads, the voters quickly bring them back to the reality of local issues. Thus, in 2004, the overly nationalist ruling party was ousted by a coalition that claimed to be closer to the people. In India, the poor constitute the political majority. Power changes hands frequently, and the press is free. Though this alone cannot wipe out corruption or the abuses of power, it never fails to reassert the primacy of the principle of harmony. Villagers can stay in their villages and make agriculture remunerative only because their elected representatives are obliged to support such initiatives. They may not add to India's might, but they do improve the lot of the deprived. And it was Gandhi who said that India's economic progress should be measured by the yardstick of the poorest of the poor.

Another major difference between the two countries is India's preference for the service sector and information technology—decentralized activities—in contrast to the Chinese predilection for industry. Is this a question of national temperament, or does it have to do with political choices? Tradition does have a part to play, but policies tend to reinforce trends. The emphasis on industry is in keeping with the Communist regime's ultimate goal of building national power. The people's welfare is secondary. The 20 percent who have benefited materially—or morally, with increased national pride—constitute China's "useful" population, the ones who can help China in its quest for power. The remaining 80 percent are human fodder.

There appears to be a relation, difficult to prove empirically, between innovation in computer technology, especially software, and political culture. The countries where creativity thrives happen to be democratic: America, South Korea, Taiwan, India, and the nations of Western Europe, versus Russia, the Muslim world, and China.

Clearly, it would be simplistic to say that India is all harmony and that China is driven solely by its desire for power. Likewise, the differences between the two countries cannot be reduced to the presence or absence of democracy. Nonetheless, if one fails to take these factors into account, it is difficult, if not impossible, to explain the differences.

In the Year of the Rooster, for the first time in its history, the Communist Party has introduced the term "harmony" in its propaganda lexicon. Perhaps the Party is anticipating social unrest. But the Chinese are not taken in. University students from Fudan University in Shanghai all tell me that "harmony" is simply another term for an old idea: no criticism of teachers and the Party. The Party can go on crying "harmony" from the rooftops. It lacks credibility and will remain forever captive to the logic of power because that is its raison d'être. The government will not transfer resources to the countryside, nor will it allocate funds for health and education. The Party may change its discourse from time to time, but its priorities will remain the same. It has condemned a billion hardworking Chinese, slaves of the power syndrome, to a life of drudgery, for power and power alone is the be-all and end-all of the Party.

Out to conquer the world

The Communist Party has made its choice between the two alternatives—a powerful China or the development of its people. Since the time of Mao Zedong, the Party has decided on a conquering China rather than on contented Chinese. From the outset, China has accorded the highest priority to the development of heavy industry and weaponry. Even in Mao's time, the majority of the peasants had already been subjugated to fulfill this ambition. The goal has not changed; only the method has been perfected. Just as in Mao's time, the Party's has never tried to hide its intent. For those who choose to listen, it is the stated ambition of the Party, expressed in a specifically Chinese code. Thus, the resuscitation of Admiral Zheng He in the Year of the Rooster to send a message to the world!

In 1405, the Emperor Ming sent Admiral Zheng He on a naval expedition with a fleet of 300 ships and 30,000 sailors. The admiral and his men spent seven years sailing around the East Indies, India, and East Africa—whereupon the Ming dynasty decided that there was no need to explore any further and closed China to the world. The Zheng He saga got buried in collective memory, and China remained inward-looking until the West forced it out of isolation with the Opium Wars of 1840. Six centuries later, the Chinese leadership thought fit to revive the expedition and its brilliant commander, a Muslim eunuch from Yunnan promoted to the rank of admiral.

So in the summer of 2005, the Chinese National Museum in Beijing's Tiananmen Square held an exhibit in commemoration of Zheng He. There was nothing, however, to display, the Ming dynasty having, for some inexplicable reason, destroyed all vestiges of his "remarkable saga." In the absence of any relic, the organizers decided to construct a model of one of the ships, a good replica perhaps but not based on any recorded historical evidence. There was also a desultory collection of recent photographs showing the places where the Chinese fleet must have cast anchor. To fill up the space were huge posters bearing the Party's pompous proclamations. This was the real purpose of the exhibition. Visitors learned that Zheng He had set sail a hundred years before Christopher Columbus, Magellan, and Vasco da Gama, that his ship was three times longer than the Genoan ships, and that the Chinese fleet had transported "30,000 men in comparison to Columbus's 88." To dispel all doubt, a poster declared Zheng He to be the "greatest navigator of all times." China had stolen a march on the West.

In addition to this technical superiority, Zheng He and the Ming dynasty showed the country to moral advantage. One of the posters said: "China was then the most powerful nation in the world. Without rival, it could have easily conquered, occupied, and colonized the lands on the route of the expedition. But it chose not do so and thereby harmed none." As China had displayed such exemplary self-restraint in the past, there was no reason why it would not continue to do so. The objective of the exhibit was to give legitimacy to China's new ambition and to emphasize the peaceful nature of its growth, a key slogan of the Year of the Rooster. The Party is faithfully keeping up the old imperial custom of rewriting history to suit one's ends.

Of course, the exhibit obscured the real reasons for Zheng He's mission. Such a large fleet could not have been sent purely to explore. The admiral's brief was to reestablish China's authority over tributary lands and to acquire fresh territory for the Empire. The Ming dynasty had only just come to power, and distant vassals were acting up. The "peaceful" nature of his mission notwithstanding, Zheng He had to wage battle in Ceylon, and ordered the king of Sumatra to be beheaded for not showing due respect to China. The commemoration did not mention this violence, no doubt inconsequential when compared with the extortion of the European conquistadors.

Was Zheng He any different from Christopher Columbus? Not really, for the Chinese were no less imperialistic than the Europeans. The Mings annexed Tibet; the Qings, Eastern Turkistan. Like the Westerners in their spheres of influence, the Chinese dynasties were convinced of their superiority over all other nations. There was one difference, however. The West exported Christian "values," which it believed universal, but China only exported goods—silk and porcelain. Nothing has changed. Even today, Westerners persist in their attempt to spread human rights. The Chinese, who make no claim to universality, are content to sell their products (after Mao, they gave up trying to export revolution). Whether this is modesty or arrogance is hard to say. Perhaps convinced of the supremacy of their values, they consider them to be nontransmittable. In a pluralistic country, the commemoration of Zheng He would have generated debate about what the country had in common with other nations and what set it apart. But Chinese policy is to avoid anything controversial.

As one left the exhibition, one wondered why the naval expeditions were stopped. No sooner had the Ming dynasty stabilized than the mandarins put an end to any further adventurism. Perhaps they found such voyages too expensive; perhaps they feared the entry of foreign ideas. Who knows? The entire record of Zheng He's seven journeys was destroyed, his prowess on the sea forgotten. The Beijing exhibition does not mention this.

What lessons should we draw from the story of Zheng He? Will China, which once surpassed the West, regain its preeminence? Will the renaissance be as peaceful as the expedition? Will China, as during the days of the Mings, seek only deference and profit? Will it withdraw into its shell once again? The odyssey of that extraordinary admiral presaged all these possibilities. Sadly, today's China will never allow public debate about them.

CHAPTER SEVEN

Shadows of Democracy

Jiren is a Tibetan shepherd who owns a thousand yaks and has a wife decked with coral and silver necklaces. He does not understand the Communist version of democracy in China. Like the other 400 inhabitants of Chala, on the upper plateaus of Qinghai Province, he has been summoned to attend an electoral assembly. The Communist Party secretary convened this assembly in Chinese, a language that Jiren can neither read nor speak, which explains his confusion.

Qinghai is part of historical Tibet, but in 1965 the Chinese government divided it into several provinces in the hope of curbing the Tibetans' pro-independence sentiment. This spring, even though the snow has begun to melt on the high plateaus, Chala shepherds obey the Party summons; some come on horseback and others, more fortunate, on all-terrain motorcycles. Not a single family is missing. If one happens to be a Tibetan in China, one has to heed the summons of the secretary. In this Year of the Rooster, Tibetans and Chinese are celebrating the fortieth anniversary of the supposedly "Peaceful Liberation" of Tibet—Communist Newspeak for colonization. Great celebrations are held to mark the event; the Tibetans, says the Party press, "were steeped in joy."

Though the Party secretary, a certain Cairang, is Tibetan, he speaks Chinese, choosing to collaborate with the regional administration. For this, the Party has rewarded him with a bank loan to buy a deep freezer and a generator, so he sells his meat and salted butter at a better price than the other shepherds, who are at the mercy of Chinese intermediaries. For as long as Cairang remains the Party secretary and toes the line, the bank will not ask him to repay his loan. His story shows how the Party uses a mixture of carrots and sticks to deal with Tibetans. Actually, it metes out the same treatment to all Chinese—only with the Tibetans, it increases the doses of both reward and repression.

Tibetans: electoral puppets

Shepherds with their wives and children sit cross-legged on the wet grass in front of the Party headquarters, the only concrete building in the village. It is covered with white tiles, the hallmark of modernity everywhere in China. There is no village as such: shepherds live in tents and mud huts scattered over thirty kilometers. The Party, an energetic organizer, plays the Chinese national anthem over amplifiers, and the Tibetans, well trained, stand up. Cairang then launches into a long speech in Chinese. The shepherds comprehend little; they whisper to one another the few bits and pieces they do understand to get the gist of what is being said. Cairang tells the villagers that Chala has attained complete democracy, nothing less, and calls upon them to elect their local committee and village chief through a secret ballot. He shows them that the wooden ballot box wrapped in red paper is empty and can be locked with a key. Next, he brandishes the voting slips: yellow for the committee, pink for the village chief. The names of candidates—six names for five seats on the committee and just one for the village chief—have been printed in advance. For the benefit of the foreign observers and journalists who have come all the way to this remote corner of China, the secretary explains that the names of the candidates were decided through prior consultation among the villagers; the shepherds look at one another, bemused. Cairang goes on to explain how the secret ballot works. Some sort of a voting booth has been set up behind a mud wall that also serves as a urinal. He asks the voters not to sell their votes, thus implying that this happens rather frequently, and introduces the two police-men who have come from the district headquarters to arrest any miscreants.

As Cairang thunders in the manner characteristic of all Communist Party dignitaries, he senses that his audience is growing restive. Women begin to chatter, men draw on their cigarettes, and bottles of liquor are passed around. Cairang turns on some music, pop versions of Tibetan tunes, to keep them entertained. Women smile and flash their gold teeth, displaying their fortunes. The election campaign can begin.

Cairang introduces the candidate for village chief supported by the Party, one Caiban, also a yak breeder and the owner of the sole car in Chala. He, too, has a deep freezer bought on credit. Dressed in Tibetan robes, he is wearing a green cap of the kind worn by Chinese soldiers in the past. The audience looks at him enviously as a cloud passes overhead, making the temperature drop fifteen degrees. Speaking in Chinese, the candidate expounds his program at length, but with such a pronounced Tibetan accent that the audi-ence seems to understand him. He makes many promises: he'll come down heavily on corruption (another way of saying that corruption is rampant), maintain accounts of all the public money he receives, pave the road that links the village center to the national highway, and do his best to settle boundary disputes, the main cause of acri-mony among shepherd families. Finally, he swears to follow the line of the Communist Party, to fight poverty, and to make progress tri-umph. No one claps; they have heard all this countless times before. The campaigning is over; the Party secretary starts distributing the voting slips.

And then Jiren throws a wrench into the works. He gets up, takes the floor without permission, says that he is delighted with the free-dom given to the Chala yak breeders, thanks the Communist Party of which he is a member, and announces that he is running for the post of village chief. He speaks simply and in Tibetan. As soon as he finishes, he sits down again and his gorgeous wife flashes a golden smile at him. The shepherds seem to like it, though it is hard to read the impassive faces that have weathered fifty years of Chinese oppression.

The Party secretary is embarrassed; he withdraws into the white-tiled building to confer with the district authorities. An hour later, all of them come back out. An announcement is made that the Chinese government respects democracy and that the voters may add the dissident Jiren's name to their pink voting slips. Few of the shepherds and even fewer of the women can write. "Those who can write must help those who can't," orders the visibly annoyed secretary. The proceedings, rehearsed for many months in advance, go awry; the official television crew stops filming the chaos. The cooks wonder what will become of the banquet of roast yak and butter tea that they have prepared for the foreign observers.

The voting begins. The slips are counted and recounted carefully in full public view so that there can no accusation of cheating. The Tibetans know the drill well; the official candidate wins with a thumping two-thirds majority. The rash Jiren manages to get a seat on the village committee. He is not disappointed: "That's democracy," he says. Order is restored.

A black limousine with tinted windows, a Buick made in China, hurtles onto the field, and a senior "cadre" descends from the car. A dark suit, white shirt, red tie, and, above all, thick black hair are the yardsticks by which status is measured in China. No Communist dignitary, irrespective of his age, is graying or bald. The cadre does not introduce himself or give his name; he is rumored to be a "director" from Xining, the provincial capital. He grabs the microphone and intones Party jargon in a martial tone, congratulating the people of China for the progress that they have made on the road to democracy in pursuance of the directives of the 16th Congress of the Communist Party. This election, he says, is one more step toward the development of China; it is a clear demonstration of the perfect harmony that exists among all its ethnic groups. He announces an exceptional grant of 3,000 yuan—a pittance, even by Qinghai standards—to be managed entirely by the village's elected committee under the local

Party secretary's vigilant eye. Before driving off, he consents to perform an old Tibetan custom: dipping his finger into a glass of fruit brandy with a layer of salt butter around its rim, he flicks three drops on the ground to bless the earth, the sky, and the family before drinking the rest. In these high altitudes, the brandy offers protection against both frost and dizziness.

The sun begins to set behind the mountains, and a snowstorm looms. Butter tea, yak roast, and giblets stuffed with herbs are all gulped down in a few seconds. The shepherds disperse in no time; entire families seat themselves on one horse or one motorcycle. Chala, one of the 650,000 Chinese villages in which the Party intends to install "democracy," returns to silence in the fading twilight.

What will become of Jiren the rebel? He will not be harmed, for he is a lightweight; the disciplinary commission of his Party will simply give him a lesson in Communist morality, and he will never get a loan from the bank to buy a deep freezer.

On the way back from Chala to Xining, our hosts from the provincial government suggest that we stop at Bird Island; located on the largest lake in China, it is a meeting point for thousands of migratory birds. Our cavalcade comes to a halt, and we take the customary photographs. The next day, we read in the international press that the dead birds on the island are carriers of bird flu, an epidemic threat to China as serious as atypical pneumonia and AIDS. The entire zone has been cordoned off, and travelers coming from there have to be quarantined. The rules are bent in our case, however, so we escape the quarantine. This is not the Party's way of getting rid of us; it is only displaying its ignorance of health hazards and its strange sense of priorities. An election planned and prepared months in advance has to take place at all costs; the honor of the Party is at stake. Not holding the elections would mean a loss of face for the Party in front of the Tibetans and, worse still, in front of the foreigners. The epidemic can wait. The Chinese press spoke of the dead birds four months after they had died.

No, the Party is not moving toward democracy

What is an election worth in a one-party country that bans opposition, passes off propaganda as information, orchestrates debates, and censures criticism? What has prompted the unelected Chinese government and the self-nominated Communist Party to hold local elections now, long after the law providing for elections in all of China's villages was enacted in 1980? And if the Party deems it proper that village chiefs and local assemblies be elected, why does it not extend local democracy to cities, where toothless neighborhood committees are nominated in utmost secrecy? Rural elections have become a top priority for the Chinese government. Even in China, people are hard put to understand why, and offer a host of interpretations, from cynical to optimistic.

Analysis becomes all the more daunting when one considers the scope of the subject: 650,000 very different villages. The director of the World and China Institute in Beijing—Li Fan, thought to be an independent observer—says that the Chinese countryside covers the entire political spectrum, from genuine pluralism to manipulation of the most sordid kind. The only possible generalization is that in the north, villagers vote on the basis of clans, divided as they are into opposing families, whereas in the south, money grants power and thus the ability to buy votes determines the outcome. Corrupt practices become more prevalent as the economic stakes rise. Elections are a low-key affair in Tibetan villages where resources are scanty; in the more prosperous provinces, however, where villages have their own enterprises, the village chief has a key role to play, as he runs these firms.

Who makes the decisions: the duly elected village chief, or the local Communist Party secretary nominated by the Party hierarchy? Here again, there is no hard-and-fast rule: everything depends on power equations, influence, and money. There are also villages—one-third of them, according to the Ministry of Civil Affairs in Beijing—where the Party secretary is also the elected village chief. Does the Party favor the principle of two posts for one man? Does it want its representatives to win legitimacy through universal suffrage?

Perhaps it is a way to legitimize the Communist Party in the countryside; perhaps the Party wants to purge its cadres by eliminating apparatchiks hated by the peasants and replacing them with others who have a little more credibility. Such a policy does seem rational. But the discourse changes from one province to the next, and the views expressed are contradictory, to say the least. At times, the Party encourages its local secretary to stand for elections so that it can win democratic legitimacy and lower local administrative costs (since the village chief and Party secretary are both paid by taxing the villagers). In other provinces, the Party discourse is totally different: the distinction between the Party and the village chief makes for less oppression and more consultation, I am told, thus leading to a genuine democratic separation of powers. There are quite a few provinces where the Party has decided not to hold elections at all, or to hold elections in some villages and not in others, according to a schedule that the Party alone knows.

The infinite variations on the ground tell us that the central government is not as strong as it seems. Though the state lays down general policy guidelines, it is the local representatives of the Party who implement these guidelines. They go about their business with an eye to personal gain, depending on how much influence they wield and the power equations in each village. Centralization in China amounts to a permanent negotiation between the authorities in Beijing and the local Communist Party potentates.

Let us assume that this sudden passion for local elections, however primitive the exercise, is because the Party has woken up to the growing discontent of 800 million peasants. It is they who sustain the army of apparatchiks camping in their villages; on average, there is one Party apparatchik for twenty rural inhabitants, a proportion growing by the day. These "cadres" arbitrarily impose taxes, fines, and duties on the peasants. The peasantry is up in arms: mutinies, sometimes well publicized by the press, at other times kept under wraps forever, testify to a real hatred for the Party. Perhaps village elections are not the foundations of democracy but rather the Party's way of telling the peasants: "Now we are ready to listen to you."

From what we have seen, the message is not getting through, for dialogue is not part of the Party culture, and the clumsily stage-managed elections are perceived as being *inflicted* on the peasantry. It seems unlikely that a Tibetan shepherd from Chala, after voting, returns with the impression that his vote counts, or feels more attracted to the Party and likely to rally around it. He probably feels, instead, that he is again being compelled to take part in one of the many rituals that the Chinese have been inflicting on him from time to time since 1949. Local elections are no different from the other campaigns—the Great Leap Forward, the Cultural Revolution, economic reforms—that have marked recent Chinese history. The elections in Tibet are reminiscent of pilot villages, model factories, and other such exemplary institutions of previous eras. Since the Sixties, only the slogans have changed; style has always prevailed over substance, music over words. The people have no choice but to submit, flexibility being the only way to survive.

This, I must admit, is a pessimistic reading of village elections. The Party has another, more promising, interpretation, known as the "process theory," a point of view shared by some China watchers, generally Western. The Communist Party has never formally ruled out democracy: the very first elections held in China—in 1954, at the time of Mao Zedong—were pluralistic. Under the influence of Stalinism and its totalitarian logic, however, Maoism was quick to abandon all pretense of pluralistic democracy and went on to proclaim a unanimous democracy. Ever since, on the rare occasions that voting takes place, it is unanimous.

After succeeding Mao Zedong, Deng Xiaoping did not exclude the possibility of China's returning to pluralistic democracy in the future—fifty years, he declared in 1981. Why such a long wait? Apart from the real fear of losing power, Deng Xiaoping put forth two arguments that form the basis of the Party doctrine. First, premature pluralism will lead to the breaking up of China, even to civil war. The result of the free elections held following the 1911 republican revolution is proof enough: country squires and local militia leaders became warlords who were responsible for ruining China and plunging it into war. Were free elections held today, would the same scenario be replicated? It seems unlikely: China is far more homogeneous than in 1913, indeed more so than ever before in its history. The provinces are well linked, thanks to the massive migrations; the various populations have intermingled; a unified economy is in place. Labor and consumer markets, television, and schools spread the national language and similar habits. Furthermore—and this is something that all champions of democracy underline—a democratic China structured along the lines of a loose confederation will be able to withstand pluralism far better than a centralized form of governance imposed regardless of the consequences.

The Party's second argument in defense of its gradualist, start-at-the-grassroots approach is that the Chinese are still not responsible citizens. This attitude of condescension is the reason for the elaborate planning and zealous rhetoric that usually accompany village elections. The Chinese were capable of voting in 1913 and 1954, so why do they need the Party to instruct them in 2005? Indians and Brazilians, in a similar situation, were not made to wait fifty years before casting their votes, nor did they require a party to tell them how to vote. It is the Chinese Communist Party and its cadres, not the people, who need a lesson in democracy and independent thinking. They also need to learn to accept electoral defeat, if such a thing ever happens.

Other observers, neither Communist nor Chinese—especially those from the Ford Foundation and Carter Center, both very active in China—feel that local elections have set an irreversible process in motion. The Communist Party will eventually lose its grip and, in the long run, be absorbed by the democratic process. For this reason, both foundations favor village elections in China; they provide logistical support and organizational know-how to the local authorities that hold the elections. This was the case in Chala, where Party cadres beamed as they told me that Tibetans were a free people. Additionally, the foundation headed by the former American president Jimmy Carter provided computers to the local government. The Chinese government is not short of computers, so who is being taken in: a naïve Carter, or Chinese communists caught up in the electoral system?

Without trying to generalize, the manner in which village elections are conducted suggests that the Party is in no mood to go any further down the road to democracy. In any case, what legitimacy can democracy have when one does not have access to information or the freedom to organize oneself?

Drops in the ocean

The landscape changes as we move away from the Tibetan plateau and travel some 1,200 miles south to Guizhou Province. Yet the farmers' poverty remains the same. The inhabitants of Chala just about make ends meet by breeding yaks and selling butter; in Maguan, families eke out a living growing rice on tiny irrigated terraces. Those dazzled by the Chinese economic miracle would do well to visit Guizhou, which has a per-capita income of one dollar a day. There is no electricity, schools are few, dispensaries nonexistent, and mechanization unheard of. Certainly the province has much to delight those in quest of the eternal China: peasants driving their buffalo, women raising small mud dikes under the watchful eyes of their ancestors, and funeral steles scattered all over the rocky mountains towering in the background. China is an immense accumulation of eras and cultures; uniformity comes from the Communist Party.

After Chala, I was made to witness another great step toward local democracy in Maguan. This time, it was a meeting of the village committee. There is one elected delegate for every thirty-five families in a total population of 30,000. So it was a mammoth assembly, somewhat like a Swiss canton, that gathered in the open public square facing the Party headquarters. As in Chala and everywhere else, this was a white-tiled building, in keeping with the bland modernity of dreary apparatchiks.

The local news is written in chalk on a blackboard: the lead items are the number of women pregnant, their names, and their states of pregnancy. This is not out of concern for the mothers of Guizhou but a means of ensuring compliance with the one-child norm; if it fails, there are informants and fines. Some of the villagers try to pass themselves off as Tibetans or Yis, ethnic minorities not bound by the single-child norm. They are wasting their time: the police know this ploy.

The "cadre" presiding over the Maguan assembly is a replica of his colleague from Chala: the same black hair, the same thundering tones, the same rhetoric, and the same triumphalism. Like almost all Party cadres, Zheng is city-born and city-educated. The Party does not reflect Chinese society in any way: only 5 percent of its 60 million members are peasants, whereas peasants constitute 80 percent of the total population; there are very few workers in the Party, and their numbers are going down; only 10 percent of the Party's members are women, and no woman holds any post of real responsibility, whether at the local or national level.

Like Cairang, Zheng is happy that the assembly will "increase Maguan's democratic awareness, take it forward on the road to progress, and eliminate poverty." The delegates look pensive, smoke, and say nothing. Zheng moves on to the special meeting's agenda. (Normally, the assembly meets only once a year, as is the norm for most "elected" bodies; in China, the purpose of an assembly is not to deliberate but to publicly endorse decisions taken by the Party in camera.)

At the entrance of the village is a pond reminiscent of the mountain landscapes depicted in old Chinese paintings. This collective property, however, has slowly become a rubbish dump. All the fish have died, duckweed covers the pond, and small plastic beer bottles float on the surface. Zheng says that the pond is an eyesore that has hurt progress and brought disrepute to Maguan; the assembly must decide its future. The Party secretary proposes that it be filled and transformed into a public garden "for the elders who deserve it." Five or six speakers raise their hands to take the floor; they praise the wisdom of the secretary; everything is going according to plan.

Then, as in Chala, a discordant note is struck. An old villager, dressed in a blue jacket of the Mao era, takes the floor without having been invited. He pulls from his pocket a poem he has written specially for the occasion. The poem is an ode to the pond that used to be the pride of the village. All that has to be done is some digging and cleaning, he says; the fish will return, and so will Maguan's former glory. Zheng is furious. His bosses, who have come especially from Guiyang, the capital, huddle together in a conclave. Zheng announces that since there are two opposing proposals, there will be a vote to decide whether the pond should be filled or restored. A secret ballot is held, but no one takes any interest in the counting. Zheng declares the result: those who want the pond filled have won. Progress has triumphed, leaving the poet in the blue jacket by the wayside. This old man can hardly be called a rebel; he is only idealizing a lost China—one that goes back to the Celestial Emperors, or to Mao Zedong, who knows? His protest is a drop in the ocean of the Party's authoritarianism. There are many like him in China; sometimes they manage to come together, causing a ripple, a brief revolt against the tyranny of the Party.

There is another unforeseen incident. Instead of the national anthem, the sound technician plays the Communist International. It is an old recording, probably from the Seventies, replete with chorus, bringing back memories of the Mao years. Delegates and villagers alike are nonplussed: should they stand up or not? Standing up for the national anthem is obligatory, but the protocol for the International is unclear, since it hasn't been played for the last twenty years. The delegates decide without much hesitation to leave the public square. The words of the International are drowned out in the cries of the traders returning to their stalls. It is market day at Maguan; the air is filled with the smell of pork, tripe, salted vegetables, and fresh straw. The next assembly will meet in a year.

All this would have been quite charming had Maguan not been one of the poorest villages in China, where local tyrants pose as democrats and pat themselves on the back for all the progress that they have made. In their own guarded way, the Maguan villagers let it be known that they were not fooled.

Some delegates, more forthcoming than others, dare to answer my questions. While they are all for democracy, they would prefer electing their representatives at the district, rather than the village, level. Their demand is not technical but political in nature. Real decisions are taken at the district level, and the villagers know that their secretary is merely a puppet. They would also like to draw up their own agenda rather than restricting discussions to what Zheng proposes. They know that the assembly is a complete sham, convened once a year to discuss trivia like the pond when the village has no electricity, roads, drinking water, dispensary, or school. They also know that the government is not short of funds, for just a few miles away, beyond the valley and mountain, is a highway running across Guizhou from east to west. Hardly anyone uses it, since only bureaucrats can pay the toll tax. Truckers prefer the old, broken roads: they are free.

Everyone in Maguan knows, moreover, that some provincial Party cadres have taken refuge in Australia after making their fortunes by siphoning off part of the money earmarked for the highway. The rumor mill keeps the villagers abreast of what is happening. There is no mention of scandals in the official press, which, in any case, no one reads. The peasants' understanding of the regime, with all its rites and subterfuges, is based on their personal experience. It is difficult for them to have a global picture of the Chinese state, given the sheer size of the country and the fragmented nature of information they receive.

"Would you like to elect your government?" I often put this question to the peasants, and silence is the only reply. Perhaps they keep quiet out of fear; it is also true that the Party discourages any attempt on their part to broaden their thinking.

Reformism, the small-step theory

We, as foreign observers, tend to analyze the situation in China through the prism of our history and our habits—so are we underestimating China's march toward democracy? Are local elections fostering the democratic spirit in Chinese peasants, the Party notwithstanding? The American foundations in China are convinced that this is the case. Some Chinese human rights activists, calling themselves "reformers" rather than "liberals," subscribe to the same view. Among these bold men are a few lawyers, a new profession in

China, just as law and its codification are recent creations. Most lawyers confine their practices to commercial cases or civil suits that pose no challenge to the political institutions; a few use the courts to advance the concept of the rule of law.

"I lose practically all the time," admits Pu Zhiqiang, an activist in Beijing who specializes in media-related cases. A few newspapers are bold enough to expose the corrupt practices of firms and Party cadres. They are harassed by the Security and Propaganda Departments; if that doesn't work, the next step is a libel suit. Either the paper goes bankrupt because of the heavy fine imposed on it, or it is banned. Pu loses his cases, but he continues to plead. A giant man with a booming voice, he is difficult to silence. His size is the subject for much mirth in media circles; the joke is that the police can't arrest him because they'd need at least ten men to hold him.

"What matters is to plead," Pu says. By taking these cases to court, he is trying to instill the notions of law, trial, and justice in Chinese society. He also hopes to stir the judges out of their inertia, caught as they are between his legal arguments and the instructions of their actual boss, the Party secretary. Pu dwells constantly on the fact that law does exist in China: there are laws, decrees, and a constitution. The problem is that hardly anyone dares make recourse to the law to get grievances redressed. Since the constitution makes mention of human rights from 2004 onward—though it does not confer any real rights on citizens—Pu never fails to invoke them. Talking about human rights and the constitution is part of his method of teaching democracy. The very fact of taking a company boss or a political leader to court, he says, is a way of bringing about greater accountability in a regime where nameless individuals make decisions. When unmasking fraud, corruption, or violence inflicted on citizens, Pu gives the names of the people involved. And sometimes he wins.

Some of the newspapers that he represented won their libel suits and received damages. Similarly, city apartment owners and rural landowners whose property was unfairly expropriated have been compensated. Pu wins because the Party has ordered it so. Doesn't that make him a pawn in the hands of the Party? Aren't his rare victories a ploy to give credibility to the legal system? Isn't this a convenient way of proving that the courts are real, judges independent, the press free, and property safe? Of course it's a game, concedes Pu. The local elections are charades, too. But this charade may just compel the Party to respect the rule of law after the people discover its virtues. Every small step in that direction is thus worth the effort.

The well-known Tiananmen dissident and workers' leader Han Dongfang is a reformist like Pu. After spending two years in a Chinese prison, he took refuge in Hong Kong. Han is often called the "Chinese Lech Walesa," since he decided in 1989 to organize a trade-union movement in China. Han rejects such comparisons. He says: "Solidarity was a political union whose main purpose was to overthrow the Communist regime." Han is more modest: he aims only to protect the rights of wage earners long held in contempt in China. From his Hong Kong base, he keeps track of labor disputes on the mainland, which he tries to resolve with the help of Chinese labor laws. Like human rights, these exist but are never applied. Working by phone, he persuades strikers to eschew violence and to go to court instead. His organization, China Labor Bulletin, has the support of Western unions and pays the Beijing lawyers' fees. Only they are independent enough to take on the provincial magistrates. (In China, 70 percent of trials have no lawyers.) Through a combination of media pressure, pleas, and negotiations, the workers manage sometimes to get redress after an industrial injury or an arbitrary layoff.

These may appear like small victories in a vast country like China, but they do bring about change in the lives of some of the complainants. Like Pu, Han exhorts their educational value. Instead of chafing and wanting to revolt, workers begin to discover the virtues of the rule of law. Are these workers, who are exploited by managers working hand-in-glove with the Party, the best disciples? It is a tenuous situation, indeed: judges have no independence, the laws are ambiguous, and Han heads an apolitical movement based outside China with foreign support. He insists that he is anchored in the Left—whether out of convenience or genuine conviction is hard to say. His Left, he specifies, is the new Chinese Left; while not hostile to the Communist Party, it wants to purge it of its "neoliberal deviation" and bring it back to genuine socialism.

Han Dongfang and Pu Zhiqiang are part of the great intellectual upheaval in favor of the rule of law. To buttress their theory, they say that a new generation of magistrates, often women, is emerging in China, determined to discharge their duties independently and to fight corruption. Stéphanie Balme, a French political analyst, compares them to the group of honest Italian judges in the Eighties who stamped out the Mafia. The comparison seems rather far-fetched, for Italy was and is a pluralistic democracy. China has a long way to go. In 2005, 97 percent of criminal cases ended in conviction; two-thirds of the accused did not have lawyers, and the only testimony recorded was that of the policemen. As things stand, the main task of the courts is not to dispense justice but to strengthen the social order.

The reformers have not lost heart, however. Wang Yi, a young academic from Chengdu, has set out their theoretical premises most explicitly. He says that though the Communist Party has no legitimacy even in China, it has no intention of giving up power or reforming the regime from the top, as Gorbachev did. Thus there are two paths for China to move toward "democratic normalcy": direct confrontation, as advocated by such "liberals" as Yu Jie, a Chinese dissident, and Wei Jingsheng, based abroad; and the "reformist" path to which he subscribes. Instead of confrontation with the Party, the reformers use all available legal means to create awareness about the rule of law and the role of civil society. As none of their actions poses a direct threat to the Party, they manage to score a few legal victories. The virtue of this reformism is that it will spare the country violence, be it that of the Party or of an angry people. At the end of this long march to the rule of law, the Chinese will have constituted themselves into a politically aware society, and the passage to democracy will thus become the natural outcome of China's modernization. How many years will it take to achieve such normalcy? About thirty, reckons Wang Yi, by which time he will have turned sixty-five, the age to assume responsibility in China.

The reformist theory is baffling, since it assumes that the relationship between the reformers and the communists will remain unchanged for the next thirty years, impervious to any new development. Moreover, it displays the same Confucian condescension toward the people. Like the communists and neo-Confucianists, Wang Yi believes that experts and intellectuals have to educate the people before they can decide democratically what is good for them.

Are we in a position to judge from the outside? The novelist Mo Yan, famous both in China and the West for his book *The Red Sorghum* and the film based on it, tells me: "We have suffered so much that any small step toward light is perceived as an immense liberation." Not having experienced the same suffering, we would do well to listen to Pu Zhiqiang, Han Dongfang, Wang Yi, and Mo Yan, as well as their brothers in arms who favor a more radical concept of democracy.

When the Chinese voted supergirl

As we look for signs of greater freedom in China, I often wonder whether we are focusing on the right things. I sometimes believe that legalism, reformism, protest, and dissidence are not the real vehicles of change. Perhaps it is coming from elsewhere: blogs, text messaging, posters, clandestine masses. And things are changing here much faster than the democratic activists and the Communist Party imagine. There is a movement away from conventional politics; a new course is being charted that does not follow any of the conventional patterns of transition from dictatorship to liberal democracy. Some think change will come from religion; I am inclined to think it will come from the mass media.

Miss Li Yuchun, aged twenty-one, may have shown the way to freedom more clearly than any intellectual or democratic activist. In the summer of this Year of the Rooster, 400 million Chinese were busy adulating Miss Li without the Party's being in the know; its censors and intellectuals had never heard of her. Li, a young girl from

Sichuan Province, was one of the 200,000 contestants in a televised singing contest based on the TV show *American Idol*. The format of this contest for amateur singers has been replicated the world over. In China, the program, known as *Supergirl*, is telecast by a satellite channel, Hunan Television, and sponsored by a private firm: the show's full name is *Mongolian Cow Sour Yogurt Supergirl*. There is hardly anything cultural or national about the contest, but it does provide a bit of spice. The number of viewers increases with each episode, with the figures crossing the 400 million mark for the final one. Viewers vote by text messaging to choose the winner. Miss Li received 4 million votes, a national score no official has ever reached, even though text-message voting is contingent on owning a mobile phone, thus limiting the number of people who can vote, and is not free.

Elsewhere, the story of Miss Li would have remained confined to the world of showbiz. But we happen to be in China. The Communist Party, shaken by the figures, decided to put *Supergirl* in its proper political and moral perspective. On the eve of Miss Li's election, an editorial in the official press said that her story was symptomatic of the deleterious effect of democracy: Miss Li was chosen "spontaneously, without any artistic education," setting "a bad example for the Chinese youth." Those who voted for her were even more to blame, because they had selected a nonprofessional "who could barely sing" and "who was not the most beautiful." Taken to task by the Hong Kong press, the editorialist, a certain Raymond Zhou, felt obliged to justify his stand. After consultations with the "cultural milieu," he said his was the "authoritative" opinion. When decoded, this means that Zhou is the mouthpiece of the Propaganda Department, on which his paper, *China Daily*, depends.

It is true that Miss Li Yuchun, with her tall, lean frame, boyish clothes, and spiked hair ("a tomboy," wrote Zhou), does not conform to the sugary aesthetic canons that public Chinese television, CCTV, inflicts on its viewers every Saturday evening. The Party saw the writing on the wall: Miss Li's election was mutiny. This is what "unprepared democracy" leads to, concluded the Propaganda Department's editorialist. Left to their own devices, the Chinese chose one of their own, not a mechanical robot, to represent them.

CHAPTER EIGHT

The Savage State

T he Chinese state is not like any other state. Yet at first glance, Western observers fail to see anything out of the ordinary. The Communist Party has taken good care to bury its revolutionary origins and to adopt the international language of economic efficiency and social order. Like any other government, it borrows from an internationally accepted political, diplomatic, and administrative lexicon. China has a president, a prime minister, an assembly, a constitution, and laws, so how is it different from other countries?

So the state has maintained appearances, but in truth Chinese laws are worthless and exist only on paper. Those in command operate behind the scenes. The Party hierarchy, the only hierarchy that matters, consists of faceless individuals. The Party's Central Committee meetings are held in the utmost secrecy; most Chinese do not even know the names of its members. The silence and elusiveness of a leadership accountable to no one has permeated from the top of the Party to its lowest levels. Local cadres terrorize the people daily. No state is ever innocent, but the Chinese Communist Party has crossed all bounds and demonstrated its extraordinary capacity to kill, steal, and lie. On June 4, 1989, Madam Ding Zilin discovered just how savage the Chinese state was.

Ding Zilin, undaunted by the executioners

It was the evening of June 3. Ding Zilin's seventeen-year-old son, Jiang Liangjie, went to meet his friends at Tiananmen Square, despite her telling him not to. Ding Zilin worked at a university. In the normal course of events, she would have eventually become a dignified, white-haired professor enjoying retired life. But on the morning of June 4, she was summoned to identify the bullet-riddled body of her son in a Beijing hospital. Sixteen years later, she is still groping for answers. Why did the Party kill her son? Who shot him and on whose orders? To date, there has been no reply.

For two years after the shooting, a distraught Ding Zilin could think of nothing but suicide. She felt guilty for not having stopped her young son from going out. She wondered whether he had been killed for doing something wrong. As any mention of Tiananmen was prohibited, Ding Zilin did not know that other parents, as isolated as she was, shared her grief and bewilderment. Two years went by before she learned that the International Red Cross had put the number of casualties on June 4 at 2,800 dead and an equal number injured. Who were these people and where did they come from? Many families never got any news of their children, their dear ones, their friends. Since most bodies remained untraceable, relatives and friends of victims were not sure whether they were dead or alive. People could not mourn for their dead, whose souls were condemned to drift in perpetuity while their relatives wallowed in despair. (The same brutality was displayed in the December 2004 massacre of Dongzhou villagers. The police removed the bodies of the victims, rendering it impossible to count the dead or ascertain the exact cause of death.)

In 1991, Prime Minister Li Peng, who had ordered the Tiananmen shootings in consultation with Deng Xiaoping, stated the Party's position, which has not changed since: in view of the families' desire for silence and secrecy, the names of the victims would not be released. Ding Zilin was outraged when she heard the blatant lie. She shed her grief and decided to fight, writing to the prime minister and telling him that the victims' families desired truth, not secrecy. A Hong Kong journalist to whom she had described her anger reported her comments. For this, the state arrested her and her husband, also a professor; interrogated, threatened, harassed, and watched them; and forced them into retirement. Their crime: "They had hurt the feelings of the Chinese people."

Ding Zilin and others of her generation have gone through far too much to be afraid. After countless horrors, exterminations, revolutions, and purges, they have nothing left to fear. And so, in spite of her limited energy, Ding Zilin is doing her best to make a list of the Tiananmen victims. This is grueling work. What makes it even harder is that most of the victims were students from other provinces whose families are scattered all over the country. Innocent bystanders, too, were caught in the shooting: passersby, laborers from neighboring worksites, peasants bringing their produce to the capital, doctors who came to the rescue of the demonstrators—all of them perished in a relentless volley of machine-gun shots. It was a massacre.

Each time Ding Zilin manages to identify a victim's family, she has a hard time getting them to talk. She asks if they would be willing to admit that one of theirs was missing and whether they actually saw the body or if it was buried furtively by soldiers. Security agents closely watch everything she does. After she leaves a victim's family, plainclothes policemen descend on them. They do not reveal their identity, nor do they state the purpose of their visit. They just barge in, interrogate, intimidate, and harass the family.

By the Year of the Rooster, Ding Zilin has managed to collect just eighty-nine names, listed in a brochure published in Hong Kong along with photographs of the missing—dead or alive—whenever available. This is the beginning of a memorial that will be built sometime in the future. The plight of Chinese parents is comparable with that of the mothers of those missing in Argentina and Chile. But while the mothers of Buenos Aires and Santiago enjoy worldwide support, Ding Zilin is waging a lone battle with little Western help. She is trying single-handedly to provide material assistance to parents of victims who have no other recourse, a particular problem for worker and peasant families that lost their head of family or eldest son. Ding Zilin is trying to collect money for them in China, but she gets very little. Do the Chinese lack compassion? She tries to find an excuse for them: perhaps they fear getting caught in a spiral of repression. With the destruction of old religious solidarity networks and the idealization of material success, the Communist regime has created a new, mean-spirited society. Aid has come from abroad. Even the modest contributions from overseas Chinese, however, were enough for the authorities to charge Ding Zilin and her husband with smuggling foreign currency and to sentence them to two months' imprisonment. Ding Zilin redistributes the proceeds to needy families. Security agents then try to convince them that their benefactor skims off a large part of the money she receives from abroad. Sadly, this smear campaign has put Ding Zilin on the defensive, forcing her to justify her actions.

The French president Jacques Chirac was among the many foreign heads of state to visit Beijing in the Year of the Rooster. He pleaded for lifting the West's embargo, imposed after the Tiananmen massacre, on the sale of arms to China. "The page has been turned," Chirac said, to justify this about-face. Not true: as long as Ding Zilin has not collected the names of all the victims and performed their funeral rites, the page will not have been turned, and the Chinese state will not be a normal state.

Family planning, another name for state intimidation

In her Beijing office, Madam Hao Lina is dismayed. Some obscure peasant from Shandong Province, Chen Guangcheng, has just shattered the national birth-control program's humane image, which China has been trying so assiduously to cultivate. To make things worse, the self-taught, thirty-four-year-old Chen has been blind since the age of nine.

The elegant Madam Hao, the international director of the Family Planning Commission, is one of the few women in China to occupy a high government position. She had nearly succeeded in winning over foreigners, if not the Chinese themselves, to China's crusade against the population explosion. Under her influence, people forgot the compulsory sterilizations, abortions under duress, and beatings inflicted on wayward parents during the Eighties. The Americans, because of their pro-life, anti-abortion stance, were the only ones to keep condemning the Chinese family-planning program. As a result, coercion has become less brutal. The single-child principle applied uniformly thirty years ago has been relaxed in certain cases. Taking into account the widespread preference for boys, the Party has made some concessions. The single-child norm now applied only to large cities like Beijing and Shanghai and densely populated provinces like Sichuan. Elsewhere, couples can have a second child if the first is a girl. The rule has been relaxed even further in sparsely populated areas, where people are allowed to have two children even if the first is a boy; ethnic minorities can have three. And Tibetans can have as many children as they like.

Coercion is a thing of the past, we are told. Instead, the government is relying on persuasion, doing all it can to encourage people to practice contraception. Now there are only financial disincentives to discourage people from having too many children. Madam Hao announces proudly that once they reach sixty, every single-child parent in rural areas gets a monthly pension of sixty yuan. When it comes to fines, however, she is evasive. She is aware that local authorities fix them as a means of extorting money from peasants.

Within the space of thirty years, she says, family-planning "education" has brought down the average number of children per family from 5.9 to 1.8, comparable with the European average. This means the Chinese population will start declining from 2033 onward. "Family planning has kept the population down to 1.3 billion; otherwise it would crossed the 1.6 billion mark," she points out. The 300 million fewer births have supposedly accelerated economic growth by 4 percent per annum. Madam Hao's statistics are precise but not necessarily accurate. They are more in the nature of victory bulletins. Official figures are rarely accurate, especially population statistics.

Western demographers put the average number of children per couple at about 2.3. Though difficult to prove, it is quite possible that population growth has not slowed down at all—contrary to the global trend of declining populations resulting from women's education, the expectation of economic betterment, and declining infant mortality. India's demographic situation is comparable with China's, even though India gave up coercion way back in 1975. It is equally hard to prove that these "300 million" fewer Chinese have hastened the pace of development, for these unborn Chinese would have grown up to be generators of wealth.

But this was not the purpose of our meeting at the Planning Commission's Beijing headquarters. The irksome Chen Guangcheng was the subject at hand. Hao Lina launched into China's population policy, knowing full well that it was Chen Guangcheng I wanted to talk about. The Chen affair had been internationalized, and this was the only reason that Madam Hao had consented to meet me.

In September, the blind peasant had taken a train to Beijing, accompanied by his wife, who acted as his guide. He was headed for the petitions office, along with a few human rights activists and an American journalist. Before he could reach it, the police intercepted him. Though his complaint was perfectly legal, no one had been willing to register it in his hometown of Linyi. Of course, what he had to say was explosive. Before Madam Hao got wind of it, the news was splashed across the front pages of the American press. Chen had done a survey in his city. He discovered that 7,000 mothers with two children each had been forcibly sterilized during the past three months and that several hundred others had been forced to undergo abortions even though they were eight months pregnant. The city's hospital staff admitted to immersing fetuses in boiling water to make sure they did not survive.

Madam Hao expressed her regret for the unfortunate incident. She had gone personally to Linyi to investigate the truth of Chen's findings. She announced a reeducation program for the local family-planning agents. "They did not understand the law," she said. She added, for my benefit, that the affair had been blown out of proportion. There had been fewer than 7,000 sterilizations, and not all of them were forced. The figures had to be seen in perspective. In relation to Linyi's 100,000 annual births, what happened seemed to be nothing more than a "regrettable lapse" on the part of the local authorities.

Madam Hao was lying. The Party has never been concerned about the truth. The Linyi affair was not a "regrettable lapse." On the contrary, it brings out the full horror of China's family-planning program in the villages, as well as our ignorance. The Linyi episode is extraordinary only because we got to hear about it. The municipal authorities had published an order directing that forced sterilizations and abortions be carried out. As justification for such an extreme step, they pointed to an unhealthy Linyi trend of producing three children. Worse still, pregnant mothers were changing their village to avoid checking. If Beijing learned that the quota had been exceeded, the local representatives' political careers would be on the line. So they had to strike hard. The Linyi police and private militias hired by the Party tracked down pregnant women and women with two children. Parents and neighbors who failed to report them were jailed, beaten, and fined a hundred yuan a day. Entire villages found themselves besieged, cut off from the rest of the world until they handed over the guilty. Husbands who resisted their wives' kidnapping were badly beaten. Herded to a hospital like sheep, the hapless women were summarily anesthetized and operated on in far from hygienic conditions. The Party cadres heaved a sigh of relief: Linyi had met its population quota, and their jobs were safe. They had not reckoned with the blind peasant.

Chen spent several years familiarizing himself with China's emerging legal system so that he could help peasants assert their meager rights. His farm became a center for legal counseling. Villagers weighed down under the burden of fines and other extortion came to him for advice. After the sterilization scandal, the foreign media had feted the local activist, much to the embarrassment of Madam Hao. How was she to get rid of him?

Chen had to be silenced. This is China's time-tested method for dealing with troublemakers. He was put under house arrest on his farm. Human rights activists from Beijing wanting to ascertain his safety are chased away and beaten by the local militia. For all Hao Lina's professed indignation, no action has been taken against those responsible for the forced sterilizations and abortions. Madam Hao is hoping that the matter will die down and be forgotten by both Chinese and foreign observers. "Aren't the French and the Chinese both committed to limiting world population and preserving our natural resources?" she says with a sudden smile.

I cannot support Madam Hao and what she is doing. To my mind, China's family-planning program serves no purpose other than to reinforce the Party's control over the people. There is nothing to prove that the draconian methods have been effective in checking China's population growth. What are visible are bureaucratic extortions and suffering parents. The preference for boys has led to female feticide and gender imbalance on an unprecedented scale. Forcible birth control will also give rise to an increasingly aging population. What will old parents do with no children to look after them? Retirement benefits prop up the aged in Europe and Japan, but a poor country like China is totally unprepared to deal with the situation. The single child is also a social problem. Only sons tend to behave like little emperors. Their social insertion is a question that has the Chinese perplexed.

Finally, family planning does not address the central question of women's position in society. Caught between their husbands' and in-laws' demands to bear sons and the dictates of the family-planning agents, Chinese women are in a bind. It is not easy being a Chinese man in the Year of the Rooster; being a Chinese woman is even harder.

The solitude of the abolitionist

In October, 2,000 schoolchildren from the city of Changsha were invited to witness an extraordinary event, the trial of six drug smugglers. All six received the death penalty and were executed soon afterward. Every year, as the National Day approaches, such dramas are enacted to remind people of the Party-State's omnipotence.

The Chinese are not against capital punishment, at least for murder. But were the six Changsha men really drug smugglers, or was it a trumped-up charge? How many executions take place every year? This is a state secret. Humanitarian organizations outside China put the figure between 3,500 and 15,000. In comparison, in the United States about fifty people are sentenced to death annually, nearly the same as in Singapore, even though America has a much larger population. In China, figures are never revealed, just as judgments and the grounds for decisions are never published. Magistrates can choose among sixteen crimes punishable by death: murder, tax evasion, panda hunting, antique-smuggling, conspiring to overthrow the government.... With the grounds for indictment so varied, judges have a great deal of latitude with respect to the law but none vis-à-vis their political mentors in the Party.

How many of the so-called political criminals actually took up arms in the course of their resistance to tyranny? How many Tibetans and Uigurs are sentenced in camera without a lawyer for supposedly conspiring against the unity of the Chinese nation? In a country where corruption is widespread and tax evasion the norm, why are some gunned down while others prosper? What is the purpose of the killings? Are they meant to serve as an example for schoolchildren, or is the Party settling scores with some rebellious faction?

Capital punishment in China is not only arbitrary but also lucrative. Dead men make some people rich. Just before the execution—not after—the condemned person's vital organs are removed and then sold. Thanks to transplants and the demand for living cells that may help the aged live longer, there is a thriving market for the organs. Once the organs have been removed, the victim is hastily stitched together before being shot or incinerated. Accounts of organ harvesting abound.

The trade doesn't stop there. In the summer of 2005, an exhibit of human bodies, coated with plastic after the skin had been removed, traveled to several American museums of natural history, as well as to Taiwan, to help medical students study anatomy. It emerged that the bodies had come from China. This recycling of dead bodies aroused indignation in the United States. The Chinese government was tight-lipped. The exhibit was withdrawn and the indignation proved short-lived. Both in Europe and the U.S., the general feeling is that a Chinese body is not worth a Western one.

Europeans seem ever ready to protest capital punishment, but their protest is halfhearted. The French media and intelligentsia have an annual petition ritual. It's the fashionable thing for Paris's literati to sign a text condemning the death penalty—in the United States. However abhorrent the practice may be, the fact is that the death sentence is not given frequently in America. It exists because of a democratic consensus and an independent judiciary. I, too, belong to the band of signatories. Over the years, I have tried hard to get the text to condemn China as well. So far, I have been unsuccessful.

Why China? they ask me. Perhaps all those who are shot down and dismembered really were guilty, they think; capital punishment, unacceptable in the United States, might be good for the Chinese; the death sentence could act as a deterrent to stem China's widespread violence. Does that mean that the Chinese government is legitimate in killing its subjects, whereas the Americans are not? Are we suggesting that a Chinese life is not worth an American life and that human rights do not apply to the yellow race? That is not the real issue, say some. We would do better to respect the cultural characteristics of the Chinese than to impose our ideas on them—even though the Chinese constitution does refer to human rights now. Between the sinophiles on the one hand and the America-bashers on the other, good sense has been thrown to the winds. Why blame the Chinese?

He Weifang is Chinese and an abolitionist for capital punishment. He opposes capital punishment in China for the same reasons as in the West: the state does not have the right to kill, and the death sentence does not dissuade criminals. In China, an additional problem arises: the police and judges are incompetent and corrupt, subservient to the Party and ready to be bought off. He Weifang has been teaching law at Beijing University for forty years. His struggle is cautious and solitary, for abolitionism does not generate much enthusiasm. Perhaps his caution comes from the experience of his forefathers, all intellectuals. His idealistic grandparents plunged into the Communist revolution only to see it degenerate into tyranny. His parents believed in the Cultural Revolution, which turned into a civil war that took their lives.

So, immune to political violence like many Chinese, He Weifang prefers to teach. Yet explaining to his students and readers of his website why the death penalty should be abolished is not simple. In fact, it is illegal to advocate banning it. The Party is willing to tinker a bit with capital punishment but not to repeal it. He Weifang must act obliquely. He draws attention to the most blatant legal errors and to executions performed without sufficient proof. He points out a procedure for the review of cases at the national level, which could improve matters because the Supreme Court judges are less incompetent and slightly more independent than local magistrates. Still, He Weifang does not trust them entirely. Unlike in the West, he says, a Chinese judge is never the guarantor of the separation of powers. He just ensures the selective application of the law. The law does not apply to the state; it is the state that lays down the law. And justice is meted out sparingly to its subjects. In such a system, no judge can afford to contradict the Party-State.

He Weifang has an uphill battle convincing even the most liberal Chinese about the universality of law and human rights. It is true, he admits, that the notion of law comes from the West and has no roots in classical China. But that does not make it any less universal or less applicable to China. The Party does concede this in principle, stating at the same time that there are two approaches to human rights. The Chinese approach favors material rights—the right to feed and clothe oneself. The Western approach, with its emphasis on abstract rights like the freedom of information or the freedom to associate, is good only for affluent nations. To impose Western standards on China is to take part in an imperialist conspiracy against Greater China—a chauvinistic argument that appeals to many Chinese taken with the idea of national dignity. He Weifang is fighting the propaganda machinery almost single-handedly to deny this moral relativism. He manages to convince small groups here and there, students and people who read his articles on the Internet. He has to measure his words; otherwise, he could end up losing his chair and the influence he derives from it. The road to reform is narrow, if it exists at all.

This serene, smiling professor, with his understated heroism, makes one feel small and humble. As travelers to China, slightly ashamed of our own helplessness, we can only listen carefully. Cocooned in Western comfort, can we be of any use to people like him? All we can do is stand firm against the communist campaign to lure Western leaders by proffering enticements. It is our duty to see that the next Paris or New York petition against capital punishment targets not only the United States but China as well.

Corruption: crucial to the Party's survival

The matter is serious. The leaders of the Central Commission for Discipline in Beijing have gathered around the conference table. There are only men, as women are excluded from decision-making bodies (their role is only to serve tea). The vice president, Liu Fengyan, is easy to spot, sitting as he is in a central position with his hair dyed jet-black. (Black hair is the fashion among Party leaders.) A large clock hangs on the wall to mark the two hours allotted for our meeting. I have been accorded a great honor. I was aware of the importance attached to the fight against corruption in the Year of the Rooster, so I had asked to meet the highest body in that fight, the Commission for Discipline. Amazingly, I managed to get an appointment, surprising everyone at the French Embassy, where one is usually obliged to stay to meet Chinese officialdom. No journalist would have been granted such an audience. Luckily for me, I am not one, which made investigation easier. In reality, the Party, desirous of "communicating" on the subject, imagined that I would be a receptive listener. I did listen, but my interpretation of the facts did not coincide with the Party's.

For two hours, the vice president read the new policy against corruption. There was no time for debate or questions. The Party believes in ramming points home, not in discussion. No one asked me what I thought of the proceedings, though I was treated courteously enough, since I was a foreign guest and not a Chinese subject. The exposé could have been briefer. There was a great deal of repetition, as we had two hours to fill. The time granted and the high rank of the members present were all meant to demonstrate to the French visitor, after the customary speech on Sino-French friendship, that the fight against corruption was a "matter of life and death" for the Party. Many Chinese would agree: corruption is one of the main reasons for the people's hatred of Party cadres.

The Central Commission for Discipline is not what we would imagine it to be in the West. We would expect it to act as an independent watchdog to check abuses of power. But in a Party-State, its role is different. It is, in the words of its vice president, a "self-regulatory mechanism against the misuse of power for personal aggrandizement." The temptation is great: local leaders, mayors, district chiefs, and governors wear many hats. They administer, legislate, run public enterprises, and provide employment at the same time. With so much power, you would have to be a saint to act disinterestedly. But the vice president refuses to acknowledge the connection between overlapping powers and the possibility of abuse. Instead he reels off statistics: in 2004, there were 162,032 cases of corruption in which 5,916 cadres were punished, 4,775 Party members tried, and 900 sentenced. This goes to show how serious the commission is about rooting out corruption. Moreover, he continues, just 900 serious cases for 60 million members is proof of the Party's probity. By 2020, he declares, "bad habits" and "bad behavior" will have been completely eradicated, thanks to the new anticorruption plan adopted this year—some 300 laws and several thousand regulations. In 2020, the very memory of corruption, an old Chinese scourge, will have disappeared because "a sense of probity will have been instilled in the entire population."

The ladies come in to serve tea. I use the occasion to interrupt his perfect speech and to ask him about the role of the press. His answer is along the expected lines: "It is useful when it condemns specific incidents but harmful when it blows things out of proportion." Even some "foreign media are prone to use the issue of corruption to destabilize the Chinese government." So far, however, no "French newspaper has taken part in this anti-Chinese conspiracy." I don't rise to the bait.

As he makes his marathon speech, replete with quotations from Marx, Mao Zedong, and Deng Xiaoping, my mind begins to wander. I look out the window at the park in which Madam Mao Zedong rode her horses when she behaved like an empress. The premises of the Commission for Discipline served as her pleasure grounds. The Party has become a little more circumspect since then, but it has not given up its doublespeak.

While Liu Fengyan extols the Party for its resolute struggle against China's old evils, we learn from the Chinese press that most of the private coal mines, very profitable because of the energy shortage, belong to the spouses or cousins of Party cadres responsible for their management and safety. Not a week goes by without the media's reporting some terrible accident caused by a total disregard for safety, with productivity taking precedence over everything. What is the Commission for Discipline doing about this? Since the beginning of the Year of the Rooster, 30,000 miners have lost their lives. Yet no inquiry has been made, nor has any cadre been dismissed.

The history of Chinese communism demonstrates that the Party's fight against corruption is as old as corruption itself. Naturally, communists deny the relationship between corruption and the Party. Westerners who do business with Chinese cadres jump to the Party's defense. Western entrepreneurs and politicians who know exactly what it takes to grease the palms of Communist leaders try to excuse the Party on cultural grounds. Corruption, they tell us, is inherent in Chinese civilization. Liu Fengyan said the same thing. Traditionally, the mandarins bought their offices and sold their services. Badly paid, they sponged off the people. The Party and its cadres are only perpetuating an age-old tradition. So a tax inspector who adjusts taxes in accordance with the bribes he gets, a cadre who buys a university degree for his son, a minister who employs his entire family in the government, an officer who gambles away his departmental budget in a Macao casino—these are publicly recorded cases that at times have been punished—are in reality the inheritors of a specifically Chinese convention. How can we be so churlish as to take offense at old customs—which, in any case, we are told, will be eradicated by 2020?

The cultural determinism argument does not stand up to scrutiny. It was precisely to fight against corruption that the Party seized power. Now corruption has become more pervasive than ever before, especially since the ethics of Confucianism no longer act as a check. When the same Chinese work as bureaucrats in Taiwan, Singapore, and Hong Kong, they are far less corrupt than their Communist counterparts. And the Chinese in China abhor the corruption of the Party cadres and do not view them as custodians of a laudable tradition.

"Corruption is efficient" is another specious argument that finds favor with Western corporations and chanceries. China is a complex society where the rule of law has yet to take root, they say. Back-door entries are quicker and save the trouble of getting lost in labyrinthine bureaucracy. What a foreign businessman can get done in a day through the back door would take an eternity through normal channels. The Chinese experience confirms the fact that corruption tempers totalitarianism. This is what people used to say about the Soviet Union, too. But the back-door route is only for the rich and powerful. The rest—those who have children to be admitted to school, are looking for a place to stay, or need an identity paper or permit—pay exorbitantly.

The third argument proffered by Western sinophiles and Chinese leaders is that corruption is a transitory phenomenon. As an economy moves from state controls to a free market, some excesses are inevitable. When public ownership moves to private hands, managers do tend to dip into bank loans and company funds to buy shares of the erstwhile public enterprises, thus becoming their owners. Once the process of privatization has been completed, these practices will cease automatically. The advocates of the transition theory say that the Chinese state, weakened by the market, needs to strengthen its power. "More state for more market" is the government's thinking.

But the transition phase has gone on for twenty-five years, and corruption shows no signs of abating. In fact, it is becoming worse, as indicated by the exemplary punishment that the Party gives its cadres from time to time. No one can get anything done in China without obtaining a host of authorizations. The State is omnipresent; how can it get any stronger? Contrary to the transition theory, the Party's privatization program makes sure that corruption persists because it is embedded in the system. Privatization in China is merely the right to grow rich granted to a private individual under the permanent tutelage of a public custodian. With the government keeping a close watch on the market and with ownership more in the nature of a grant, the Party ensures that its concessionaires remain beholden to it. This brings us back to our initial hypothesis: corruption is crucial to the Party and has been so since the beginning.

From the outset, the Communist Party intended to acquire political and economic power in China so that it could maintain its hold over society and ensure the prosperity of its members. From its first "base," set up from 1934 to 1949 at Yanan in Shaanxi Province, the Party has been self-sufficient, relying on its own enterprises to meet its members' needs. Mao Zedong rejected any distinction between economics and politics, never wanting civil society to generate wealth. He encouraged Party cadres to get rich by all means, including contraband. The Party's greed for lucre is as old as its condemnation of it. In 1946, Huang Kecheng, a general of great integrity, said, "All the cadres want is the decadence and luxury of the city." They got both when they reached Beijing in 1949. Mao Zedong led the way, building huge palaces and collecting a bevy of courtesans. His wife, Jiang Qing, did not lag far behind. Yet in 1963, the very same Mao Zedong, using the kind of metaphor that the Party favors, ordered that the "tigers and lice"—in other words, the big and small alike—be exterminated to stem the rot. The Party was thus to have a split personality: indulging in every kind of corrupt practice itself, it was to mount a crusade against corruption at the same time.

Indeed, why does one become a Party member, if not to live off it? From the peasant soldier of the early days to the modern ambitious student, economic security is what prompts people to join the Party. How many of its 60 million are members because of their ideals? And what ideals can they have when the Party is geared for only one thing: individual prosperity?

This obsession for amassing wealth has put the Party in a dilemma. How can it motivate people to "throw themselves into the ocean of business" without the cadres, who are in charge of applying this policy, getting rich themselves? The Singapore solution is to pay officials the same salaries as those of company executives, while punishing any form of corruption. But Singapore is a small country with few bureaucrats, and monitoring is easy. Besides, the British inculcated a sense of law in them. In Communist China, implicit corruption is the implicit answer: the Party cadres rallied around the "free-market revolution" because they saw that it was to their advantage. Did Deng Xiaoping have any other choice? None of the ex-Maoist cadres resisted privatization, because they all stood to gain from it. The Party has been supporting liberalization for the past twenty-six years without any protest, for the main beneficiaries are the cadres and their families, who have either become entrepreneurs or are on their payrolls.

At the same time, the Party must condemn corruption, a ritual as essential as corruption itself. Since 1949, it has launched an anti-corruption campaign every two years. The propaganda managers have shown great inventiveness in naming this campaign: in 1980, it was a campaign against official privileges and unhealthy trends in the Party; in 1982, it was a fight against economic crimes, and in 1983, against "spiritual pollution"; 1988 saw a campaign to build a "clean government"; in 2005, the motto was "little eyes against big eyes"—in other words, children should tell on their parents. The government keeps publishing manuals, rules, case studies, and posters on how to fight corruption. There are 300 laws, Liu Fengyan tells us.

All these campaigns, manuals, orders, and posters are part of an expiatory ritual to convince the people that the Party does not treat corruption lightly. The sensational trials of a few Party leaders, with the death sentence thrown in at times, make appearances all the more credible. Like the propaganda campaigns, the trials are not meant to eliminate corruption but to contain it within limits tolerable for the people and acceptable to the cadres. Going too far would be suicidal; it could disband the cadres and incite them to revolt against the liberal reforms.

Do reforms and corruption go hand in hand? Is it possible to move from socialism to a market economy without the subornment that supposedly eases the transition? In all the countries of the former Soviet Bloc, privatization has helped Communist apparatchiks turn themselves into entrepreneurs. But the privatization was real, and when it had been accomplished, the Communist Party generally made way for an administrative bureaucracy on the one hand and a new class of entrepreneurs on the other. This is not the case in China. The Party has not become an administration, and the rule of law has not replaced clientelism. In the absence of any democratic changeover, the Party continues to prevaricate with no other check than its own goodwill.

The manner in which the Nanjing municipality proceeded is a good case in point. In May of the Year of the Rooster, it ordered Party cadres to report their extramarital relationships to an office set up for the purpose. The ostensible reason given was that 95 percent of the cadres accused of corruption also had a mistress (the Party has a fetish for precise figures). The local government therefore decided to take this step in the hope of eliminating corruption, or at least of detecting it. The *People's Daily*, the official newspaper of the Party, made it a front-page story: "When fighting corruption, the Party scales new heights of creativity." In order to strike fear into the cadres and please the public, the newspaper recalled that, in 2000, the Party had not hesitated to execute the former vice president of the National People's Congress. He was the highest leader ever to get the death sentence for corruption—and he had had several "second wives."

Chinese individuals decide marriage and divorce freely, so a few Beijing jurists questioned the legality of the order. The reply of the Nankin municipality was that legal niceties were extraneous in the fight against the scourge of corruption.

During the Year of the Rooster, not a single confession had been recorded so far at the Nanjing office for extramarital affairs. Had cadres turned chaste—and honest—overnight? Did the leadership in Nankin really believe that such a measure would yield results? There must have been some who did, or else the constant rehash of the sixty-year-old anticorruption campaign would be meaningless. The democracy advocates aver, tongue in cheek, that the Communist Party will vanish under the weight of its own contradictions. This is wishful thinking; the Party has both political and economic clout and has no intention of giving up either.

The Voice of Big Brother

"Obesity, the new threat to China": this was the editorial in the *China Daily* on August 10 of the Year of the Rooster. The *China Daily* is one of several newspapers that are mouthpieces of the Communist Party's Propaganda Department. Reading it tells us nothing about the real China but provides an insight into the nature of the state.

On August 10, the Propaganda Department discovered—or, to be more precise, decreed—that 12 percent of the Chinese were obese and had to watch what they ate. The nameless editorialist—articles are usually churned out at Party headquarters—called for yet another campaign, this time against dietary excesses, one of the few pleasures the Chinese can indulge in. Frugality and chastity are the buzzwords of Communist discourse, a way of reining in people suspected of being individualistically hedonistic. That the Party cadres are hardly frugal or chaste in their private lives is of little consequence. Plainly, the obesity threat was a piece of pure fabrication to make us believe that China was now suffering from a problem of surfeit. There are 100 million undernourished people living in nearly faminelike conditions (the figure has been given in various scientific journals), and yet the Party denies their existence, just as it down-plays the devastation caused by AIDS and other pandemics. A good Chinese communist must always live in a state of euphoria.

That week, another *China Daily* editorial recalled "the tradition of Chinese leaders of placing the people's interest above their own." Three centuries before Christ, Mencius wrote: "The people come first, land and grain second, and the sovereign last." This tradition of self-lessness, continued the nameless editor employed by the same office that invented the obesity epidemic, was brought up to date by Sun Yat-sen, who decided that the focus of the 1911 revolution would be on "the three principles of the people": *minsheng*, the welfare of the people; *minzu*, the people as a nation; and *minquan*, the power of the people. Finally, Mao, with his principle that the "service of the people is the sole reward of the leader," transformed once and for all the relationship between the state and the nation.

This nonsense, reproduced here faithfully, is so far removed from the reality of China that the expression "service of the people" has become a common joke. The moment you say it, your audience bursts into laughter. How can the press continue to churn out such gobbledygook day after day when nearly everyone in China laughs at it? Does the Propaganda Department think that by repeating something ad nauseam, it will succeed in brainwashing its readers? The effect seems to be just the opposite: fed up with official false-hoods, the Chinese have become inured to ideology. "Journalists," especially editorialists who toe the official line, behave like members of a secret sect: they believe in what they write, though their articles are divorced from reality.

Espionage, too, hit the headlines that week. We learned that the China correspondent of the Singapore daily *Straits Times*, who held a British passport issued in Hong Kong, had finally confessed after being arrested by the police and kept in solitary confinement for four months. There wasn't the shadow of a doubt: Ching Cheong was a spy in the pay of foreign agencies—in other words, Taiwan. He admit-ted receiving "large sums of money for his spying activities." In prison and without a lawyer to defend him, Ching Cheong never got an opportunity to tell his side of the story. From the Hong Kong press, one gathers that he had managed to get hold of documents revealing divergences between the Party's hardliners and its more liberal elements. The *China Daily* wrote: "Long oppressed by British colonialism, it was only with the transfer of Hong Kong to China that journalists became free and thus tend at times to abuse their newfound independence."

In fact, under British rule, the Hong Kong press was one of the freest in the world; since the transfer of power to the Communist government, it has lost a little of its freedom. Do the "journalists" of the Propaganda Department really believe anything of what they write, be it about obesity, the selflessness of the leaders, Ching Cheong the spy, or Hong Kong? There is only one plausible explanation: Big Brother believes what Big Brother says. No one else does, except for some Western sinophiles who perhaps have a vested interest in doing so. Not one asked for Ching Cheong's release, thereby giving credence to the charge of spying. How many excesses will the Party have to commit before China's Western friends wake up and protest?

A chronicle of everyday repression

Here are some more stories that appeared in local newspapers or on the Internet during the Year of the Rooster. They did not make it to the front pages of the Western press. Perhaps they were too ordinary, or perhaps they were not what the West wanted to hear about China.

Zheng Enchong, a fifty-four-year-old Shanghai lawyer, was sentenced to three years' imprisonment for revealing state secrets. Actually, he was helping families draft a complaint against a promoter close to the Party who had taken their land illegally. Zheng is being kept in a high-security area and is not allowed to meet a lawyer.

The Chinese minister of construction said that in the first six months of 2005, 4,000 associations and 18,000 individuals had complained against the illegal confiscation of their land. In September, 30,000 petitioners whose land had been confiscated were arrested in Beijing.

The police used rubber bullets to disperse a group of peasants in the Shijiahe village of Henan. They were protesting the confiscation and illegal destruction of their houses. The police hired "antisocial" elements to help out.

The Shanghai police department set up an emergency cell to deal with "political threats." All eighty people working at the cell have been provided "high-tech surveillance equipment."

The Luwan court in the Shangcai district did not allow a group of complainants seeking damages from a real-estate promoter—who, they claimed, had destroyed their locality illegally—to enter the courtroom. In their absence, the court decided in favor of the promoter.

The state telephone company China Mobile banned twenty-two text-messaging services for allowing users to send "pornographic messages." Sending such messages by text or through the Internet is punishable by life imprisonment. Software to censor text messages, with a vocabulary of about a thousand words, was developed. Apart from sexual terms, the software flags expressions such as *Falun Gong, Tiananmen, political prisoners, correction centers, Taiwan, Tibet, Xinjiang, Sino-Russian border, corruption, ultranationalism,* and even *truth* and *idea.*

The day before the Dari Rulai Xingyuan Buddhist temple in Inner Mongolia—restored thanks to contributions from abroad—was to reopen, the police arrested the spiritual leader who was to have presided over the ceremony. He was charged with "inciting the people to superstition."

Du Hongqui, a worker at the Mingguang factory in Chongqing who had protested against layoffs, received three years' imprisonment for "disrupting social order."

The police arrested a group of baby-traffickers in Fujian Province. Fifty-three boys were recovered. Each boy had been bought from his parents for 2,000 yuan and then sold for 15,000 yuan. The same gang also sold girls of various ages to work as wives, prostitutes, or domestic servants.

Xiao Weibin, editor in chief of the magazine *Dong Zhou Gong Jin* in Canton, was fired for publishing an article by a former Communist Party chief who favored political reform based on Western-style separation of powers.

Ten thousand people retired from the textile industry demonstrated at Bengbu in Anhui Province against the decrease in their pensions and the absence of medical coverage.

The *China Daily* calculated the wages that public and private enterprises have still not paid to migrant workers at about 360 billion yuan. The Changzhou court sentenced Huang Jinqin to twelve years' imprisonment for "subversion." The journalist had circulated material in defense of human rights on the Internet.

Authorities closed down the Internet discussion forum of Beijing University, YiTaHuTu ("Good Disorder"). The participants had brought up sensitive issues such as corruption, human rights, and Taiwan.

The public office for "reducing poverty" awarded a prize for poverty elimination to nine deserving private organizations. The government announced that poverty would be eradicated from China in ten years.

A piece of good news at last! The supreme court prosecutor charged 1,780 officials and magistrates with human rights violations: property theft, illegal detention, torture, atrocities committed on prisoners, acts causing death, electoral fraud. The charges came after an amendment to the constitution in 2004 protecting human rights. The beginning perhaps of a new dawn.

CHAPTER NINE

The End of the Party

Is the Chinese regime still Communist? Is the Party really Communist? People asked the same questions about the Soviet Union. The distinction between ideal communism and real communism, the idea that the latter was a distortion of the former, enabled the preservation of the ideal. All those who suffered under the Soviet regime were unequivocal, however: there can be no communism other than that which exists. The Soviet Union was as Communist as it claimed to be, and China remains Communist because her leaders draw their inspiration from Marxism and Leninism.

Her economic takeoff does not make China any less Communist, for development is the raison d'être of Marxism. The negation of individual freedom has always been part of the Marxist-Leninist credo; so have dictatorship and the single party. Besides, the Party is not contemplating changing its name; nor is it giving up its ideology or its monopoly. Its cadres continue to study Marxist-Leninist thought, learn its catechism, and attend regular refresher courses held in Party schools. What do these schools teach? Officially, the cadres are supposed to learn how to manage modern China. In 2005, the Leadership and Management Academy was launched in Shanghai; the English name was intended to give it a global flavor. Here cadres would learn "the latest methods of international and innovative leadership." The Academy would teach them how to "coordinate the development of the economy and society." Do the courses offered at the Academy and other Party schools meet these goals? Sadly, the answer is no. They merely regurgitate Marxist-Leninist jargon. We have to accept the fact that the Party functions like a sect, not like an inculcator of "international and innovative leadership."

The art of mastering jargon

There are few places in the world where Marx and Engels continue to be presiding deities. For many years, portraits of both men adorned Tiananmen Square. But they blocked the traffic and got swept away by an endless stream of cars. Today, the only portrait in Beijing is that of Mao Zedong. Giant granite statues of the two old bearded philosophers, however, still stand before the glass façade of the Party School in Shanghai. I ask Chen Xichun, the director of studies, what subjects are taught so that the cadres can "coordinate the development of the economy and society." I have drawn the question from one of the course titles. Because I have no desire to be branded an enemy of China, I take great care to use the official terminology and whenever possible to follow the official mind-set.

The director appreciates this. With his closely cropped gray hair and small, round, steel-rimmed spectacles, he looks more like a military officer than an academic. He thaws somewhat and thanks me for "taking an interest in the Party's pedagogy." In a hopeful tone, he asks me whether I like the Party. "Do I like the Party?" I remain vague, disappointing Chen, who nonetheless decides to rid me of my "honest doubts."

He tells me that the cadres, tainted by excessive exposure to reality, have to come back to school every two to three years "to improve their understanding of Marxism" and to take a refresher course in ideology. Does modern management in China require a better understanding of Marxism, I ask? Yes; I have understood correctly. Is Chen not worried that China's reality, very different from what Marx and Engels wrote in the nineteenth century, no longer corresponds to the original vulgates? This is an important question, he replies. Evidently,

I am a worthy interlocutor, even though I have made Chen waste his afternoon. I have been invited in the name of Sino-French friendship, so he cannot avoid meeting me. Before answering my question, he convenes three other professors and has tea served.

"The teaching at the Party School," Chen explains, "allows cadres to find the right Marxist response to new societal demands." Societal demands? "You can't imagine how demanding the Chinese have become toward the Party," Chen says. "They want the Party to represent them and satisfy their demands." All this would be quite normal in a democracy. But China is a dictatorship. Yet Chen feels that the principle of authority no longer suffices.

"The Party has three answers to the two popular demands." This is typical of Communist ideology and an old Chinese tradition. Everything serious is enumerated; at times, the enumeration is more important than what is being enumerated. In response to the first demand—for representation—the Party proposes former president Jiang Zemin's theory of "Three Represents." Every Chinese has heard of the Three Represents; they know there are three, just as they knew during the Cultural Revolution that they had to "smash the four olds" (old thoughts, old customs, old habits, and old traditions) and, with Deng Xiaoping, to engage in the "four modernizations." But hardly anyone in China will be able to tell you just what the Three Represents or the Four Modernizations are. "One center, two bases" is a popular saying, but those who use it have forgotten that it was originally one of the Party slogans in 1987: development was the center and opening to the world the two bases. Chen maintains that the Three Represents have resolved "once and for all" the contradictions between the Party and society. "The Three Represents are a very important thought," he says. In every medium, in every speech, the words "very important thought" are compulsory after the words "Three Represents."

Before the Three Represents, the Party *represented*—repetition is integral to indoctrination—the avant-garde of the peasants, workers, and soldiers. At the time, the Party was a revolutionary party but did not represent society as a whole; it neglected the "avant-garde experts." I don't bother to ask what an "avant-garde expert" is; I know the answer. He is the owner of a private enterprise to whom membership was denied by the old statutes of the Party. Now that the Party is banking on these "capitalists" to develop China, how are they to be integrated? The Three Represents have resolved the problem. The Party has moved from the representation of the revolutionary pioneers to the representation of the most advanced "productive forces" (read: "owners"), the "most advanced culture" (heaven knows what this refers to, given the miserable state of culture in China—teachers, probably), and the "fundamental interests of the largest number of the Chinese people." Thanks to the Three Represents, the Party now represents—the repetition is hallucinatory—the "avant-garde," the "experts," and the "interests of the entire nation." I have summarized in a few lines what Chen took one hour to explain.

At the school, Party cadres listen to these lessons all the time, lulled by the humming of air conditioners. Let us continue. The new entrepreneurial class, thanks to the Three Represents, can henceforth "participate fully in the construction of the Party." In a nutshell, owners are swelling the ranks of the Party while the number of peasants and workers is dwindling. The Party can heave a sigh of relief. Owners are certainly not going to ask for democracy. The status quo suits them, prospering as they do on account of the Party. What about women? They have never had anything more than walk-on parts. This long-winded discourse fails to address the Party's metamorphosis into a technocratic machine and the replacement of the Reds by experts. Chen's conclusion: as the Party henceforth represents society as a whole, "It is here to stay." And since it represents everyone, there is no need for any other party. So a multiparty system would not represent anyone? That's right; I have understood correctly, Chen tells me.

Having dealt with the question of democracy through the Three Represents, the Party then had the task of "listening to the people's demands in order to satisfy them." Chen calls it a "question of good governance," and once again the Party has found the right answer. The three professors Chen has gathered around him light up. "At last, we're going to talk about the petitions office, the perfect solution of a good government in a complex society," they think.

These days, every administration has a petitions office where dissatisfied citizens can file petitions. The petitions are recorded in computers: China never ceases to amaze us! If a petitioner does not obtain satisfaction at a lower level, he can seek redress at a higher one—sending his petition, for instance, from the commune to the district or even to the city level. The professor of petitions, a certain Wang, suggests that his students do a training course at the petitions office. He himself spent six months at the Shanghai office, whereupon he concluded that 90 percent of the petitions were genuine. He also concluded that the Chinese "like their administration and the Communist Party." How does he know? "If the citizens didn't trust us, they wouldn't come and complain to us." I am dumbfounded.

How many citizens dare to file petitions? How many petitions are registered and how many redressed? Now that the topic has come up, we might as well examine it thoroughly. Wang finds my questions excellent: they deserve to be studied "at length." In fact, the Beijing Academy of Social Sciences has just published a study on the subject, finding that all the petitions are well-founded but that only 0.3 percent wind up redressed. Wang has not heard of this study. He doubts whether it is scientific, since it doesn't correspond to his own experience. Do the cadres really undergo training at the petitions office, as he suggests? Unfortunately, they are "too busy," Wang says.

But we are getting lost in details. The main thing, says Chen, taking charge of the discussion once again, is that the Party has found the right ideological response to an obvious social issue: the Chinese are protesting more and more. Chen talks of the "important" and "spontaneous" demands of the people. I look skeptical. China has become a "society of citizens," he tells me. "But the Party remains as strong as ever, because it has been able to adapt, thanks to the Three Represents and the petitions office." Wang adds: "And because it has understood the changing nature of society, the Party will rule for a long time."

My interpreter, who translates this drivel word for word, is privately surprised to see me taking notes. I tell her later that the Party's real thinking and the training that it imparts have less to do with content than with the incessant repetition of these circumlocutions. "Do they really believe what they say?" she asks me. The same question is asked of all totalitarian regimes. Though one joins the Party more out of ambition than out of conviction, once inside, one begins to think along sectarian lines and believe blindly, so thorough is the ideological brainwashing.

"Do you have any other questions?" Chen's tone suggests that it is time for me to leave. But I do have one more query: I want to know about human rights in China. Chen tries to play for time. We need to freshen up a bit. June in Shanghai is unbearably hot. We are given wet towels. We mop our faces and hands and rub our necks energetically.

But Chen, aware of the European obsession with human rights, is ready for my question. He has an expert at hand. Master Yang introduces himself: he is a professor at the Party School, a lawyer, an expert on human rights, and an AIDS specialist. Yang represents China at all international forums where AIDS is discussed. China is not doing much to contain the disease, yet Yang always heads a large delegation whose very size precludes any criticism.

"As you know," begins Master Yang, convinced that Westerners are totally ignorant about China, "human rights have been enshrined in our Constitution." This happened in 2004, to the great satisfaction of Western governments. But Yang says that this concession to European humanists did not cost the Communist Party anything.

I ask whether a Chinese citizen who believes that his individual rights have been infringed upon can lodge a complaint at the petitions office. Can he cite the constitution in court? Yang observes that I know nothing about China. He will try to help me nonetheless. The constitution, in China, is the "mother of law," yet it is too sacred to be invoked. What is its purpose, then? It "shows the way to legislators." Do human rights form part of any other legal text that may be invoked? Not yet: "It is far too early." China is in transition. I had forgotten about this universal justification for everything—including our credulity.

In this room where visitors are received, there are Chen, Wang, Yang, and Deng, who has yet to utter a word. He is the youngest, about forty; the others are gray. His silence indicates that he is the school's real boss, the Party secretary who keeps watch. It is the same in all institutions. Chen turns respectfully toward Deng and asks him to conclude. As a mark of deference to his elders, Deng assumes an air of false modesty, murmuring his inability to do so. I recognize the mannerisms of the chief, the same everywhere in China. There is no doubt: Deng is the secretary. He begins speaking. The others speak only Chinese, but Deng's English is excellent. "You are loath to admit it," he says, "but the Party has anticipated all your objections. We don't need democracy because we are ahead of your democracy. The Party listens to the people and addresses all their concerns. Western-style democracy would mean going backward for China."

There is nothing more to say; the interview is over. We bid one another a curt farewell, with Sino-French friendship a notch lower.

How to make a career in the Party

It is commonly said in the West that all Chinese look alike. The Chinese think the same about Westerners. The fact remains that all the Communist Party's cadres do resemble one another. One obvious reason is that there are no women among the students at the Party School, as far as I can tell. There may be one or two, but they are discreet and could be mistaken for the ladies who serve tea. As for the men, they have all adopted the Western suit, which in China is the symbol of modernity. The suit is always black, even in summer; it is worn with a white shirt and tie. Outside the Party, not many people wear suits. Perhaps the suit and tie will one day become the uniform of the Communist Party.

It is also easy to recognize a cadre by his body language. He has a way of asserting himself while remaining in the background; he is arrogant and calculatedly modest, excessively polite—politeness is the exception in China—while making it amply clear that he represents power. These clonelike attitudes cannot be learned; but they are quickly acquired through constant repetition. This is one of the purposes of the school: teaching cadres to look alike, to form one body.

Exchanging business cards is another obligatory ritual. Everywhere in China, in powerful circles, cards are exchanged at the beginning of any meeting. One is always running out cards. You have to be well stocked if you don't want to be taken for a boor. At the Party School, cards are exchanged at a feverish pace, a way of building a network— the Party is both a sect and a network—and increasing one's social stock, or *guanxi* (one's influence and capacity to get things done). Thanks to *guanxi,* the cadres can bypass hierarchical circuits; through it, they prosper. A cadre with *guanxi* is respected by his subordinates, his colleagues, and the people he administers. If he doesn't have enough *guanxi,* no one will listen to him, and he will become an object of ridicule. By resolving the problems of his department, a cadre proves he has *guanxi. Guanxi* gives him an aura of invincibility. So one goes to the Party schools to be reprogrammed ideologically—what the Party calls "being at the avant-garde"—and to accumulate *guanxi.* In a country in which laws are not worth the paper they are written on, *guanxi* can get things done; administrative and legal decisions depend on it. This is openly admitted. There are three more career principles, not stated but known to the initiated. I got to know about them from a Party renegade—a rare species, for it is not easy to leave the sect. When one joins the Party, one takes the following pledge: "I wish to become a member of the Communist Party to support the Party line, respect the Party statutes, ... apply the decisions of the Party, work with all my might and fight all my life for the cause of communism, ... remain faithful to the Party, keep the secrets of the Party, and never betray the Party." So the Party has its secrets.

"To move up in the Party, you have to stick to three principles," Cao Siyuan explains to me. Cao, who used to have a great deal of influence in the Party, is a jurist and the author of China's first law on the bankruptcy of enterprises. He was nicknamed "Cao the

Bankruptcy," a nickname of which he is proud, for the 1988 law enabled the restructuring the public sector. The first principle, says Cao, is "to love one's chief": love him and he will love you. You must always say yes to the boss, agree with him, never criticize him, never contradict him; your duty is to admire him. You must speak to him in a low voice and be duly modest. The second principle is to give discreet gifts to the boss. Generally speaking, "It is recommended that you apply principles one and two to everyone close to the boss, his friends, his family." Cao comes to the third principle and has a nice way of putting it: he calls it the "boss has a headache" principle. The boss doesn't want any trouble, he doesn't want to hear about anything, and he doesn't want his bosses to hear about him. To keep the boss from suffering a migraine, his subordinates make sure that no protest or petition reaches him. The area committees are there, backed by the police, to see that the people keep mum. No one in the Party is particularly bothered about the methods used, provided the bosses don't get to hear of it. By applying these three principles, a cadre can climb to the top.

Cao is right. At the Party School, I had been told that a cadre's career depended on the number of petitions recorded at the various offices. If the number is small, you get a good score. The teachers at the school view this as proof of the department's having been well managed. Cao says it shows only that the cadre has been terrorizing people so much that they don't dare lodge a complaint. Which is true? Cao's version, undoubtedly.

How the Party is getting Americanized

While criticizing this farce of an education to a leader of the new generation, Westernized and with an apparently modern outlook, I was surprised to see him share my analysis. True, the training of the cadres had failed to keep up with the needs of the times and the complexity of new Chinese society. He suggested that I visit another avant-garde educational establishment, an illustration of the modernized Party's radiant future.

The Leadership and Management Academy is the school that will lead the Party's elite, the governors, the mayors, and the heads of ministries, into the twenty-first century. The Party expects the Academy to transform it into a modern and global technocracy. Just like the École Nationale d'Administration (ENA), the director says, a veiled compliment to France. I dare not tell him that we in France are trying to dismantle the institution. The Academy is located in the Pudong area, a new Shanghai locality, on the right bank of the Huangpu River. A French architect, Antoine Béchu, was chosen to design it, no doubt on account of this fascination with the ENA.

With its office and residential towers and network of highways, it is a kind of slapped-together Manhattan, a theatrical representation of the Party as conceived by a Westerner. The central building housing the conference rooms is built under a red steel table. Red is the color of dynamism, and the table represents the man of letters, I learn. The office tower looming over the monumental complex is supposedly the brush pot of the learned man. An American name, French architecture, the fusion of modernity with quotations from the classics—all this is part of an expensive symbolism. One dare not ask the price of this "creation" set amid Chinese landscaped and formal gardens. So much for the outer shell—a vision of the Party as it sees itself in the future. But inside, no one knows what purpose it serves. Such is the passion for building that you build first and then ask why you've built. A case in point is the Beijing Opera, designed once again by a French architect, Paul Andreu. Yet another example of mindless construction: the building first, the program later.

In spite of the Academy's international name, I didn't come across anyone who spoke English or any other foreign language, except the man in charge of public relations. The students have passed the age of learning; they are all senior cadres with successful politico-administrative careers. What is the point of the training, which lasts no more than a few weeks, imparted to leaders who are very busy with their administrative duties? The unspoken vocation of the Academy, it appears, is to cast the cadres in the mold of modernity, a task at which the Party's schools have failed. Here they learn how to behave like Westerners, get rid of their provincial habits—clearing one's throat or pulling up one's trousers to cool oneself in public, for example—and become initiated into Western ways. To acquire a cosmopolitan veneer, provincial cadres interact with company managers and senior officials in Shanghai. Chinese and modern, they are good models to emulate. As part of their training, cadres visit enterprises and public offices and take inspiration from their "avant-garde" style. "Avant-garde" is the politically correct term, though "American" would be more appropriate. For the cadres, there is only one model: America—the American way of being, the American style of management. The Party makes no bones about it.

Won't a mayor from a western province get overawed by the lavishness of the Academy and the opulence of Shanghai's public offices and enterprises? The Academy's director, apparently unaware of the Marxist concept of alienation, tells me that the very purpose of the Academy is to impress provincial cadres so that they, too, emulate Shanghai and Pudong. Thus the Academy functions along exactly the same lines as the model villages and factories that have characterized Communist education since the Maoist era. Yesterday, one had to imitate the brave workers of the Daqing oilfields; today, one has to copy the Americanized managers of Pudong. Learning to think for oneself is out of the question.

I expressed my uncertainty about the cadres' ability to manage social movements before they turned violent. The Academy had provided for this eventuality, I was told. Just outside Shanghai was the model village of Wuyiang, where Party cadres successfully managed the "peaceful coexistence" of peasant demands and modernity. Groups of students are taken to see this showcase.

The director of the Academy invited me to give a few lectures. When I asked what he would like me to speak on, he said it hardly mattered. The main thing was that the cadres from the provinces would get to see what a French speaker looked like. I thought to myself that on the appointed day I would have to pay more attention to what I wore than to what I said, for evidently people wouldn't come to listen to a speaker but to look at him. If what the Party wants

to become is so much like what it used to be, it has no future, I concluded—somewhat hastily, perhaps.

The Party in search of a lost legitimacy

The history of the Party is the story of its constant search for legitimacy, a legitimacy that has become weaker and weaker over the
years. To begin with, it posed as a patriotic movement fighting
Japanese invaders and the corruption of the nationalist state. The
truth is less heroic, Mao's army avoiding as far as possible direct confrontation with the Japanese, which would have been disastrous for
his troops. When he seized power in 1949, the Party restored law
and order and promised democracy. As in Eastern Europe after
Soviet colonization, liberal movements supporting the Party believed
that the communists would keep their promise of free elections. But
Mao changed his discourse: like the Soviet Union, China needed an
authoritarian regime to modernize herself. But the Great Leap
Forward proved to be an unmitigated disaster. First liberation, then
second-wave industrial modernization, and finally permanent revolution were to provide legitimacy to the regime. Mao Zedong began
the systematic elimination of old China and its elite. On his death,
the Revolution was suspended, and Deng Xiaoping took control. He
provided the fourth legitimization for the dictatorship through the
credo of individual prosperity.

Will economic development be enough to guarantee the Party the
eternity that it seeks? Westerners, who underestimate the desire of
the Chinese people for freedom and justice, are ready to believe that
it will. But the Party, taking note of the rising number of religious
protests, worker demonstrations, dispossessed peasants, and petitions of intellectuals, has concluded that development alone will not
suffice—all the more so since it doesn't benefit three-fourths of the
nation. The Party is now trying to invent a fifth reason for its own
legitimacy. It could well be nationalism and war, the invariable culmination of belligerent nationalist discourse.

How are the Chinese to be made nationalist? Left to themselves, they are hardly so. In this traditionally agrarian empire, solidarity is first and foremost with the family, the clan, the village, or the province. Being Chinese is an enduring phenomenon not requiring aggressive assertion. The past few centuries' massive migration is testimony to the precedence that people give to individual and family welfare while remaining very much Chinese, even far from national territory. There is the nationalism of the elites, which first appeared after the Opium Wars in 1840. A mixture of humiliation and revanchism is the common theme running through contemporary history until the rise of the Communist Party. In the nineteenth century, China, as a sovereign state, was close to annihilation. "A corpse ready to be dismembered, putting itself before the scalpel" is how Paul Claudel, France's consul at Fuzhou in 1897, described her in his diplomatic correspondence. Claudel, who was looking to expand the French empire, seemed to be caught between regret and jubilation.

The official history of the Party in school textbooks holds the West squarely responsible for all the country's woes. There is no attempt at critical analysis to find out why the Empire fell so easily or how the corrupt Chinese leaders failed to modernize their country. Conversely, every xenophobic—or nationalist, depending on how you view it—revolt, especially the Boxer Uprising, is sanctified as a redeeming moment, a precursor of the 1949 "liberation." It was the Party that avenged the affronts of the Japanese and the Americans and even the Taiwanese. A noncommunist Taiwan is the betrayal of nationhood, for communism is the nation.

Now the Chinese had to be taught this rewritten history. Every ideology requires a starting point. The new nationalism, it was decided, began at Xian, the first capital of the Chinese Empire twenty-two centuries ago. The Empire was founded by Qin Shi Huangdi, one of the worst tyrants history has ever known.

The invention of nationalism

As the legend of Mao falls apart, Emperor Qin gains in stature. In the 1980s, schoolchildren and pilgrims from all over China would stand in line for hours at Tiananmen Square in Beijing before being allowed to enter Mao's mausoleum. Pushed by guards, they had only a few seconds to walk around the refrigerated glass coffin in which the Great Helmsman lay, with long lines outside clamoring to get in. They did not have time to observe that Mao dead bore little resemblance to Mao alive. The Vietnamese embalmers, we are told, made a mess of the mummy. The face was an unhealthy pale green, but the famous wart under the chin was preserved. The mausoleum has now become a palace visited only by the wind. Schoolchildren and pilgrims—the same or their descendants—are now packed off to Xian in central China. Here, archaeologists and architects have restored (or, to be precise, reconstituted) the necropolis of the first emperor.

Every public monument is a political manifesto. The colossal dimensions of Qin's tomb, its grandeur, underscore his newfound legitimacy. The founder of the Empire has ousted the father of the Revolution. Qin was no more a humanist than Mao. This barbaric warrior, who descended from the upper plateaus of Tibet or the Mongolian steppes, conquered all the kingdoms in China in the third century B.C., amalgamating them into a single empire. In the north, he built the Great Wall, in the construction of which a million enslaved masons are said to have died, their bones mixed with the lime. He ordered the burning of all books written before his time, thus fixing the first year of a new era. He decreed that all Chinese belonged to the same race and nation, the beginning of the ethnic myth of the Han people. When he died, several thousand soldiers and servants were buried next to him to escort him to the nether land. The troops were depicted in clay as well. In the 1990s, inspired by massive Communist monuments in Russia and North Korea, huge granite and marble porticos were built to overhang the necropolis. The first emperor was to become the new national cult figure. For this purpose, the Beijing government roped in its quasi-official film director Zhang Yimou, the Chinese Leni Riefenstahl. In his epic movie *Hero*, a propaganda masterpiece, Qin is shown venerated by his enemies, yet misunderstood by his own people, for having unified China.

The visitor is invited to Xian to celebrate the might of China, before which, his individuality annihilated, he feels no bigger than an ant. Tourists, untroubled by this Chinese fascism, take photos of themselves: the Chinese, they think, are not individuals but a great yellow mass. Overwhelmed by the giant statue of Qin in white stone, I was lost in thought when a tourist guide who spoke a smattering of English accosted me. Before melting into the crowd, he murmured: "Qin was like Stalin."

Qin, the emblem of China, is also the symbol of all its instability. He claimed to have founded a dynasty that would continue for "10,000 generations." Two years after his death, his inheritors were overthrown. Thereafter, imperial power passed to twenty-six successive dynasties, often non-Chinese. The Party would do well to keep its distance from this founder.

Looking for a scapegoat: Japan

In the spring of 2005, as the sixteenth anniversary of the Tiananmen Square uprising approached, foreign journalists noted, as they did every year at the same time, the heavy buildup of police. It was difficult to approach the square, and any gathering, no matter how small, was dispersed. Each year, the Party fears a commemoration that could reignite the democratic movement, but for the past sixteen years the only people to gather here have been members of the Falun Gong. Crowds did assemble in Hong Kong to commemorate the June 4, 1989, repression.

Protest came from an unexpected quarter: "students" carrying anti-Japanese banners marched in procession not just in Beijing but also in Shanghai and Shenzen. They attacked Japanese consulates and destroyed goods bearing the Japanese trademark (even though they were made in China and belonged to the Chinese). Were they really students, as the media claimed? They seemed very young to me, and those leading them, too old. Were these demonstrations spontaneous? That was the official version. Anti-Japanese associations supposedly had convened their members through the Internet and text messages. Knowing how closely everything is monitored in China, including electronic messages, I found it unlikely that the authorities were caught by surprise. The demonstrations went off without any major trouble, under the benevolent eye of the antiriot police. No demonstrator was arrested. The "students" returned in waiting buses. The agitation went on for three weeks before the government decided to end it. University professors were called upon to calm their students. The demonstrations stopped as "spontaneously" as they had begun.

No more than 20,000 people in the entire country had taken part, but the effect was spectacular—for, as a general rule, no one demonstrates in China. Demonstrations in distant provinces remain invisible. Journalists and diplomats posted in Beijing wondered about the significance of the events. Were they spontaneous? Had the Party been involved? Was it the instigator or the moderator of popular sentiment? Were we witnessing the beginnings of a civil society that had escaped vigilant eye of the Party?

The debate among China-watchers was facetious. The Party watches over everything; it was unthinkable that the anti-Japanese demonstrations had escaped its notice. It must have orchestrated them, and the anti-Japanese message was intended more for the outside world than for the Chinese nation. That message was clear: the Chinese people are angry; fortunately, the Party is there to contain their anger. The idea behind the revival of Chinese nationalism was to cause concern in the West and to reassure it at the same time that the Party had things well in hand. It was the Party's way of making everyone believe that a strong Party was good for all—the Chinese, the West, and the Japanese. Without it, there would be fascism and war all over Asia. The Western media, especially in France, swallowed the bait. Our columnists concluded that the Party was maintaining order in Asia, keeping the people's anger in check.

Anyone in China at the time could see the Propaganda Department's obvious manipulation. You had only to go on the Internet to be greeted by a flood of anti-Japanese slogans and images of the Nanjing massacre. In 1937, at the start of its second war with Japan (the first broke out in 1894), the Chinese alleged that Japanese soldiers cold-bloodedly massacred 300,000 civilians in Nanjing. Public exhibits about the massacre were held in all the large cities of China, displaying the same horrifying pictures found in all school textbooks of Japanese soldiers piercing Chinese children with their bayonets. At the National Museum of History in Beijing, a commemoration highlighted the number of victims. Posters reminded viewers that there were 300,000 victims and not 240,000, as the Japanese claimed. Just as the tension began to abate, the Beijing government raked up the issue again and decided that December 14 would be a national commemoration of the "First Day of the Nanjing Massacre." No one in Japan denies that the massacre occurred. Historians dispute the number of victims and what led to the slaughter, but they are clear that there were no attenuating circumstances. Still, in China it was anti-Japan time, and every news bulletin referred to the Nanjing massacre and the glorious resistance of the Communist army against Japanese fascism. These reminders were all the more necessary as Mao had never fought the Japanese, preferring to save his forces for conquering China.

How justified is the Chinese government's anti-Japanese tirade? The pretext for the demonstrations during the Year of the Rooster was the publication of a textbook in Japan that played down the Nanjing massacre. That the textbook was never distributed hardly mattered. Japanese leaders, including the emperor, have apologized to the Chinese people on several occasions for the atrocities. The Chinese authorities say that this is not enough, and whenever the Japanese express their regret, it never gets reported in the media. A Chinese who does not have access to the Internet is thus convinced that the Japanese have never acknowledged the massacre and that their schoolbooks deny it, which is untrue. The Party accuses the Japanese of refusing to "face up to their own history." Coming as this does from the Party, the criticism is bizarre, to say the least. When has the Party ever faced up to its own history, or the Chinese people to theirs? It was left to the maverick Yu Jie to point out in the Hong Kong press in August 2005—when China was commemorating the sixtieth anniversary of "the victory of the Communist Party against Japanese fascism"—that "Mao Zedong had killed far more Chinese than the Japanese army."

True, the Japanese did not go as far as the Germans in their self-criticism, but they refused to be compared to the Nazis and confess to genocide. Indeed, there is little comparison between Japanese imperialism and German Nazism, and the Nanjing massacre is certainly not the equivalent of the Holocaust. The Japanese also point out that they have given the Chinese considerable development aid as reparations. Not enough, says the Chinese Communist Party. Nothing will ever be enough—because it is not just the Nanjing massacre but the fact that Japan is a humiliating reminder of all that China could have become but didn't. Japan, a small country that borrowed so much from China—script, Buddhism, architecture, court etiquette—has successfully synthesized identity and modernity without any revolution or civil war. Contrary to Marxist theory, it did not require a single party to develop or external enemies to fortify itself. For the Chinese leadership, Japan is intolerable. Were the people properly informed, they would no doubt take a more balanced view. While the anti-Japan demonstrations were going on, many academics tried to dissuade their students from taking part, condemning the Party's manipulation of a complex history. A student in Beijing told me, "I hate Japan, but I don't know why." Yet many degree-holders want to work in Japanese companies in China, and 500,000 Chinese, qualified for the most part, are currently settled in Japan.

In a more enlightened China, xenophobia would be on the decline, but it is not in the Party's interest that the Chinese become enlightened. The Party does all it can to fuel hatred of Japan, to build a patriotic ideology. Japan is necessary for its fifth legitimization.

Why Japan and not the United States? There is little danger in attacking Japan; the worst that can happen is that tourists will stop coming and investments will dry up—but the shortfall will be made up by others. The United States, however, is far too dangerous an enemy. American support remains indispensable for what in 2005 the Party called "peaceful growth."

Neo-Confucianism is not an alternative for the Communist Party

"When the Party disappears, it will not be replaced by democracy. I will not let that happen." Pan Wei, not quite forty years old, is a professor of political science at the Tsinghua University in Beijing. He doesn't appear to have the stature to influence the course of history, but then, didn't Mao Zedong start out as a librarian? On the Tsinghua campus—modeled along the lines of an American university—students dress like young Yankees. Most of them say they want to pursue their studies in the U.S. and settle down there. Every year, 60,000 Chinese students leave for the U.S., of whom only half return to China. The ones who return are vociferously anti-American and delight in anti-American demonstrations. History has been rewritten in Chinese textbooks. They speak of a hidden American hand behind the nineteenth-century colonial adventurism of the British and the French. Is the Party preparing young minds for a future clash?

Pan Wei belongs to a generation caught between two contradictory pulls. He is part of a breed of new intellectuals who have returned to China after spending ten years at Berkeley. Having learned "in the U.S. what was useful for China," he came home with a political project called *The Myth of Democracy*, a critique of both the Party and democracy. Pan Wei says that democracy is chaos. Many Chinese think the same. They have been encouraged by the Propaganda Department to do so, and the widespread acceptance of this belief is its greatest achievement. Pan is categorical: "Democracy has led to chaos in Russia, India, the Philippines, Indonesia, and Taiwan." What about Japan? "It is an orderly country but not a democracy." He talks of Japan, Russia, and other countries without any real understanding of them, as if they were names on a map. A common refrain in China is that Russia plunged into chaos because democracy came too soon, political reform preceding economic reform. Evidently, such discourse is intended to prove the superiority of the Chinese way.

My interlocutor is emphatic, assertive, and not open to discussion. He is a self-confessed neo-Confucian; I am not. Confucius saw things in black and white. Shades and humor were not for him. So Pan Wei doesn't believe in smiling. He says: "The Party must quit for two reasons. The first is corruption, a supreme form of disorder in the Chinese tradition. And the second is the faulty economic model it has chosen. China is lagging behind the West." Pan Wei points to his computer. It has been assembled by Chinese workers and runs on American software. "Even if we managed to copy this software, Microsoft would come out with a new one better than our fake." If the Chinese are to catch up with Western creativity, "they must be free to use their critical faculties." I can't but agree. However, Wei's apologia for freedom does not include democracy. The years he spent studying in a Western institution convinced him that Western superiority was based not on democracy but on the rule of law. The Chinese are confusing the rule of law with the mode of selecting the ruling elite. China needs the former, but elections serve no purpose. From time immemorial, the Chinese have drawn their elite from the universities, a far more efficient method.

Democracy may not always guarantee the best leaders, but doesn't it have a tempering effect, assuaging passions and ensuring the peaceful transfer of power? Pan Wei has heard all my arguments before. They aren't relevant in the Chinese context: "The Chinese are a homogeneous people, without the class distinctions found in the West." Concepts such as majority and minorities are not applicable to China, he says. Elections as a means of arbitration between social groups may be of some use in the West but are superfluous here.

"All you have to do is look around you," Pan Wei says. "You will see that the brightest children in China come from all social strata and all provinces. They have sacrificed their youth to pass their university examinations and reach this point." When the leadership of the future has been decided, what is the need for elections? But examinations are a test only of one's book knowledge, not of one's capacity to think independently. The same holds true for course content. Teachers do not tolerate contradiction; students must listen, not question. Consequently, Chinese universities are producing efficient robots rather than creative individuals.

Pan Wei remains unfazed. For him, society is a machine to steer in the right direction, not a body tormented by passion. Evidently, his elitist project is inspired by the mandarins who governed imperial China. The sinologist Étienne Balazs has given a wonderful description of this "celestial bureaucracy" that exercised absolute power: "officialdom." Balazs writes: "Without the mandarins, the Chinese civilization would have faded away; but the peoples they condemned to live together may have been better off had they gone their own separate ways." One could argue endlessly about the pros and cons of a celestial bureaucracy. It can, however, rule only over a closed universe. The moment it was exposed to the outside world in 1840, it crumbled.

How can one call oneself a neo-Confucian a hundred years after the fall of the Empire? The ideology to which Pan Wei subscribes is widespread in university circles, among company managers, and in the leadership of the Communist Party. Confucius is a much-misunderstood philosopher, indeed. First, he was the fountainhead of the Empire; then, under Mao Zedong, the cause of China's backwardness, only to be rehabilitated by Deng Xiaoping. Confucius would not have been able to identify with the Empire's Confucianism any more than with today's neo-Confucianism, whose Chinese credentials are, in any case, dubious.

In the seventh century of our era, during the early Qing dynasty, the first neo-Confucian movement took place, a revolt of the educated classes against the authoritarianism of the Manchu Empire. Basing their ideas on the writings of Confucius, the neo-Confucians wanted the sovereign to abide by the rules of good conduct and respect local autonomies. The movement, from which some modern-day democrats draw inspiration, was in essence liberal and directed against an empire that already rejoiced in its own efficiency. But Pan Wei and other neo-Confucians—rather, neo-neo-Confucians—have been selective in their borrowings from Confucius, taking only his ideas of a moral order and hierarchism. In truth, their ideology is made in America: its high priests are Chinese academics at American universities, especially Professor Du Weiming of Harvard and Professor Theodore de Bary of Columbia, and it borrows something of the fundamentalism of the American New Right. Neo-Confucianism offers a middle path between liberalism and Marxism. By subscribing to Confucianism, the neo-Confucians can criticize the Party in relative safety, criticize corruption—all the Chinese do—and reject liberalism as foreign. The middle path has the advantage of letting the new mandarins bypass democracy—which would only confer power on uneducated rustics, scorned by academics and apparatchiks alike.

Even if we accept Pan Wei's project of a technocracy chosen on the basis of a competitive examination—after all, we in France have our mandarins, too—who would assume the role of leadership in a regime neither hereditary nor democratic? Mencius, a disciple of Confucius, suggested three methods that, Pan Wei maintains, remain valid for modern-day China. The sovereign can be nominated by a college of wise men. Pan Wei would lead this assembly of philosophers, of course; though hardly forty, he has studiously cultivated an older look and the grave mien of a scholar. The second method is for the chief in power to designate his successor. Co-optation is already the rule in the Communist Party, I point out. Yes, but it hasn't been successful because Mao Zedong, the founder of the lineage, was Marxist, not Confucian. Mao's error was to have introduced "foreign thinking in China." A coup d'état is the third method: a bad sovereign is eliminated and replaced with a good one. Pan Wei, who has no wish to be behind bars, finds this superfluous, as the Party is not "all bad." It has guaranteed social stability, reunified China, and won it international recognition. All that remains is to transfer power from the Communists to the neo-Confucians.

The ideal transition would be an interregnum, during which Communist leaders would willingly withdraw in favor of a college of philosophers. This college would nominate a good ruler to rid China of the deadwood of superfluous ideology and policing. A good ruler would not need to protect his regime, because the people would identify with him. Property would be privatized, for a good leader would not need a state-run economy. The public sector and planning are Western, not Chinese, ideas. The press could be free, religions acceptable, and the right of association recognized, for a good sovereign would have nothing to fear from freedom of expression. This wonderful project assumes that the Chinese people are inclined to unity. Does this mean the Chinese are distinct from the West? Pan Wei is clear: Chinese society wants to reconstitute itself into a virtuous community.

What will happen to rebels in a neo-Confucian regime? Implacable minorities will exist, but if the sovereign is good, they will remain minorities. Too many rebels are a sign of the sovereign's failure to act. The example of Singapore comes to my mind: the great neo-Confucian apologist Lee Kwan Yu and his family continue to rule there, the opposition having been reduced to a single seat in Parliament. But the very mention of Singapore is an insult to Greater China: Pan Wei does not deign to answer.

Our conversation is turning sour. Fortunately, we manage to part ways courteously, neither of us losing face. We agree that under the Party, China combines the worst of socialism with the worst of capitalism. We also agree on three likely future scenarios: perpetual communism, liberal democracy, and neo-Confucianism. But what Pan Wei calls neo-Confucianism is called fascism in Europe. In both cases, adherents express themselves in the name of a superior order with the emphasis on morality and chastity. Is the neo-Confucian ideology more Chinese than socialism or liberalism? That is what Pan claims, but it is his way of staving off criticism. It will come as no surprise if the Communist Party embraces him in the name of the Three Represents. Like nationalism, neo-Confucianism poses no threat to the Party; it is just one of the masks that the Party wears.

The nostalgia for Maoism

Is He Qing a nationalist, a neo-Confucian, or a leftist? The Party calls him a leftist, though he describes himself as a conservative. This young man, who has authored a series of philosophical essays published in France and Hong Kong, teaches the history of art at Hangzhou. He Qing is sweeping in his critique of the Communist regime. He accuses the Party leadership of entering into a diabolical alliance with multinational companies, sacrificing the welfare of the majority and Chinese civilization itself for the prosperity of a few. His words sound bombastic, yet they reflect a widespread sentiment among the post–Cultural Revolution generation of intellectuals. And so we must give He Qing a patient hearing.

In his analysis of China, he borrows a few elements from Confucianism and a great deal from Marxism and from the fashionable writers Pierre Bourdieu and Samuel Huntington, whose articles have proved useful to Chinese intellectuals seeking to deconstruct power. From Huntington, He Qing has taken the "clash of civilizations." The different nations of the world will not converge toward democratic synthesis and world peace; the ultimate reality will be, instead, the differentiation of civilizations and their inevitable clash. Huntington has already foreseen a Sino-American war. In opening China to a global economy, the Party is ignoring the unique nature of Chinese civilization: capitalism runs counter to her value system. Which values are we talking about? Westernization, He Qing says, leads to materialistic individualism and contempt for the Other, whereas there is no place for egoistical efficiency in Chinese civilization, which stresses the relationship among subjects. Such inter-subjectivity is specific to the Confucian idea of the clan, the family, and the nation. Globalization will end up making the Chinese schizophrenic, since they will be forced to become efficient, as defined in the West, while remaining deeply Chinese at heart. For a fistful of dollars, the Party is selling the soul of the people.

Taking up the conspiracy theory dear to sociologist Bourdieu, He Qing says that globalization is no accident. Capitalists with vested interests have imposed it on China. But don't the Chinese also stand to gain from it? The gains are only material, and they accrue to the city dwellers at the expense of the peasantry. In comparison with this restricted material gain, the spiritual destruction is incalculable. Is China not making progress? He Qing rejects the Western notion of progress. Chinese civilization is based on harmony, not progress. Westerners introduced the notion of progress to China in the nineteenth century, making the Chinese ashamed of their so-called backwardness. Ever since, the Chinese elite has struggled to ape the West and catch up with it. This course will prove suicidal. If Chinese values are to be restored and China cured of her schizophrenia, it will have to abandon the Party's materialistic ideology, not the Party itself. To China's great misfortune, says a distressed He Qing, the Communist Party is progressive and materialistic. Its rejection of culture and spirituality makes it genuinely communist.

As the history of China can't be rewritten, He Qing feels the least that can be done is halting its irrevocable march. He is actively advocating—through the force of his pen, nothing more—a more inward-looking China, based on its traditional values and the domestic market. How does he propose to achieve this? He rejects democracy, saying that the Chinese do not know what it means; their demands are not political but spiritual. What are the immutable Chinese values? He Qing identifies Chinese civilization with Confucian thought. Not unlike our Jesuit missionaries, he dismisses Daoism and Buddhism as superstitions. His attempt to reconstruct an ideal regime is even more astounding: there is no difference between his model and Maoist discourse. The peasantry, economic autonomy, and fierce national independence were its mainstays, though of course it paid only lip service to them. What Mao really wanted was to transform China into an industrial power, and to achieve this he was prepared to sacrifice the peasantry. He failed in his mission, but those who followed him succeeded. How could a scholar confuse Maoist mythology with the real history of Maoism?

Yet the confusion is common, not only among those nostalgic for the good old days but also among the so-called enlightened generation.

The Chinese people see no contradiction between respect for collective values and the obligation to assume their individuality. It is the inability of the elite to come to terms with their own history that is the real cause of their schizophrenia. The Communist Party's opposition to an honest appraisal of twentieth-century China can only add to the national schizophrenia. He Qing is quite right: schizophrenia is a painful condition for both the individual and the nation.

The last days of the Communist Party

China is like a movie out of sync. The soundtrack is the voice of the Communist Party telling us that all is well, that the nation is marching ahead, stable and harmonious. The pictures alternate among economic achievements, the affluence of the parvenus, and the poverty of the vast majority. "We are going through a phase of *transition*," the soundtrack says, while we see images of hundreds of thousands of despairing peasants, worn-out migrants, workers out of jobs, the old and the infirm left by the wayside. This yawning gap between what is said and what actually happens has, in the past, led to the fall of the emperors. At the time of the Qin dynasty, the last to rule China, the court sought refuge in Confucian ritualism while the people were marching ahead into modernity. When in 1912, after 2,200 years of imperial rule, the Chinese got to elect their leaders for the first time in history, they voted for the Republican Party.

If the history of China has any lessons to offer, then the Party has cause for concern. Twenty-two centuries witnessed the fall of twenty-six dynasties, and each time the end was violent. The history of the Party has been no less brutal. Ever since it came to power, its leaders have constantly changed course, the series of about-faces reflective of internecine struggles within the Party. After the Great Leap Forward, the Cultural Revolution, and reform, has inner Party strife finally come to an end? Hasn't the Party been consistent in its stands since 1979? This is not certain. Co-optation being the Party's only mode of succession, there is always the possibility of factional conflicts. The Party has stayed on course, but the path that it has chosen has left the great majority unhappy. Within the Party, one faction, leftist, is hostile to economic liberalism; another, nationalist, opposes the Americanization of society. There is a permanent power struggle between the two. The Party has no room for compromise or dialogue. This is also true of the Party's relations with the nation. Village elections and the petitions office, the only Party-authorized forums where people can vent their ire, are inadequate to cope with the demands of the majority. The Party is not prepared to listen and refuses to negotiate. A totalitarian monolith, it can't move forward. It knows only how to repress, prohibit, and incarcerate. Power is in the barrel of a gun, said Mao Zedong in 1930. It still is.

The people and the Party are moving at two different speeds. Will economic growth be able to satisfy the people's needs? In all likelihood, disparities will increase. Without the countervailing effect of democracy, the rich will become richer and the poor will have nothing left to lose. A single uncontrolled mutiny, a rumor of bankruptcy, a pandemic—and millions of Chinese will begin clamoring for the Party's dismissal. How will the army react? Instead of one Tiananmen, will there be ten, twenty, or a hundred massacres in every city? Wei Jingsheng, the democrat exiled in Washington, predicts that the army won't fire. Even in 1989, though the People's Army obeyed the Party, the massacre of fellow citizens divided officers and soldiers alike. If a fresh revolt breaks out, the army could well break away from the regime. As Mao Zedong aptly put it: in a tyrannical regime, "if you don't shoot, you're dead!" When Gorbachev hesitated to give the order to shoot Baltic and German demonstrators, he signed the Soviet Union's death warrant. The West neither foresaw nor analyzed that—and despite the precedent, it displays the same blindness toward China. As for France, which boasts the largest number of friends of the Communist Party, only our ideology can explain our affinity for despotism.

Sinomania: a French ideology

Chinese archives remain closed. Pictures are rare and films nonexistent. The great massacre of the Chinese in the twentieth century will remain invisible, unregistered in our collective conscience. So the French infatuation for China continues unabated. Once the diplomatic mourning for Tiananmen was over, successive French governments displayed the same admiration for the Communist Party as they did in the past for the Chinese emperor, hailing it for maintaining peace and ushering in a new era of prosperity. That social order has been imposed by a police state, and the fear of civil war hardly matters to the French leadership. In 1995, Alain Peyrefitte said that a vast nation like China could be ruled only with an iron hand. China as a confederation, which is what most Chinese democrats are proposing today, was inconceivable to him. When asked about democracy in China, former president Valéry Giscard d'Estaing, who claims to be no mean sinologist, continued to raise political and cultural objections as late as 2005: "China is too big to organize elections"; "the polytheistic Chinese do not understand the meaning of individual freedom or democracy."

Will the Canadians and the Brazilians stop voting because their countries are too big? Should the Indians, even more polytheistic than the Chinese, abandon democracy? Why does French diplomacy use the cultural-differences argument only in China's case? It is unfair, our diplomats say, to impose human rights on the Chinese, because they are not like us. This policy of cultural relativism—China is wonderful but the Chinese are to be looked down upon—draws its inspiration from French sinology. For the last three hundred years, it has been harping on the timelessness of China.

The French sinologists Édouard Chavannes, Marcel Granet, Henri Maspero, Paul Demiéville, and Étienne Balazs produced an immense body of work on Chinese thought, which their students went on to study in a completely ahistorical manner. Scholars in French universities quibble over Pierre Ryckman's (Simon Leys') translation of Confucius, which he did in Australia, holding forth as if time had stood still and Confucius was a contemporary, not 2,500 years old. In 2005, François Jullien, a philosopher among sinologists and a sinologist among philosophers, wrote that to understand modern-day China, it was necessary to be acquainted with Confucianism as revealed by him. It is true that there can be no understanding France without some knowledge of Christianity—but somewhat far-fetched to say that we would be able understand modern-day France just by reading the Gospels. Similarly, Confucius's *Analects*, adapted to suit all tastes, are by no means a compendium of modern-day China. Besides, why should the study of China be the sole prerogative of specialists in classical Chinese whose achievements, in any case, are unexceptional? Are we to infer that just by learning English and German, we can understand the United States and Germany?

Along with this academic sinology, however, there is a more recent school, guided by teachers and researchers such as Jacques Pimpaneau, Marie Holzman, and Jean-Luc Domenach, that makes a distinction between the museum China and the living China. Regrettably, this school does not enjoy the same kind of political and administrative backing as the other school, represented by influential spokesmen like Alain Peyrefitte. French diplomacy is, by and large, a reflection of classical sinology, because it has a vested interest in it: French mandarins are at ease with Chinese mandarins. The Gaullist tradition—from which French foreign-policy makers, leftists and rightists alike, have drawn inspiration for over fifty years—shows a marked preference for government-to-government dealing, tending to avoid thorny issues like human rights. Finally, the dominant cultural-diversity discourse has proved helpful in emphasizing the fundamental difference of the Chinese, while leaving to America the more distasteful task of defending universal values, such as democracy and human rights.

Luckily, more and more people are learning Chinese, and a new generation is viewing China from all angles: sociological, economic, demographic, environmental, and theological. China is ceasing to be the preserve of sinologists, though the Communist Party is doing its best to block factual research. Sinologists taken with Confucius will always be welcome, because they advance the cause of the authoritarian regime. By contrast, sociologists and economists looking to study conditions on the ground, especially if they become too curious, are not permitted to work in China and have to confine themselves to the periphery—Taiwan or Hong Kong. Journalists, in particular, are closely watched. If they are too explicit in their criticism of the regime and its atrocities, they are expelled. Apart from the pressure of the Chinese authorities, they also have to deal with the censorship of their own managements, which filter dispatches in order to placate China and safeguard short-sighted economic interests. It took the Dongzhou massacre in December of the Year of the Rooster for the French press to take note of China's rebellions. Needless to say, political observers interested in Chinese human rights and democracy have a hard time getting visas. The purpose of the alliance between classical French sinology and the Chinese Communist Party is to project a certain image of China, rather than China as it really is.

While on an official visit to Beijing in 2005, the then–French president Jacques Chirac said, "In China, time flows more slowly than elsewhere." This elegant formulation, which could be applied elsewhere, was music to the ears of sinologists and sinophiles, a legitimization of their defunct research. The Communist leadership was pleased, too. "Things take their own time in China" is how it explains away its own shortcomings. Deng Xiaoping said that it was too early to evaluate the results of the Communist Revolution. We are going through a phase of transition, the Communist cadres answer in chorus to anyone who dares to be critical. But the transition never seems to end. The endless willingness of Chinese Communists and French sinologists to wait bridges our own ideological divisions. The Left in France is not particularly concerned about human rights. The social realists are disciples of Henry Kissinger, who fears that Chinese elections would bring to power a nationalist party far more dangerous than the Communist Party—leading us to believe that the Communist Party is harmless. This is not true. It is dangerous to its own people, who live in fear; it is dangerous to the Tibetan and Uigur minorities that it has annexed; it is dangerous to its neighbors Taiwan, Korea, and Vietnam, on whom Beijing has made territorial claims. How can we say that a democratic government in China would pose a greater danger?

Are we to understand that in France, leftists and rightists both prefer enlightened despotism to democracy? Are we to assume that because they don't have the right to democracy, the Chinese are different from us? If so, how? As for the transition, it has no meaning. The time will never come. What are we to say to a billion Chinese who have been living so long in a phase of transition in hope of "a thousand years of happiness"? Shall we tell them to come back later, for the time is not yet ripe?

That the French intelligentsia and political leaders persist in this ahistorical view of China is perplexing. What interests them is not the flesh-and-blood Chinese but a supposedly eternal Chinese ethos. China itself, it appears, will change faster than they will.

CHAPTER TEN

The Republicans

I n Taiwan, a hothouse of all China's cultures, it is customary to
arrive early for an appointment and very early for a meal. Li Ang,
however, is late.

Li Ang has arranged our meeting in a noisy, crowded bar in the
heart of Taipei. The atmosphere is suddenly lighter than in Beijing.
It feels good to breathe the air of democracy. The Chinese here can
talk publicly without the fear of arrest, and I can wait, secure in the
knowledge that no one is following me. People who live in a democratic system tend to take their freedom for granted, not realizing how
lucky they are not to have to think twice before speaking. A little deprivation is perhaps a good thing; only then do we realize the true
value of freedom.

At last Li Ang appears. Slender, out of breath, her eyes red, her
hair disheveled, she has come straight from a demonstration in support of Chinese lesbians. No, Li Ang does not have lesbian leanings;
her novels and private life, equally tumultuous, are proof enough.
Most Taiwanese women are fashion-conscious, but Li Ang looks as
though she has dressed in a hurry. Her eyes are her striking feature,
fiery with a lurking glimmer of irony. Her friend Wuer Kaixi, the
Tiananmen student leader who has settled in Taiwan, has warned
me, "She'll eat you alive."

Li Ang owes her reputation as a man-eater to her novel *The
Butcher's Wife*. Published in 1968, when she was twenty-five, the

book won her instant acclaim. It tells the story of a peasant woman forced to marry a butcher with two passions: raping his wife and cutting up pigs at the village abattoir. He himself ends up like the pigs, dismembered by his own wife. Based on a small news item, the novel is her metaphor to describe women's position in society. Would she write such a novel again? "Certainly not," she says. "Democracy in Taiwan has freed politics and given women freedom, in fact and in law"; now they can vote and make their voices heard. "We have secured all our feminist demands," she adds. But don't Taiwanese husbands still keep a second wife without telling the first? They can't afford it any more, she tells me laughingly. The hard-core bigamists have to go to the mainland for their home away from home. They use business as an excuse to set up a mistress who is easy on the pocket.

But the issue of lesbianism remains to be resolved. Male homosexuals dominate Taipei's cultural life and cinema, but lesbians are still looked down upon. Ang has devoted her last book to them. She also demonstrates in front of newspaper offices and television stations, which shy from tackling the issue. "But I'm all alone," she complains. Lesbians don't dare come out in the open and join her protest, for fear of repercussions at home and at work.

A woman, free and Chinese

Is lesbianism the last of Li Ang's crusades? Are we to understand that she has won her other battles? Undoubtedly, Chinese men and women cannot be freer than they are in Taiwan. They are free to say what they want and take a stand on just about anything—except, of course, lesbianism. After Li Ang's book, this, too, will no longer be taboo.

I tell Li Ang that many Europeans still believe that the Chinese, not predisposed to liberty, don't know what individual freedom is. She is indignant: "Do we really have to prove to the world that we are human?" And she has a contention with European feminists, especially two of the movement's leading lights: Maria-Antonietta Macciocchi and Julia

Kristeva. The former, who enjoyed considerable moral stature in her time in France and Italy, saw in Mao's China the hoped-for revolution that the Stalinists betrayed. In 1971, she wrote: "At last, we are witnessing the end of discrimination between material and intellectual labor, nothing short of full equality." She called Mao a "genius" and viewed the Cultural Revolution as "ushering in a thousand years of happiness after three years of trouble." Her book *About China*, in which she reproduced word for word the monotonous drivel of her Communist mentors, has faded into oblivion.

Kristeva, a psychoanalyst and writer of repute, thought that Mao's China had found the true answer to the "eternal conflict" between the sexes. Madam Wang and Madam Zhao, the heroines of her book *About Chinese Women*, work in a factory by day and are artists by night. Their husbands are conveniently absent. Kristeva sees this as liberation, forgetting that the husbands are being reeducated in labor camps. First published by Éditions des Femmes, this book, too, would have been forgotten had Kristeva not allowed a reprint in 2001, without changing a single word. She says in the preface that nothing has changed. She herself "had not seen any violence" during her stay in China. She did not exclude the possibility of Mao's China being totalitarian, but she left the task of denunciation to others. Her main concern was women's liberation, which had made more progress in China than in Europe.

Li Ang is just as outraged by Kristeva's remarks in 2005 as she was in 1974. How could Kristeva not have realized that the "liberated" Chinese women she met at the time were acting on orders from the Communist Party, simply playing a part? In the seventeenth century, the Jesuits were equally blind; Kristeva was following in their footsteps, though, unlike them, she couldn't claim to have built Western pavilions in the Summer Palace or translated a vast body of work in Chinese and Manchu. Li Ang can perhaps understand the Kristeva of 1974 being taken in. After all, she was not quite thirty, and she was under the sway of Roland Barthes and Philippe Sollers, both sympathizers with the Cultural Revolution. What she finds hard to swallow is that thirty years later, Kristeva allowed a second reprint of her work without changing a word. Did she *still* not know that Chinese women living in Taiwan were free?

What next, I ask Li Ang? She seems to have run out of causes. I suggest that she raise her voice on behalf of Communist China's millions of prostitutes. Mass prostitution is an unexplored feature of the new China—"the socialist China with Chinese characteristics," to use Party jargon. Young girls fleeing the poverty of the countryside can make money in the city only by selling their bodies. They are taken in hand by the Triad, with the connivance of the police and Party cadres. Is this a socialist trait or a specifically Chinese one, one wonders? Li Ang promises to think about it.

Taiwan is a hive of artistic activity. Li Ang, the best known of the Chinese novelists, is not alone. This country of 22 million has made significant contributions to Chinese literature, cinema, the fine arts, and cuisine. They are far more prolific than their 1.3 billion counterparts on the mainland. The Communist regime promotes grand shows to keep up the myth of a glorious, unchanging, immutable China. Contemporary artists can only survive at the fringes of society. A few prosper because of recognition from the West. Had Li Ang lived on the mainland twenty-five years ago, it is doubtful that she would have been able to publish *The Butcher's Wife*. She might get away with it today, but afterward she would either keep quiet or be imprisoned. Had he not been living as an exile in France, Gao Xingjian could never have published his Nobel Prize-winning novels, or written the opera and theater productions that are staged in France and Taiwan. One of the many unfortunate consequences of tyranny is that it denies thousands of artists and potential artists the possibility of self-expression.

While the Communist regime has kept down many Li Angs and Gao Xingjians, it has squandered enormous sums of money on theaters and halls that don't produce anything. In 2005, the Shanghai Opera had nothing to offer except Broadway musicals. We will have to wait for the Beijing Opera to be completed before we learn what its schedule will be. Designed by Paul Andreu, it looks like a gigantic titanium UFO sitting next to the Forbidden City. The European cognoscenti, those great aficionados of Chinese culture, head straight for Beijing. They seem to have forgotten Taipei.

Is Taiwan really Chinese?

Is Taiwan less Chinese because it is democratic? Must it be tyrannized by an emperor, dictator, or commissar to become truly Chinese? Is China's greatness dependent on its homogeneity? Does it have to be ruled by an iron hand in the velvet glove of Confucianism or Marxism? Will those who disagree with this image of China always be branded dissidents or secessionists?

The Communist regime would like Westerners to believe that uniformity and tyranny are Chinese characteristics. The Party's collusion with Western politicians and businessmen rests on a lie; Chinese leaders project themselves as the custodians of a culture that they have, in fact, done their best to destroy. Li Ang explains: "The authorities play on words, using interchangeably *zhong guo* and *zhong hua*, the two Chinese words for China." *Zhong guo* refers to the Chinese state, and *zhong hua* to the Chinese civilization (*hua* means "essence"). In awe of the Great China, as they call it, Western businessmen and politicians venerate the state for fear of offending the civilization. This suits the Beijing leadership, which accuses the Taiwanese of betraying the Chinese civilization, when all they are doing is refusing to be the slaves of a state that they consider illegitimate.

The Chinese themselves are not fooled. Whether in Beijing, Taipei, Paris, or San Francisco, Li Ang and any other Chinese are perfectly justified in asserting Chineseness while refusing to bow down to Beijing. In fact, an educated Li Ang in Taipei is more Chinese than the ignoramuses who rule in Beijing and fly into a rage whenever anyone questions their monopoly on Chinese civilization.

We have to learn to distinguish between China the state and China the civilization. And within the Chinese civilization, we have to learn to tell the various nations apart, distinct by virtue of their history, language, or culture. China can be better compared with Europe as a whole than with a single country. Just as a Westerner may be French or Italian, Christian, Jewish, or Muslim, so a Chinese may be Daoist, Buddhist, Confucian, Muslim, or Christian, speaking Cantonese or Shanghai Chinese (the difference between Mandarin, the official language of the north, and Cantonese is like that between French and Italian). Li Ang is truly Chinese, since she speaks both Mandarin and Taiwanese and is an agnostic—though she believes in ghosts, like everyone else in Taiwan, especially in July. As she speaks English as well, she is also part of a cosmopolitan culture.

Religion in democracy

To the north of Taipei is the large port city of Keelung, in whose cemetery lie hundreds of sailors, sent in 1885 by Jules Ferry and Courbet to conquer Formosa. Master Chen, who lives in Keelung, explains to me why he gave up his pharmacy to open a temple. He realized that the clients in his modest locality needed spiritual solace more than medication. So, on the third floor of the building where his pharmacy used to be, he arranged a pantheon of Daoist gods and collection of ritual objects. Dressed in ceremonial robes that confer magical powers on him and give him great presence, Chen receives the faithful in distress, directs them to a suitable divinity, and suggests appropriate prayers. He has acquired this understanding and knowledge of rituals from his father. For every wish, whether for health, work, or love, there is a special formula. Master Chen tells me that he doesn't take any money in advance. When devotees make a wish, they also make a pledge—in general, a gift—which they fulfill when the wish is granted. The master clarifies that he deals only with the living, redirecting families who come for funeral ceremonies to the Buddhists. Roles are neatly distributed between Daoists and Buddhists, then, but the entente with the shamans who abound in Taiwan is not so cordial. "They have no theological training," Chen expostulates. Yet the Taiwanese value the services of these masters who can communicate with the dead in a trance, charlatans or not.

I question Master Chen about compassion and the lack of it in Chinese society, an issue that has struck me, as it has many Westerners. I ask about the place of commiseration and charity in Daoism. My question catches him unawares. He takes his time answering. At last, he gives me what he considers a convincing example of the Daoist spirit of compassion: "Under the Tang dynasty, when China was ravaged by the plague, Taoist priests performed the exorcism rites without any compensation. The plague went away." Didn't the Tangs rule a thousand years ago? Master Chen thinks for a while before coming up with a more recent demonstration of Daoist compassion. In 2002, when SARS or atypical pneumonia threatened Taiwan, "Daoist priests once again invoked the gods for the common good, free of charge."

His answer is far from satisfying, no doubt because Chinese religions are not prompted by the impulses of the Christian West. In principle, one's feelings and the Christian love of one's neighbor govern Western behavior. Chinese religions set little store by feelings and love, both of which are ephemeral. They would rather abide by rules. In the West, to do good is to love; in China, it is to obey the rules. This could explain why cruelty has come to dominate social relationships in Communist China, where rituals have been destroyed and the quality of love is not valued.

On the mainland, Western visitors are happy because religious freedom has been restored after fifty years of repression. But when compared with what obtains in Taiwan, the extent to which this freedom is limited and controlled becomes obvious. A truly free China would be like Taiwan, with her masters, priests, and shamans. Almost all Taiwanese visit temples, pray, and invoke their gods. They do not make any important decisions without consulting the oracles, immortals, and shamans. Then there are the Catholic, Protestant, and Pentecostal churches where the faithful go with requests as practical as those of the Taoists. The gods have to compete with one another in Taiwan, and the Taiwanese address them with same familiarity as the Indians do their gods. Left to themselves, the Chinese are mystical—believers or superstitious, depending on the value judgments we make about their religions.

Economic modernization has not sapped these religions. On the contrary, successful businessmen cherish the idea of building temples bigger and brighter than the old ones. As in ancient China, trade guilds are often housed in temples, which act as business and credit centers from which devotees set out to conquer world markets.

Taiwan, like Japan, Korea, and the United States, has shown that it is not progress but anticlericalism that destroys religion. The religiousness of the Taiwanese brings them closer to the Americans than to Communist China. Like the Americans, they communicate directly with the gods. The shaman in Taiwan is what the preacher is in America.

The Western traveler determined not to see the gods can find support with Confucians, who exist even in Taiwan and look down on popular superstitions. One such gentleman, the Taiwanese ambassador to a European country—Confucians are generally high officials—asked me to visit a dog temple in northern Taiwan. "Can you believe it, these people actually worship a dozen pet dogs that they have turned into gods," he sneered. I went to the shrine, which faces the sea. I saw devotees burning incense sticks before the idol of a dog. It is the tradition to write your wish on a piece of paper and then rub it against the bronze statue, each part of the dog's body fulfilling a different kind of wish. The ears are rubbed for health, the mouth for a house, and so on. Yet it is not so much the statue but the thought behind it that makes the temple for loyalty and dogs special. The story goes that the statue is of a dog that followed his master, a drowning fisherman, to his watery grave.

It is possible to read China's history as an endless conflict between Daoist rebels and Confucian bureaucrats. It is also truly amazing that not a drop of blood was shed in the name of religious beliefs. The peaceful coexistence of several worldviews is the starting point of political pluralism.

How a democracy is born

Ma Ying-jeou has decided to give me a lecture on democracy in China. One visit to the mayor's office in Taipei is enough to tell you, in case you don't know, that his name means "horse" in Chinese. It is crammed with every possible kind of horse artifact: paintings, sculptures, horse-shaped table legs, tapestries. The mayor owes his election, for the most part, to female voters. The sixty-year-old Ma has the reputation of being Taiwan's most attractive politician. And he does not take kindly to being interrupted.

Ma launches into the diversity of democratic models in the different Chinas. He breaks up democracy into three constituent elements: freedom, the rule of law, and universal suffrage. In none of the countries of the Chinese sphere can the three be found together. Hong Kong, for example, has the rule of law that the British established. In spite of its transfer to Communist China in 1997, the freedoms of speech and of the press remain inviolable, as does the right to do business. But the Hong Kong government is not elected. It is appointed by Beijing. The assembly—half of which is elected through universal suffrage—is only a consultative body. So Hong Kong is not a full democracy.

Singapore is another British legacy. The rule of law exists there, too. But both the right to do business and freedom of the press are limited. Though the government is elected by universal suffrage, the conditions are such that there can be no opposition. A single party has been at the helm of affairs since the state's creation in 1963. Democracy in China is always relative, Ma says.

Where does Taiwan figure on this scale? All political offices, local and national, are elective. The party once in power, the Kuomintang, has lost its monopoly. Elections are by no means free of corruption, but they are nonetheless closely contested. On the economic front, there is complete freedom. What about the press? Ma, who brooks no questions, says: "It is too free!" Does the rule of law exist in Taiwan? Not yet. Deception, corruption, and feudal relationships prevail. Traditional solidarities—the clan, the family—count far more than the law. For Ma, these are not specifically Chinese traits, but a lapse on the part of the authorities. Since assuming the mayoralty, he has done everything to correct it. People obey the traffic rules because the police are vigilant and the fines are stiff. Ma concludes that the Chinese are no different from anyone else. They won't cross the street on a red light if they know they'll get caught. It has nothing to do with Chinese culture.

As for mainland China, there are no elections, no freedom, and no rule of law. So there are as many variations as there are Chinas. Democracy, or its absence, assumes different forms. This rules out the theory of cultural determinism. The democratic reflex does not come naturally, Ma adds; it has to be learned.

Conventional wisdom, one would say, if Ma hadn't been Chinese. China has a different conception of order, in which the individual's behavior is subordinated to the leadership's morality. It is enough for the sovereign to be just for society to become harmonious. Classical China, the existence of which is not certain, forms the ideal for a group of sinophiles who see in it an alternative to Western order. According to this Orientalist scheme of things, in the West order is imposed from the outside, but in China it is internalized. It could be an interesting philosophical debate, but few would participate in it in today's China. Ma Ying-jeou has acquired the reputation of an honest politician trying to weed out corruption. He can't conceive of any order outside the Western framework of the rule of law. This is a universal construct, irrespective of where it originated. One could even claim that the notion of law has always been present in China because penal laws were decreed by the emperor in the past. What really matters, Ma says, is that China has been in sustained contact with the West for over a hundred years, so necessarily she has to be part of a community shaped by the West. There is no realistic alternative to this model.

Is Ma Ying-jeou the harbinger of democracy? I had met him in 1986. At the time, he was a young secretary of the Kuomintang. Now he has become its president. He has forgotten the previous interview, but I have preserved my notes. In 1986, all the attention was on

Taiwan's economic miracle. Democracy was a secondary issue. What made Taiwan interesting was that it had succeeded in overcoming poverty while mainland China stagnated. Taiwan did not use any magic formula; it relied on the time-tested methods of private ownership, openness to the global market, freedom to do business, a moderate tax rate, and a stable currency. My analysis followed that of the agronomist René Dumont. The founder of the ecological movement in France, he had just completed a book on agrarian reforms in Taiwan (thirty years late). In his book, he said that the Third World would do well to emulate the Taiwanese example. The agrarian reform imposed by the Americans and implemented by the Kuomintang was of liberal inspiration. The large estates were confiscated, but their owners were well compensated and they took to industrial enterprise. The land so released was handed over to peasants who had to buy it on credit. Thus, they learned to appreciate the economic value of land and to cultivate it on rational lines. This policy, extolled by Dumont, contributed significantly to Taiwan's economic, agricultural, and industrial development. It was implemented at the same time as the collectivization of land and the mass murder of landowners in Communist China. The liberal Taiwanese model has won international acclaim—except, of course, in mainland China, which continues to reject private ownership, especially of land.

When I first met him, Ma Ying-jeou had just returned from the United States. He would preface all his sentences with "Dr. Sun Yatsen says," very much like Confucians who quoted their master and Maoists who quoted *The Little Red Book*. He said that there was only one truth, based on the somewhat ambiguous thoughts of the Kuomintang's founder. Repelled by Mao Zedong's army from mainland China, the Kuomintang fell back to Taiwan, imposing its dictatorship on the local population—90 percent of whom were of Chinese origin, their forefathers having immigrated several generations ago. There were several revolts against the occupiers, but they were brutally suppressed. The last revolt took place in 1979 in Kaohsiung. Though the Kuomintang has been the dominant party, it was never the only party, for its basic creed has always been republican. Thus in 2000, the opposition candidate from the Popular Democratic Party defeated his Kuomintang rival to be elected president of the Republic. Since then, the once dominant Kuomintang has converted into a democratic party. Ma, who successfully ran for the post of mayor of Taipei, is likely to be the next presidential candidate. The Republic of China has accepted the simple principle of the changeover of political power between parties.

Will this happen in mainland China? Will Beijing see a Ma Ying-jeou emerge from a new generation of reconverted communists? Will he stand against a liberal opponent in a fair election under the watchful eye of a free press? Can what happened south of the Formosa Strait be replicated north of it?

How dictatorships come to an end: the Taiwanese precedent

It is pleasing to think that mainland China will move to democracy as Taiwan has, in the culmination of a natural process leading to greater economic and political freedom. This gives history a sense of direction, reassuring to Westerners. In anticipation of such a happy transition, engagement with Communist China becomes morally correct. It was through sustained trade that democracy came to Taiwan and Korea. The same argument was advanced for the Soviet Union. Trade, we were told, would bring down the Berlin Wall. This did not happen, either in the erstwhile Soviet Union or in the countries of Central Europe. It was American military pressure that finally brought down the dictatorships. There is little likelihood that Taiwan's experience will be reproduced in Communist China. There is no comparison between the authoritarianism of the Taiwanese regime and the totalitarianism on the mainland. An authoritarian system has the potential to move toward democracy: Pinochet's Chile, Chiang Kai-shek's Taiwan, and South Korea are all cases in point. A totalitarian regime (Nazi, Soviet, Baathist) is rigid and will crumble only under external economic or military pressure.

Chiang Kai-shek was not Mao Zedong. He may have been impervious to the demand for Taiwanese autonomy, but except for the single-China dogma, the Kuomintang had nothing in common with the Communist Party. Civil society in Taiwan was never destroyed. The country has always had a free-market economy, based on private ownership, trade, and enterprise. Artists are free to create, unencumbered by ideological compulsions and official aesthetic canons. The religious activities of the Buddhists, Daoists, and Christians were never in any danger. Several churches, especially the Presbyterian Church, worked actively for democracy without facing harassment. Chiang Kai-shek could hardly repress churches when he himself was Christian and an ally of the United States. The church in Taiwan played the same modernizing role that it did in South Korea and Hong Kong. It strived for social justice, provided succor to the poor, and promoted literacy and health care.

Even when a dictatorship ruled Taiwanese society, it managed to preserve its autonomy and some degree of freedom. Was the passage from dictatorship to democracy the natural outcome of the generation of wealth? That's what happened in South Korea. Yet the theory of an inevitable transition to democracy, once a certain per-capita income threshold has been achieved, does not hold in the case of Singapore, a prosperous China, which is still not democratic. Nor does it explain why India, a poor country, is a democracy. The truth is that the Taiwanese managed their transition successfully because of pressure from the United States. With the American government's recognition of the Chinese Communist regime in 1976, the only way Taiwan could survive was by transforming herself into an exemplary democracy, a moral China versus a totalitarian one. Chiang Kai-shek's son and successor was quick to grasp this. At the same time, the dictators in South Korea, too, realized that the United States would not support them against North Korea unless they came out clearly on the side of freedom.

Another factor that proved decisive was the training that young Taiwanese received in the United States. Ever since the Sixties, the elite had begun to acquire a taste for democracy. Will the mainland

Chinese get bitten by the same bug? It is hard to say, because most of them stay in the U.S., and the few who return are not old enough to assume political responsibility. In another twenty years, perhaps the cadres of the Communist Party will think of changing the Party from within. Many in China are counting on such a natural evolution, but, for the moment, it is only wishful thinking.

The economic, social, and religious conditions of Taiwan cannot be compared with those of mainland China. The Chinese Communist Party has nothing in common with the Kuomintang. So far, no one is putting the least pressure on the Beijing government to give up its tyrannical ways. If anything, the opposite is true. In the name of international stability, the Chinese Communist Party and Western producers have forged a convenient de facto alliance to exploit Chinese rural labor. It was imperative for Taiwan and South Korea to adopt democracy, but the Chinese Communist Party is under no such compulsion. The happy metamorphosis of the Communist chrysalis into a pluralist butterfly seems improbable in Beijing.

Asian values: a myth

The Taiwanese feel that they have been shortchanged in their conversion to democracy. Western governments treat them like pariahs who don't matter. Even the Vatican, which one would imagine to be a bastion of morality, is preparing to break diplomatic ties with Taipei for the sake of setting up an apostolic nuncio in Beijing. Celebrating mass in Beijing is reason enough, or so it seems, to make short shrift of human rights. The Taiwanese ask themselves what they have received in return for democracy. On the domestic front, there is a sense of disenchantment with politics. Corruption persists, particularly at election time, and when the members of the Taipei parliament don't come to blows, they are trading insults with one another. Beijing television never misses an opportunity to telecast these shouting matches.

Are the Taiwanese disappointed with democracy because they expected too much? The Chinese, brought up on Confucian values,

tend to idealize their leaders, so perhaps the Taiwanese were not prepared to accept the mediocrity of democracy. "They will get used to
it," says Shih Ming-teh. "It is just a question of time."

Relatively unknown in the West, Shih Ming-teh is an icon in Asia.
He belongs to the pantheon of freedom fighters that includes Aung
San Su Ki in Myanmar, Benito Aquino in the Philippines, and Wei
Jingsheng in China. He is for Taiwan what Nelson Mandela is for
South Africa and Lech Walesa for Poland: a dissenter, a symbol, a
destiny.

When he was twenty, Shih Ming-teh was accused of conspiring
against the Kuomintang dictatorship, tortured, and sent to jail. In fact,
he was a student like any other who participated in the discussion
groups of young people feeling the oppression of dictatorship. On his
release, Shih Ming-teh was forty-nine. He left prison a changed man,
having used his enforced leisure to educate himself. He became the
symbol of Taiwanese resistance, the inspiration behind the
Democratic Party that went on to dislodge the Kuomintang. I asked
him the same question that I had asked Wei Jingsheng: How had he
managed to survive the torture, the solitary confinement, and the
hunger strikes? He said that his faith in Christianity proved helpful.
But he left Catholicism for Protestantism, for the Catholic Church
refused to support him, whereas the Presbyterians defended his
cause. "Besides," he says, "I prefer speaking to God directly, rather
than through the priests, who know less than I do." Shih Ming-teh
held out because he "loves life." Even in his most difficult moments,
he never once doubted that life was good.

When he was released, he decided to make the most of every
moment. Unlike Mandela or Walesa, Shih Ming-teh did not take up
any political office. Elegant, a bit of a dandy, and surrounded by a
bevy of appreciative young women, he looks more like a film star than
like a republican hero. When I tell him that he looks good at sixty-
four, with his jet-black hair and unlined face, he laughs. Nineteen
years in cold storage, he says, have preserved his appearance.

But Shih Ming-teh is more than a flamboyant playboy. His
struggle continues, though in a new form. "Democracy must be an

exhilarating experience," he says. The Taiwanese have won their freedom to enjoy it. It is important to talk loud and clear, say what you think, do all that was forbidden in the past and remains prohibited in the People's Republic. It is also important to forgive. "I forgive you": these were the first words that he uttered on his election as a legislator in 1995 to the representatives of the Kuomintang, once his persecutors, now his vanquished rivals.

Does forgiveness come easy because he is a Christian? Shih Ming-teh finds my question silly. "Westerners are constantly harping on the relationship between history and culture, religion and democracy. In Asia, we want democracy because it works irrespective of where one comes from: the West, India, Japan, Korea."

During his exile in the United States, Wei Jingsheng had said the same thing about the People's Republic. Asian democrats want democracy because it is efficient, though some in the West persist in the belief that democracy is not compatible with "Asian values." When we talk of a cultural predisposition for democracy, we are falling into the hands of despots who tout Asian values, telling beatific Westerners that Orientals think differently. We would do well to heed the words of Shih Ming-teh and Wei Jingsheng. They know far better what is good for their fellow citizens.

Shih Ming-teh does not deny that his countrymen are caught up in a climate of gloom and disappointment. They do not doubt the merit of democracy, but they do question its institutional framework. Taiwan blindly copied America's presidential system, which is totally unsuited to local conditions. Taiwanese society is divided along ethnic lines, while in a mature democracy, public opinion is divided along ideological lines. Elections in Taiwan pit native Taiwanese against mainland Taiwanese. They may be best described as a kind of tribal war in which race is far more important than class. The Democratic Party, on the other hand, represents the interests of the native Taiwanese. Clamoring for independence from mainland China, it takes great care to preserve its folksy character. The Kuomintang, on the other hand, flaunts its Chineseness, clinging to the idea of an eternal China. Such conflicting identities mean that only a parliamentary system can bring both parties to the negotiating table. The presidential form of governance has steered the country on a collision course.

This is not an argument about technicalities. Democracy has failed in several countries that imported democratic institutions from the United States without taking into consideration local attitudes and issues. Democracy per se can't be dissociated from the nature of the regime—presidential or parliamentary, federal or unitary. Wei Jingsheng believes that democracy in China can only be federal, while for Shih Ming-teh, it has to be parliamentary. In a parliamentary arrangement, ethnic belonging would take a backseat to economic and social issues. Does he think that Taiwan should have a Right and a Left? Shih Ming-teh bursts out laughing: "No one can be a leftist in Taiwan." The left means socialism—in other words, communism or Beijing.

Will the Republic of China fade away?

Is there any democracy in the world whose very existence is as threatened as Taiwan's? Yes, Israel—which is why so many Taiwanese identify with it. Israel's enemies want to wipe it off the map; Beijing wants to annex Taiwan, not annihilate it. But the Taiwanese see no difference, living as they do under the constant threat of Chinese missiles pointing at them from Fujian Province, just 300 kilometers from their shores.

Instead of worrying about the military threat to Taiwan and Asia, we need to examine the validity of Beijing's claim. Legally, it is worth little. From the fifteenth century onward, Taiwan was gradually occupied by mainland Chinese before becoming a Japanese colony in 1895. In 1945, the Japanese ceded Taiwan to the government in Beijing. The question is, which government: the nationalist government of Chiang Kai-shek, or the Communist Party of Mao Zedong that came to power four years later? In reality, Taiwan had been developing as an autonomous nation over the years. Chinese, yet with a distinct identity, it had never been ruled by Beijing. The

Chinese demand for reunification thus rests more on symbolic than on legal grounds. There is the determination to settle scores with the Kuomintang army and to regain the art treasures of imperial China currently housed in a Taipei museum. There is also the megalomaniacal assertion of Communist power over Greater China that already encompasses the Tibetans and the Uigurs. Beijing's claim to Taiwan, like its claim to Tibet and Xuijiang, is the expression of its desire for an empire. Had the Beijing regime not been communist, it would have probably ceased to be imperialist or looked for a more accommodating form of imperialism. An American- or a European Union—type of confederation, as suggested by the Chinese democrats, would abandon military threats in favor of civilized negotiation. Such a possibility, however, is remote.

So how real is the Chinese threat? Undoubtedly, the People's Army has the capacity to destroy Taiwan, but it can never conquer it. The Taiwanese pin their hopes on this distinction. Chinese missiles could devastate the island, yet the Chinese fleet would not be able to capture it. The Communist army is equally incapable of containing a people should it choose to rise against it. This is an optimistic view. The communists have no interest in destroying Taiwan because they could never colonize the island; all they can do is harass the Taiwanese, and their saber-rattling may wear down Taiwanese nerves but it can cause the Republic no real danger. Communist China is a virtual reality rather than a dangerous neighbor at the doorstep—and this attitude, which most of the Taiwanese hold, keeps them going.

Such sanguine thinking will prevail only if Beijing remains rational. Currently, it is being cautious because it knows that an attack against Taiwan would strip Beijing's China of all credibility. Having said this, we would do well to recall that the Communist government has not always behaved predictably. The Red Army launched military campaigns against India in 1962 and Vietnam in 1979 with the sole purpose of intimidating them. The Vietnam campaign was a fiasco. In the Year of the Rooster, Beijing's army chief stated that in case of a conflict with Taiwan, he would not hesitate to paralyze the United States through a nuclear attack. How is one to read this statement? Those who believe in the rationality of the Communist Party say that growing Chinese provocation and military expenditure are not a cause for concern. China's "modernization" of defenses is aimed solely at protecting the coastal regions where its economic activities are concentrated. The Chinese army's arsenal of missiles is the modern-day Great Wall of China. Throughout China's long history, the Wall has served as a protective rampart, nothing else. But who are the new barbarians China fears: the United States, or the democrats, the barbarians from within? After Tiananmen, Deng Xiaoping, who had ordered the massacre, thanked the army officers, calling them "the great steel wall of China."

There is another optimistic viewpoint. The Chinese army is acting provocatively only to get the world to take China seriously. Though China is a permanent member of the Security Council, its word does not carry much weight in international relations. The general impression is that unlike the United States, Europe, and Russia, it does not have the military might to back its position. As diplomacy and defending national interest are the main purposes of the Chinese army, it does not pose any serious threat.

A reassuring analysis, indeed, but one that assumes that the army functions along rational lines. This has not always been the case, and no one can tell what will happen in the future. The analysis also overlooks the nature of the army, firmly established both at the country's center and in the colonial periphery. The army is a powerful entity in its own right, not dependent on the Party. As in 1989, it continues to be the Communist regime's ultimate protection against its citizens. Someday the Party may endanger the survival of the entire planet; for the moment, it is crushing its own citizens, the Chinese, the Tibetans, and the Uigurs. Fortunately, Japan and the United States are there to safeguard the freedom of the Taiwanese, but who is going to protect the Tibetans, the Uigurs, and the Chinese against their own army?

Instead of worrying about China's invading the free world—the danger is theoretical and remote—we should ask why the free world has chosen to support a communist-military complex that is holding 1.3 billion people hostage.

CHAPTER ELEVEN

A Moral

I had spent the first day of the Year of the Rooster with Wei Jingsheng, the exemplary democrat. On the last day, I was in Beijing, talking with China's most popular novelist, Jiang Rong. For the second year running, his only novel, *Wolf Totem*, was the Number One bestseller, selling 14 million copies, of which 13 million were pirated. This high priest of subversion took ten years to write his 600-page magnum opus. Jiang Rong has been at loggerheads with the Party since his early youth. His pen name, "Barbarian from the North," is deliberately provocative, a slighting of classical China. The only reason why his book has not been banned is its overwhelming success, which has forced the Party to take note of it. Jiang Rong does not give any interviews in China and never appears in the media.

Wolves and dragons: two chinese totems

Why has *Wolf Totem* received such widespread acclaim? At first glance, it appears to be a collection of stories about wolf hunting in the Mongolian steppes. Young Jiang had been sent there in the Sixties to complete his education among the masses. But the lessons he learned from his ten-year stint among the last of the Mongolian nomads were not those that the Party had in mind. There he came to know that there was not one but two Chinese civilizations: the nomadic (the official term is "barbarian") civilization and the peasant one. Like their totem, the wolf, the nomads are "cunning, free, dignified, and independent." The others, the "sheep," are passive peasants trapped in an ideological prison, first Confucian and then Marxist. The totem of the Chinese peasant is the dragon, the mythical animal that brings rain vital for crops.

On the basis of what he saw and experienced, Jiang constructed a literary epic, an Odyssey through China in which he rewrote her dual history. He tells us that when the Chinese behave like wolves, China holds its head high; when they behave like sheep, it falls prey to the first barbarian invader, whether Western, Japanese, or Communist. The author, avowedly anti-Marxist, believes that the fate of a nation hangs on its culture, not on its economics.

Is Jiang Rong a Chinese Solzhenitsyn? His book is both a legend about the wolves of the steppes and an exaltation of the wolf as a totem of freedom. It is a eulogy of the nomadic culture as against the sedentary peasant tradition. The clash between these two conceptions of man, the wolf and the dragon, is the true history of China, he says. This explains the author's success, especially with young readers who willingly identify with the wolf.

There are countless websites on this mythical battle, where eager readers use metaphorical allusions to get past the censors. Jiang Rong feels that the tremendous enthusiasm for *Wolf Totem* is because the Chinese have rediscovered their true nature. "The dormant wolf in the Chinese sheep has been aroused." To change from a sheep into a wolf, all one has to do is discard the sheep's garb of Confucianism and Marxism.

I tell Jiang Rong that the wolf is not kindly viewed in the West. In the past, he used to eat up little girls. Today, he stands for "savage neoliberalism." Jiang Rong sees nothing wrong with neoliberalism, the market economy, and globalization. In point of fact, the "wolf culture," which frightens Europeans and elderly Chinese, holds great attraction for his readers. No doubt the Communists would prefer a society of sheep, but the younger generations, dreaming of freedom, have other ideas. The fact that they chose Miss Li as a she-wolf is ample proof, says Jiang Rong.

Who is Miss Li? Jiang is all praise for the amateur singer who won the *Supergirl* contest on a Hunan television station in August 2005. Jiang is a fan of Li Yuchun, and so is his wife, also a writer, who did not miss an episode of what became the most popular program ever televised in China. *Supergirl* and *Wolf Totem* were the two major events of the year. This, too, is part of globalization. Jiang Rong sees a link between the two. If we want to know where the real China is heading, he says, we have to look at popular fads and understand their significance. *Supergirl* was the democratic victory of an ordinary Chinese girl. The Party-ordained public television announcers' vapid baby-doll look didn't stand a chance against Li's liberated image and the raw energy that she exuded.

And so the Year of the Rooster came to an end to make way for the Year of the Dog. With this conversation about wolves and dragons, my last in China, it was time to say good-bye. The interview took place at a venue chosen by Jiang Rong: McDonald's, the symbol of new China. Located in a parking lot, the restaurant faces the Summer Palace. Jesuit architects designed the imperial abode in 1750 along the lines of Versailles; English and French troops ravaged it in 1860. For many years now, China has ceased to live on another planet. She is very much a part of the world we live in. Her people may use different forms to express their aspirations and conflicts—a story about wolves and dragons, for instance—but they are not fundamentally different from the rest of us. The Chinese are not the Other; neither are they elsewhere. They are very much here and now. Their desires, joys, and sufferings are no different from ours. We have no right to condemn them to Otherness; nor do we have any right to deny them their ordinary desires, be it bad coffee at McDonald's or the freedom to express themselves. China is no longer exotic; only the Communist Party is. For how long, who can say?

Which way will China go? Four scenarios, from revolution to status quo

Rather than prophesy about a country as elusive as China, let me merely outline the four future scenarios—all, apparently, highly unlikely—that dominate contemporary sinology, as well as a fifth, which could in fact come about, but has yet to be described.

Rebellions are breaking out all over China; I have described those that occurred over the last year. Will all these local revolts add up to a revolution? If so, it will be the third in a hundred years, after the overthrows of the Empire in 1911 and of the Republic in 1949. This is the visionary's scenario. Though people are simmering with discontent, rebels have no means of communicating with one another and are unable to constitute themselves into a single movement with a common leader and agenda. The Party has succeeded in dividing them. That they will be able to shake the Party seems very unlikely. Nor are they powerful enough to take on the army and the police.

Do religious movements pose a serious threat? The historical precedent—a regime overthrown on account of a groundswell of mystical fervor—is not likely to repeat itself. Religions and sects active in Chinese society are fulfilling the desire for individual salvation or collective solidarity; they do not constitute a millenarian threat. The Party's crushing of the Falun Gong shows its determination not to be destabilized by apocalyptic projects. Once again, its mastery of the instruments of repression has given it the upper hand, at least in the immediate future. Moreover, people are mortally afraid of violence, making a revolution seem even less likely. The Chinese fear of civil war is far greater than the Chinese hatred of the Party. Though people are convinced that nothing could be worse than the present regime, they can't conceive of an alternative. No one—neither rebel nor revolting peasant nor striking worker nor candidate for religious martyrdom—has dared to suggest an alternative. And the Party has seen to it that the desire for liberal democracy is confined to intellectual circles.

After discarding the first scenario, we turn to the second: bankruptcy. China will not be able to maintain its current pace of growth because natural bottlenecks and poor management will lead to shortages of electricity, water, and qualified manpower, as well as pollution and pandemics caused by too many people packed together in unhygienic conditions. Besides, the Party has no real control over the two engines of Chinese growth: American consumer demand and Chinese savings. Should the Americans move away from the Chinese market and should Chinese savers invest in foreign banks, there would be general bankruptcy and the country would plunge into chaos. (Theoretically, it would be possible to develop the economy on a surer footing—by stimulating the domestic market—but this would happen only after a long period of transition. Meanwhile, the Party would have lost the legitimacy that it derived from growth.)

Could this second scenario lead to democracy? The far greater likelihood is the rise to power of a military regime to end anarchy, prevent provinces like Tibet and Xinjiang from proclaiming their independence, and stop others such as Fujian and Guangzhou from moving toward Hong Kong and Taiwan. In any case, the second scenario seems just as improbable as the first, for the simple reason that the world needs its Chinese workshop. Should the workshop lose momentum, Westerners would have to pay much more for scarcer items of daily consumption. In all probability, international interdependence is what is going to save the Party.

The third scenario, more moderate, is a gradual, structured transition to democracy—an idea that will find favor with most people both in and out of China. The Party, faced with growing social turmoil and increasingly complex choices, will of its own accord accept the need for dialogue. The principle of negotiation will triumph over the principle of authority. The Communists will organize themselves spontaneously into different streams, liberal and socialist, which will give rise to new political parties. In this way, the Party will have successfully transformed itself for a third time, from a totalitarian to an authoritarian to a liberal democratic body. Don't local elections, the emerging judiciary and legal systems, social debates in the media, and the white paper published in the Year of the Rooster all point in this direction?

Alas, this rosy picture is not likely to materialize because the Party refuses to make any firm commitments or set any deadlines. Democratization has been subordinated to vague notions such as "Chinese characteristics" and other "transitions"—in short, pretexts for prevaricating and not doing anything.

That the Party would willingly set forth on a path that would lead to its extermination is doubtful, to say the least. Democratization would mean replacing the present lot of technocrats with peasants' representatives, who would then be a majority; it would also mean reorienting economic choices, giving up the current obsession for national power for more people-oriented strategies. Finally, the transitional phase has always been the most perilous to an authoritarian government, a fact that history has vindicated time and time again, from Louis XVI to Mikhail Gorbachev. So why should the Party fish in troubled waters? Reform is wishful thinking and will remain so.

The fourth scenario, conceivable, is authoritarian status quo. You can hate the Party, fear its all-consuming desire for power, take umbrage at the way it despises its own people, but you have to admit that it has pursued its objectives with a cold-blooded rationality. Its first objective is to stay in power. In the normal course, a dictatorship dies with the dictator or because there is no clear mode of succession. The Chinese Communist Party has become a nonhereditary dynasty in which one generation smoothly replaces the next. It is equally adept at changing its positions, moving from utopia to development, militancy to technical expertise, all the while honing its managerial skills to control the economy, national defense, and social movements. The Party's second objective is to enrich its members. It has shown a remarkable talent for increasing its power and wealth in the process of making a powerful China.

Are these reasons strong enough for us to be in awe of the Party? No one doubts its efficiency. What is frightening is its unbridled ambition. Its aims are certainly not those that ordinary Chinese would enunciate if they were allowed to. What the people want is clear: greater individual welfare, schools for their children, hospitals for their old age, a decent wage without being uprooted, freedom of speech, and less corruption and military spending. But the people don't have a voice. They go unheard both in their own country and outside. They are the a billion people of silence, the victims of the Party's ruthless efficiency.

Yet the Chinese, except those who stand to gain directly from the current system, remain steadfast in their demands. Whenever they can, in Hong Kong, Taiwan, and overseas, they choose liberal democracy, proving that the Communist model is not a universal one. In fact, it is not even suited to the Chinese—whereas so-called Western values remain a valid point of reference for all peoples, regardless of who they are and where they come from.

Human rights: what the West must do

The fourth scenario, authoritarian status quo, is probable but intolerable for the vast majority of the Chinese. It is thus outside China that the future of the Party will almost certainly be decided. It depends for its legitimacy on the outside world, which treats it with all the deference due to the Chinese nation—precisely because the world seems to have forgotten that the Party is not China.

Should the West refuse to trade with China, as some democrats in exile are advocating? No, because it is important that China continue to develop. Thanks to trade, a billion human beings will someday be able to escape from the clutches of poverty and rebuild their civilization. Economic and cultural globalization will also benefit the West. The question, therefore, is how to act in a way that fosters the development of the majority of the Chinese, not just the Chinese army and technocrats. Is there anything we can do—and if so, what?

If we believe in dignity for all, we must be consistent in our behavior and listen to what Chinese democrats have to say. At the time of the Soviet Union, supporting Russian dissidents, linking trade to human rights, and containing the Soviet Union's military aggressiveness were considered both normal and moral. So we would do well to boycott Yahoo until Shi Tao is released. He has been sentenced to thirteen years' imprisonment only because he sent prodemocracy e-mail, condemning the Chinese police through the American server. Are we going to allow ourselves to be taken in by the Chinese ethos humbug? Are we going to abandon all that we believe in and let the Party continue suppressing the rights of the Chinese? We should listen to the people of silence and show the same solidarity that we did with the Soviets not so long ago. If we turn a deaf ear, then we should give up the pretense of being the embodiment of humanist values.

For politicians and businessmen, such an approach may seem unrealistic. But it is no more unrealistic than our support for human rights movements in Russia and Central Europe, oppressed by the Communist Parties of their countries. Besides, is it always necessary to justify a moral choice and duty? The time has come for action. The Olympic Games will be held in Beijing in 2008. Will they prove to be another Berlin, or will they revive the spirit of Seoul? In Berlin in 1938, we remained mute spectators to the triumph of Party, dangerous not just for its own people but for the whole world. Will it be the same in Beijing? Or can the impossible happen: freedom of speech restored to all the Chinese, as in Seoul in 1988?

It all depends on what we do: the government in Beijing is very sensitive to its image in the West, as investment from abroad determines the growth rate. Mobilizing support for human rights in China is effective: the Chinese are our brothers.

Paris-Beijing,
January 2006

Acknowledgments

T he *Empire of Lies* is a personal inquiry that I conducted in China from January 2005 to January 2006. Before embarking on this project, I had been going to China each year from 1977 onward and had written about its economic development (*La Nouvelle Richesse des nations,* published in Paris in 1987 and Beijing in 1989), its religions (*Les Vrais Penseurs de notre temps*), the economic and political reforms in mainland China and Taiwan (*Le Capitalisme, suite et fins,* 1991), and the relations between China and its neighbors (*Le Monde est ma tribu,* 1997).

Among the many people who guided me in the course of my research, I would like to thank in particular Claude Martin, François-Marcel Plaisant, Jean-Paul Réau, Gérard Chesnel, Pierre Barroux, Nicolas Chapuis, Paul Jean-Ortiz, Daniel Blaise, Bruno Cabrillac, Christian Thimonier, Wang Hua, and Chen Deyan.

Zhao Fusan, Theodore de Bary and Du Weiming, and Kristofer Schipper initiated me to the religions of China; Pierre-Étienne Will and Yves Camus helped me discover contemporary sinology.

My numerous meetings with Alain Peyrefitte, both in China and France, helped me clarify my thoughts.

Yang Hangsheng, Ouyang Zantong, and An Sha accompanied me in my journeys.

Marie Holzman and René Viénet helped me prepare the final manuscript.

Brian Anderson, editor of the Manhattan Institute's *City Journal*, introduced me to the American audience of his magazine and to Roger Kimball at Encounter Books.

Bibliography

This is a selective bibliography that helped me verify the information I had gathered in the course of the inquiry. The works are classified alphabetically according to the names of the authors and refer to the various chapters of the book.

Prologue: The Myth of China

Bergère, Marie-Claire, Lucien Bianco and Jürgen Domes, *La Chine au XXe siècle, de 1949 à aujourd'hui,* Fayard, Paris, 1990.

Domenach, Jean-Luc, *L'Archipel oublié,* Fayard, Paris, 1992.

—— *Où va la Chine?,* Fayard, Paris, 2002.

Étiemble, René, *Quarante ans de mon maoïsme (1934–1974),* Gallimard, Paris, 1976

Fairbank, John K., *The Great Chinese Revolution, 1800–1985,* Harper & Row, New York, 1986.

Fairbank, John K., *China, a New History,* The Belknap Press of Harvard University Press, Cambridge, Mass., 1992.

Granet, Marcel, *La Pensée chinoise,* Albin Michel, Paris, 1968.

Guillain, Robert, *Dans trente ans la Chine,* Seuil, Paris, 1965.

Huc, Père, *L'Empire chinois,* Éditions du Rocher, Monaco, 1980.

Ladany, Laszlo, *The Communist Party of China and Marxism, 1921–1985: A Self-portrait,* Stanford University Press, Stanford, Calif., 1988.

Lecomte, Louis, *Un Jésuite à Pékin: Nouveaux mémoires sur l'état Présent de la Chine, 1687–1692*, Phébus, Paris, 1990.

Leví, Jean, *La Chine romanesque: Fictions d'Orient et d'Occident*, Seuil, Paris, 1995.

Leys, Simon, *Essais sur la Chine*, Robert Laffont, Paris, 1998.

Pasqualini, Jean, *Prisonniers de Mao: Sept ans dans un camp de travail en Chine*, Gallimard, Paris, 1973.

Peyrefitte, Alain, *L'Empire immobile ou le choc des mondes*, Fayard, Paris, 1989.

—— *La Tragédie chinoise*, Fayard, Paris, 1990.

—— *Un Choc des cultures, le regard des Anglais*, Fayard, Paris, 1998.

Short, Philip, *Mao Tsé-toung*, Fayard, Paris, 2005.

Spence, Jonathan D., *Chinese Roundabout: Essays in History and Culture*, W. W. Norton, New York, 1992.

—— *The Chan's Great Continent: China in Western Minds*, W. W. Norton, New York, 1998.

Tsien Tche-hao, *L'Empire du milieu retrouvé: La Chine populaire a Trente ans*, Flammarion, Paris, 1979.

Verdier, Fabienne, *Passagère du silence, dix ans d'initiation en Chine*, Albin Michel, Paris, 2003.

Chapter One: The Dissenters

Bastid-Burguière, Marianne, *L'Évolution de la société chinoise à la fin de la dynastie des Qing, 1873–1911*, Éditions de l'École des Hautes Études en Sciences Sociales, Paris, 1979.

Che Muqi, *Beijing Turmoil: More than Meets the Eyes*, Foreign Languages Press, Beijing, 1990.

Fang Lizhi, *Abattre la Grande Muraille: Science, culture et démocratie en Chine*, Albin Michel, Paris, 1990.

Holzman, Marie and Bernard Debord, *Wei Jingsheng, un Chinois inflexible*, Bleu de Chine, Paris, 2005.

Lian Heng and Judith Shapiro, *After the Nightmare: A Survivor of the Cultural Revolution Reports on China Today*, Alfred A. Knopf, New York, 1986.

Lou Sin, *Nouvelles chinoises*, Éditions en langues étrangères, Beijing, 1974.

Sabatier, Patrick, *Le Dernier Dragon, Deng Xiaoping: Un siècle de l'histoire de Chine*, Jean-Claude Lattès, Paris, 1990.

Spence, Jonathan D., *Emperor of China, Self-portrait of K'Ang-His*, Vintage Books, New York, 1988.

Wei Jingsheng, *Lettres de prison*, Plon, Paris, 1998.

Wu, Harry, *Laogai, the Chinese Gulag*, Westview Press, Boulder, Colo., 1992.

Zhang Jie, *Ailes de plomb*, Maren Sell, Paris, 1985.

Chapter Two: Wild Grass

Buck, Pearl, *Peony*, Mayer Bell, New York, 2004.

Haski, Pierre, *Le Sang de la Chine, quand le silence tue*, Grasset, Paris, 2005.

Johnson, Ian, *Wild Grass: Three Stories of Change in Modern China*, Random House, New York, 2004.

Kristeva, Julia, *Des Chinoises*, Pauvert, Paris, 2001.

Kristof, Nicholas D., and Sheryl Wudunn, *China Wakes*, Random House, New York, 1994.

Li Zhisui, *La Vie privée du président Mao*, Plon, Paris, 1994.

Shang Yu, *Ripoux à Zhengzhou*, Philippe Picquier, Arles, 2002.

Chapter Three: The Mystics

Aikman, David, *Jesus in Beijing: How Christianity Is Transforming China and Changing the Global Balance of Power*, Regnery, Chicago, 2003.

Bary, Theodore de, *Asia Values and Human Rights: A Confucian Communication Perspective*, Harvard University Press, Cambridge, Mass., 1998.

Chapuis, Nicolas, *Tristes automnes: Poétique de l'identité dans la Chine ancienne*, Librairie You Feng, Paris, 2001.

Chesneaux, Jean, *Sociétés secrés secrètes en Chine*, Juilliard, Paris, 1965.

Ching, Julia, and Hans Küng, *Christianisme et religion chinoise*, Seuil, Paris, 1988.

Claudel, Paul, *Correspondance consulaire de Chine (1896–1900)*, Presses Universitaires de Franche-Comté, Besançon, 2004.

Éloge de l'anarchie par deux excentriques chinois, polémiques du IIIe Siècle, translated and presented by Jean Lévi, L'Encyclopédie des nuisances, Paris, 2004.

Entretiens de Confucius, translated from the Chinese by Anne Cheng, Seuil, Paris, 1981.

Gernet, Jacques, *Le Monde chinois*, Armand Colin, Paris, 1972.

—— *L'Intelligence de la Chine, le social et le mental*, Gallimard, Paris, 1994.

Herrou, Adeline, *La Vie entre soi: Les moines taoïstes aujourd'hui en Chine*, Société d'ethnologie, Université Paris X Nanterre, 2005.

Hsia Chang, Maria, *Falungong, secte chinoise: Un défi au pouvoir*, Autrement, Paris, 2004.

Ladany, Laszlo, *The Communist Party of China and Marxism, 1921–1985: A Self-portrait*, Stanford University Press, Stanford, Calif., 1988.

Lévi, Jean, *Le Rêve de Confucius*, Albin Michel, Paris, 1989.

Needham, Joseph, *La Science chinoise et l'Occident*, Seuil, Paris, 1989.

Palmer, David A., *La Fièvre du Qigong: Guérison, religion et politique en Chine, 1949–1999*, Éditions de l'École des Hautes Études en Sciences Sociales, Paris, 2005.

Schipper, Kristofer, *Le corps taoïste*, Fayard, Paris, 1982.

Schipper, Kristofer, and Franciscus Verellen, *The Taoist Canon*, University of Chicago Press, Chicago, 2004.

Shang Yang, *Le Livre du prince*, Flammarion, Paris, 2005.

Spence, Jonathan D., *Le Chinois de Charenton, de Canton à Paris aux XVIIIe siècle*, Plon, Paris, 1988.

—— *The Search for Modern China*, Hutchinson, New York, 1990.

Ter Haar, Barend J., *The White Lotus: Teachings in Chinese Religious History*, University of Hawaii Press, Honolulu, 1999.

Tu Weiming, Milan Hejtmanek, and Alan Wachman, *The Confucian World Observed: A Contemporary Discussion of Confucian Humanism in East Asia*, Institute of Culture and Communication, the East-West Centre, Honolulu, 1992.

Yang Huilin, *Christianity in China*, M. E. Sharpe, New York, 2004.

Yuan Bingling, *Chinese Democracies: A Study of the Kongsis of West Borneo (1776–1884)*, CNWS, Netherlands, 2000.

Chapter Four: **The Dispossessed**

Bernstein, Thomas, and Xiabo Lu, *Taxation without Representation in Contemporary Rural China*, Cambridge University Press, City 2003.

Bianco, Lucien, *Jacqueries et revolutions dans la Chine du XXe siècle*, Éditions de la Martinière, Paris, 2005.

Bobin, Frédéric, and Zhe Wang, *Pékin en movement*, Autrement, Paris, 2005.

Fei-Ling Wang, *Organizing through Division and Exclusion: China's Hukou System*, Stanford University Press, Stanford, Calif., 2005.

Scott, James C., *The Moral Economy of the Peasant: Rebellion and Subsistence in Southeast Asia*, Yale University Press, New Haven, Conn., 1976.

Theroux, Paul, *Sailing through China*, Michael Russel, Salisbury, 1983.

Chapter Five: **The Downtrodden**

Cohen, Philippe, and Luc Richard, *La Chine sera-t-elle notre cauchemar?*, Mille et une nuits, Paris, 2005.

Izraelewicz, Erik, *Quand la Chine change le monde*, Grasset, Paris, 2005.

Jung Chang and Halliday, *Mao: The Unknown Story*, Jonathan Cape, London, 2005.

Chapter Six: **Skewed Development**

A Cheng, *Le roman et la vie*, Éditions de l'Aube, Paris, 1995.

Bastid-Bruguière, Marianne, *Aspects de la réforme de l'enseignement en Chine au début du XXe siècle*, Mouton, Paris, 1971.

Cayrol, Pierre, *Hong Kong, dans la gueule du dragon*, Philippe Picquier, Arles, 1997.

Economy, Elizabeth C., *The River Runs Black: The Environmental Challenge to China's Future*, Cornell University Press, Ithaca, 2004.

Godement, François, *Dragon de feu, dragon de papier: l'Asie a-t-elle un avenir?*, Flammarion, Paris, 1998.

The Korean Association for Communist Studies, "China's Reform Politics, Policies and Their Implication," *Study Series No. 5*, Sogang University Press, Seoul, 1986.

Ma Hong, *New Strategy for Chinese Economy*, New World Press, Beijing, 1993.

McGregor, James, *One Billion Customers: Lessons from the Front Lines Doing Business in China*, Free Press, New York, 2005.

Oshima, Harry, *Economic Growth in Monsoon Asia: A Comparative Survey*, University of Tokyo Press, Tokyo, 1987.

Qiu Xiaolong, *Mort d'une heroine rouge*, Points, Paris, 2003.

Scalapino, Robert, *The Politics of Development, Perspectives on Twentieth Century Asia*, Harvard University Press, Cambridge, Mass, 1989.

Smil, Vaclav, *China's Past, China's Future: Energy, Food, Environment*, Routledge Curzon, London, 2004.

Xie Baisan, *China's Economic Policies: Theories and Reforms since 1949*, Fudan University Press, 1991.

Chapter Seven: Shadows of Democracy

Balazs, Étienne, *La Bureaucratie céleste: Recherche sur l'économie et la société de la Chine traditionnelle*, Gallimard, Paris, 1968.

Béja, Jean-Philippe, *A la recherche d'une ombre chinoise: Le mouvement pour la démocratie en Chine (1989–2004)*, Seuil, Paris, 2004.

Macciocchi, Maria-Antonietta, *de la Chine*, Seuil, Paris, 1971.

Chapter Eight: The Savage State

Attané, Isabelle, *Une Chine sans femmes?*, Perrin, Paris, 2005.

Chen Lichuan and Christian Thimonier, *L'Impossible Printemps: Une anthologie du printemps de Pékin*, Rivages, Paris, 1990.

Courtois, Stéphane, et al., *Le Livre noir du communisme*, Robert Laffon, Paris, 1997.

Link, Perry, *Evening Chats in Beijing: Probing China's Predicament*, W. W. Norton, New York, 1992.

Mo Yan, *Red Sorghum: A Novel of China*, Penguin, New York, 1994.

Nathan, Andrew, and Perry Link, *The Tiananmen Papers: The Chinese Leadership's Decision to Use Force against Their Own People*, Public Affairs Books, New York, 2000.

Sharping, Thomas, *Birth Control in China, 1949–2000, Population Policy and Demographic Development*, Routledge Curzon, Oxon, 2003.

Xiaobo Lü, *Cadres and Corruption: The Organizational Involution of the Chinese Communist Party*, Stanford University Press, Stanford, Calif., 2000.

Xiran, *Chinoises*, Philippe Picquier, Arles, 2005.

Yan Sun, *Corruption and Market Relations in Post-Reform Rural China. A Micro-Analysis of Peasants, Migrants and Peasant Entrepreneurs*, Routledge Curzon, London, 2003.

Chapter Nine: The End of the Party

Balme, Stéphanie, *Entre soi, l'élite du pouvoir de la Chine contemporaine*, Fayard, Paris, 2004.

Dillon, Michael, *Xingjiang—China's Muslim Far Northwest*, Routledge Curzon, London, 2004.

Écrits édifiants et curieux sur la Chine au XXIe siècle. Voyage à travers la pensée chinoise contemporaine, supervised by Marie Holzman and Chen Yan, Éditions de l'Aube, Paris, 2003.

Griesttays, Peter, *China's New Nationalism, Pride, Politics and Diplomacy*, University of California Press, Berkeley, 2004.

Mitter, Rana, *A Bitter Revolution, China's Struggle with the Modern World*, Oxford University Press, City, 2004.

Nathan, Andrew, and Bruce Giley, "China's New Rulers: The Secret Files," *New York Review of Books*, New York, 2002.

Wang Hui, *China's New Order*, Harvard University Press, Cambridge, Mass., 2003.

Chapter Ten: The Republicans

Ang Li, *The Butcher's Wife*, Peter Allen, New York, 2003.

Bergère, Marie-Claire, *Sun Yat-sen*, Fayard, Paris, 1994.

Bo Yang, *The Ugly Chinaman and the Crisis of Chinese Culture*, Allen & Unwin, London, 1980.

Cabestan, Jean-Pierre and Benoît Vermander, *La Chine en quête de ses frontières: La confrontation Chine-Taiwan*, Presse de Sciences Po, Paris, 2005.

Campbell, William, *Formosa under the Dutch*, SMC Publishing, Taipei, 1903.

Chee Soon Juan, *To Be Free: Stories from Asia's Struggle against Oppression*, Monash Asia Institute, City, 1998.

Chen Ruoxi, *The Execution of Mayor Yien and Other Stories from the Great Proletarian Cultural Revolution*, Indiana University Press, Bloomington, Ind., 2004.

Chu His-Ning, Chu T'Ien-Wen, and Chu T'Ien-Hsin, *Le Dernier Train pour Tamsui et autres nouvelles*, Christian Bourgois éditeur, Paris, 2004.

Dumont, René, *Taiwan: Le prix de la réussite*, Seuil, Paris, 1987.

Gao Xinjiang, *Le Livre d'un homme seul*, Éditions de l'Aube, Paris, 2004.

K. T. Li, *The Experience of Dynamic Economic Growth on Taiwan*, Mei Ya Publications, Taipei, 1976.

Kuo, Shirley, Gustav Ranis, and John C. H. Fei, *The Taiwan Success Story: Rapid Growth with Intense Distribution in the Republic of China, 1952–1979*, Westview Press, Boulder, Colo., 1981.

Martin Ahern, Emily and Hill Gates, *The Anthropology of Taiwanese Society*, Caves Books, Taipei, 1981.

Peng Ming-Min, *A Taste of Freedom: Memoirs of a Formosan Independence Leader*, Taiwan Publishing Co., 1972.

Scobell, Andrew, *China's Use of Military Force*, Cambridge University Press, City, 2003.

Chapter Eleven: A Moral
Gordon, Chang, *The Coming Collapse of China*, Random House, New York, 2001.
Hu Ping, *La Pensée manipulée, le cas chinois*, Éditions de l'Aube, Paris, 1999.
—— *Chine: À quand la démocratie? Les illusions de la modernisation*, Éditions de l'Aube, Paris, 2004.
Author, *State and Society in XXIst Century China: Crisis, Contention and Legitimation*, published by Peter Hays, Gries and Stanley Rosen, Routledge Curzon, London and New York, 2004.

Reviews:
Chinese Cross Currents, published by Macau Ricci Institute.
Perspectives chinoises, published by the Centre français d'études de la Chine in Hong Kong
Website: www.hrichina.org (Human Rights in China)

Transcription of Chinese names: we have adopted the Pinyin system currently in use—Mao Tsé Tung becomes Mao Zedong. Canton become Guangzhou, and so on.

Value of the yuan: ten yuan are worth about one dollar.

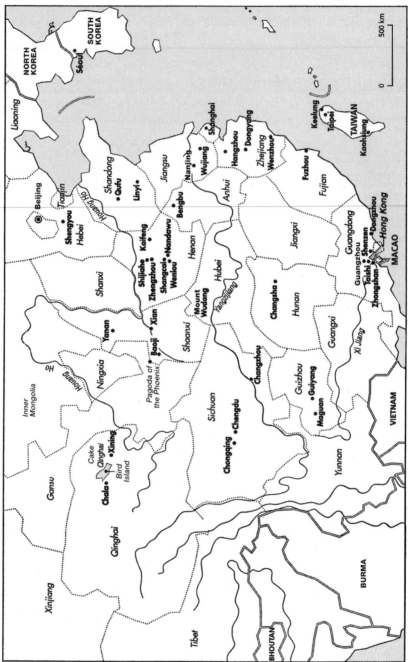

Guy Sorman

The Year of the Rooster

Throughout 2005, the Year of the Rooster in the Chinese calendar, China was rocked by a series of rebellions: peasant revolts, religious uprisings, workers' strikes, petitions by democratic activists, and environmental movements. As China opens up to the world, its people are becoming more aware, thanks especially to the Internet, and they are rebelling against the tyranny of the Communist Party. More and more Chinese are disenchanted with the growing injustice, corrupt officials, censorship, permanent surveillance, propaganda, and repression of the system. Both the educated classes and the billion peasants who have been bypassed by Party-driven industrialization are protesting loudly.

Who, in the West, is listening to the voices of these Chinese up in arms? Statesmen and businessmen, as if mesmerized by the Party and its supposed successes, prefer dealing with it and ignoring the advocates of democracy. Such an approach is dangerously short-sighted, as it fails to take into account the reality of the country and makes a mockery of its future.

Guy Sorman spent the Year of the Rooster in China, listening to these rebels in their quest for freedom; he let them speak during his journey into the innermost depths of China, its villages and provinces, far removed from the usual circuit.

Guy Sorman lives in Paris and has published some twenty books on a wide range of issues confronting the contemporary world, including *The Genius of India* (2000); *The Children of Rifah: In Search of Modern Islam* (2003); and *L'économie ne ment pas* (2008). He is a contributing editor of *City Journal* and a columnist for Project Syndicate.